Lost Vegas

The Redneck Riviera, Existentialist Conversations
with Strippers, and the World Series of Poker

By Paul 'Dr. Pauly' McGuire

Cover designed by Kat Goodale

Cover photo by Getty Images

Author's photo by Kym Bracken

Edited by Jeremiah Schupbach and Dr. Ken Friedman

Printed in the United States of America

First Printing: June 2010

ISBN: 978-0-557-50007-9

For Derek, Señor, and K.B.

Part I

"As far as men go, it is not what they are
that interests me, but what they can become."

- Jean-Paul Sartre

Chapter 1

June 2005.

The cookie-cutter buildings with pink stucco and adobe seemed pleasing to the eye, but I knew better. You cannot judge a zoo by what it looks like from the outside. You have to inspect all the animals in their cages. One by one.

"Didn't they catch the Ohio highway serial sniper in one of the Budget Suites in Las Vegas?" I asked Flipchip.

"I wouldn't doubt it," he said, "It might have even been this one."

Flipchip had a camera slung over his shoulder. He tried to blend into the background while taking photos by wearing black all the time, a distinct contrast to his perfectly messy white hair. In his 60s, Flipchip was a man of few words because his son, the Poker Prof, did most of the talking. The Prof lived in an undisclosed bunker somewhere in the Nevada desert, and rarely left his computer compound even to visit the Las Vegas Strip, which may have explained his pale complexion. On rare occasions when he did venture out in public, the Prof also wore all black. Black shoes. Black socks. Black pants. Black t-shirt. Black long-sleeve button-down shirt or sometimes a black mock turtleneck. He looked like the freaky Goth kid from high school who hung out alone chain-smoking cigarettes in the corner of the cafeteria.

Flipchip and the Prof owned LasVegasVegas.com, on which they authored a blog about the Las Vegas poker scene. They had successfully covered the 2004 World Series of Poker (WSOP) and were looking to expand their coverage team in 2005. Flipchip had been snapping pictures at the WSOP since its infancy at Binion's Horseshoe in downtown Las Vegas in the early 1970s.

Three months earlier, the Prof and I sat at the bar near the newly renovated sports book in Caesar's Palace. Our conversation turned into a job interview on a noisy Saturday night in Las Vegas as a boisterous crowd cheered on a hot roller at the craps table. The Prof and Flipchip were both fans of my poker blog, Tao of Poker, and the Prof had sought me out to write articles to accompany Flipchip's photos.

"Do you want to cover the World Series of Poker?" the Prof asked as a flock of gorgeous women in high heels and cocktail dresses sauntered by with a swarm of drunken frat boys on Spring Break chasing them down. "You'd have to move to Las Vegas for two months."

I desperately needed some sort of direction in my life, so when the Prof offered me an all-expenses-paid writing assignment, I dove head first down the rabbit hole and accepted his offer. I didn't even bother to ask about the finer points. After all, I was in my early thirties and supposed to be a writer but all I had to show for it were four unpublished novels and a really bad Project Greenlight screenplay.

The Prof's enticing offer sounded amazing because up until that point, I had been writing articles for a couple of poker websites, but those low-paying gigs barely covered my staggering ganja habit. In addition, with no place to live, I had been crashing on my brother Derek's couch in the Bronx. I had $450 in cash in my pocket and $1,000 in an online poker account at Party Poker. I was severely debt-ridden with a school loan and a couple of maxed-out credit cards. I played low-stakes online poker and frequented different underground card rooms in Manhattan, but I was nowhere close to good enough to make a real living as a professional poker player.

Besides needing to solve my money problems, I also desperately needed a break from an ongoing volatile relationship with a drug-addled Upper East Side-heiress to an elevator-button fortune. I had no more outs and was on the verge of swallowing my pride and asking my friend Señor for a job at his father's brokerage firm. A real job, as they say, one of those nine-to-five gigs where I'd have to wear a suit and sit shoulder to shoulder on a rush-hour subway with CrackBerry-addicts.

I was so excited that I didn't think about the fact that the opportunity of a lifetime might have fallen into my lap. I was more concerned about surviving two months in Las Vegas, and I hoped I didn't blow every paycheck on strippers and betting on baseball.

Las Vegas lures you to shed moral responsibility and piss away your money on indulgences like decadent food, entertainment, gambling, and sex. If you don't enjoy these pastimes, then what's the point of visiting the land of compromised values? Where else can you get a cheap steak, crash a Mexican wedding, get cold-decked in blackjack by a dealer named Dong, play video poker for thirteen straight hours, drink piña coladas out of a plastic coconut, bum a cigarette from an 85-year-old woman with an oxygen tank, speed away to the Spearmint Rhino in a free limo, get your dick rubbed by a former Miss Teen USA, puke in the back of a cab driven by a retired Navy SEAL, snort cheap cocaine in the bathroom at O'Sheas, and then catch a lucky card on the river to crack pocket aces and win a poker tournament? Only in Las Vegas.

Every day new dreamers arrive in Las Vegas hoping to fulfill their destiny. I moved to Vegas because I had no other place to go.

* * * * *

My new digs at the Budget Suites were in the shadows of the Las Vegas Strip on Tropicana Avenue across the street from the Wild Wild West Casino. This extended-stay hotel, which specialized in short-term housing, rented furnished apartments by the week. Transients lived there to save enough money for a nicer and safer place while the more downtrodden were trapped in purgatory.

I lived in one of twelve identical three-story generic motel buildings made up of sixty units. A concrete walkway separated my apartment from a small patch of grass and a couple of desert plants. A carport topped with flimsy pieces of metal shaded the cars parked in the row closest to the building. My front door stood ten feet from a pink-painted metal staircase which accessed the second and third floors. A white guardrail wrapped around the upper floors creating external hallways.

Two hundred bucks a week paid for a one-bedroom apartment that reeked of stale cigarette smoke and bleach. My sparse flat included a worn out wall to wall grey carpet with dozens of spill stains, leaky shower, kitchenette, tiny table with cigarette burns on the surface, two wobbly chairs, TV (with the remote control missing the #7 button), and a lumpy couch that could barely fit a sleeping child let alone an adult. The coffee table had a huge bite mark on one side. Too big to be a human. Must have been a dog. I hated to think it was a rat.

A thin wall separated the bedroom from the tiny living room. A bare mattress showed an odd-shaped stain that looked like the outline of the state of Florida. If you sent the mattress out for lab testing, God knows how many urine, feces, and semen samples you'd discover. When I called the front desk to ask about the missing linens, I found out that such luxuries ran an extra $8 a week. The room came with a phone that included free local calls, but no wi-fi or high-speed internet access, which meant I was stuck using a dial-up connection.

I immediately tested the air conditioning and was relieved that it worked – AC is critical for surviving Las Vegas summers. Somewhat satisfied that I found a place to call home for a while, I unloaded all my gear: a large black backpack with a sparse collection of clothes, and a smaller book bag that held my laptop, iPod and digital camera.

After the few minutes it took me to settle in, I headed out in search of local food options. These constituted a mini-mart in front of my complex, a 24-hour coffee shop across the street inside the Wild Wild

West Casino, and a hodgepodge of greasy fast food restaurants including my long-time favorite In-N-Out Burger.

Satisfied with my culinary recon mission, I loaded up on necessities – Gatorade, a jug of bottled water, and rolling papers. On my way back to my new home, I caught a glimpse of a family three doors down in apartment #1061 that apparently kept their door wide open at all times. I nicknamed their living room, "Michael Jackson's wet dream" because six kids, dressed only in underwear wrestled with each other over video games. Their hopeless mother stood outside chain-smoking a pack of Reds while groaning about losing her alimony check the previous night at the slot machines.

A skinny shirtless mulleted hooligan whizzed by on his skateboard almost knocking me over.

"Fuckin' little punk," I muttered.

He stopped and whirled around. "What building do you live in?"

"I don't live here," I lied, "I'm visiting my friends upstairs."

"Oh, the sexy strippers on the second floor?" the skateboard punk asked. "My mom said to stay away from those crackheads."

Chapter 2

June 2005.

Every day at high noon, young and eager gunslingers arrive on the outskirts of Las Vegas ready to take down the established pros and grizzled locals. This is not the plot to a John Ford western, rather, it is the World Series of Poker, where millions of dollars are on the line, new stars are born every few hours and the souls and dreams of many are crushed in the Darwinian process that is high-stakes tournament poker.

For almost seven weeks every summer, the Rio Hotel and Casino transforms into poker's version of Mecca. Tourists and media types from all over the world converge on the Rio to witness the world's largest and most prestigious poker tournament while hopeful players arrive with one thing in mind – a WSOP bracelet. These bracelets are badges of honor to the established pros and a measuring stick the media used to distinguish high-caliber players from average schleps.

The eternal flame of the American Dream had dulled to a flicker. Millions of lost souls found themselves sleepwalking through life, unexcited about the things, the places, and the people around them until a mild-mannered accountant from Tennessee by the name of Chris Moneymaker became the focal point of the gambling world. He was a living Cinderella story after winning a seat in the $10,000 Main Event via a satellite on PokerStars.com. He parlayed that $39 investment into $2.5 million.

Under the bright lights of downtown Las Vegas, Moneymaker's run at the Horseshoe Casino in May 2003 captivated an international audience as he survived an epic heads-up battle against local high roller Sammy Farha. In terms of physical appearance, Moneymaker looked like any guy in your home game. Clad in a PokerStars-branded golf shirt and hat, Moneymaker wore a pair of Oakley sunglasses as he stared down the slick Farha, who was clothed in an expensive black dinner jacket with his trademark unlit cigarette dangling from his lips. ESPN's cameras caught one of the greatest bluffs of all time from Moneymaker as he battled Farha for the championship. That moment revved the competitive juices inside every average Joe Six-Pack online poker player sitting at home watching the amateur defeat the Vegas fat cat.

Chris Moneymaker singlehandedly revitalized the American Dream and ignited the "poker boom." His victory inspired players to sit down and take a shot at the big time. Two years later, prize pools at the

2005 WSOP were the highest they had ever been as more players than ever dove into the orgiastic frenzy.

Spectators flocked to the Rio en masse to watch their favorite professional poker players and celebrities in nonstop action twenty-four hours a day. They gawked on the rail, pestered pros for autographs, and spent ungodly sums of money on garish paraphernalia. And these were the sober ones.

A wave of energy engulfed me as soon as I took my first step inside the Amazon Ballroom at the Rio. Larger than a football field, the overwhelming size of the tournament room resembled an airplane hangar. Hundreds of tables were illuminated by some of the brightest lights I had ever seen. The tables were filled with players from all over the world listening to their favorite hipster bands on iPods while others sported sunglasses to hide their timid eyes. More than a few fresh fish had that "deer caught in the headlights" look after finding themselves seated across from vets nicknamed Texas Dolly, Devilfish, Men the Master, and Johnny 'Fuckin' Chan.

From the corridor leading up to the poker room you could hear the clamor of clattering chips, a distinct sound that would not stop until a new WSOP Champion had been declared. Over the loudspeaker, a woman's voice told players when their seat to a specific cash game became available. Cocktail waitresses cautiously balanced trays as they delivered cheap beer, water, and Red Bull to the players. Chip runners sprinted from the cage to the cash game tables and back again trying not to knock over the waitresses.

Random displays of extreme anger, frustration, and jubilation could be seen throughout the ballroom from players weathering a sickening beat or surviving a desperate all-in attempt with a short stack. Floor managers refereed disputes between players, often giving them a ten-minute penalty for unruly behavior or excessive profanity.

In media row, writers from various news outlets exchanged gossip and chip counts on different players. In the hallways and in the bathrooms you could overhear players recounting their bad beat stories and other depressing tales of how they lost all of their chips. In the cash game section, pros pulled out bricks of $100 bills ready to take on other pros, hopeless suckers, and random celebrities with deep pockets who dropped by to see if they could hang with the big dogs in games that lasted past sunrise.

The long-shot dreamers could be found hanging out at the far end of the poker room in an area reserved for satellites. For as little as $50, you could try to earn your $10,000 seat in the Main Event by winning a series of smaller buy-in single-table tournaments. The satellites were filled with plenty of dead-money players from all walks of life: doctors from Long Island, building contractors from Virginia, college dropouts from California. The amateur piranhas fed on each other around the clock, hoping to turn their limited bankrolls into a chance to become the next multimillionaire at the WSOP.

Media row in the Amazon Ballroom became my office with a front-row seat to the action. In the past, I had worked at amazing locations such as the floor of the New York Commodities Exchange (in the former World Trade Center) and at the Metropolitan Museum of Art. The trenches of Wall Street have their own unique charm, to be sure, but I found myself preferring the quirks of my new working arrangement in media row. Flipchip and I set up next to the final table area where credentialed reporters and photographers clustered. Flipchip's seat remained largely unoccupied. He spent most of his time afield with his camera and mammoth lenses, using his ninja skills to pop up when and where you'd least expect.

441 Productions, the crew responsible for taping and producing ESPN's WSOP program, erected a television stage where the final tables were played out. Media row was draped in black cloth and the film crew encouraged us to wear dark clothing to blend into the background. We had the benefit of a large-screen TV that was hooked into the flop camera so reporters could view the board cards without stepping onstage to interrupt the filming process.

The Swedes from Poker Listings sat at the end of media row. They mostly kept to themselves and worked efficiently in tight shifts. Mike Paulle, a mountain of a man with a bushy white beard and long grey and white ponytail, worked for Poker Pages. With the exception of Flipchip, no one on media row had more seniority than Paulle, who was once the WSOP media director.

John Caldwell, the editor of Poker News, sat behind me. The former music industry exec had an impressive resume and headed up Hootie and the Blowfish's record label in South Carolina during the 1990s. As the road manager for the Stone Temple Pilots, he had the formidable task of keeping lead singer Scott Weiland out of trouble. Caldwell had traded rock and roll for poker.

The reporters from Card Player sat to my left. Walk into virtually any poker room in the country (Foxwoods, Tunica, Atlantic City, Los Angeles, Las Vegas) and you'll find a courtesy copy of Card Player magazine. It's the one poker magazine that just about everyone has read. BJ Nemeth had been working for Card Player as its lead tournament reporter for a year. He provided hand-for-hand coverage of the final tables in addition to taking photos and updating chip counts for the Card Player website. A lanky guy with a beard, BJ was always clad in a dress shirt with a Card Player logo over the front pocket. He was a one-man operation who worked insane hours. His stamina made more sense once I found out he ran marathons in his spare time.

Poker Wire employed two female reporters, Jen and Heather, who typically set up shop next to BJ. Poker Wire was a subsidiary of Full Tilt Poker, itself a relatively new online poker site determined to go all-out for the 2005 WSOP by aggressively expanding its brand. All of the pros affiliated with the site (including Phil Ivey, Howard Lederer, and Chris "Jesus" Ferguson) wore their own sports jerseys with their names on the back. As a part of this massive marketing campaign, Full Tilt created Poker Wire as a promotional tool to provide real-time chip counts of their sponsored and featured pros, as well as other notables in the field. On a daily basis Jen and Heather functioned as a well-oiled machine providing rabid fans with updates.

Jay Greenspan, a writer with an extensive vocabulary, was a fellow New Yorker from the mean streets of Greenpoint, Brooklyn. He had started a poker website several years earlier and then sold it for a nice chunk of change as the poker boom began ramping up. He decided to use the money to travel and play poker all over the country and the material he collected in those games became the meat of a book called *Hunting Fish*.

I nicknamed Greenspan "Big Shot" because of the sweet gig he landed writing final table recaps for Full Tilt. Tilt put him up at the Rio and paid him a generous daily rate that earned him more in a week than I would make the entire summer. I was insanely jealous and at the same moment in deep admiration of both his lofty accomplishments and poker skill. He would often disappear into the playing area only to return a short time later with a triumphant smile having won yet another single-table satellite.

The press room was located at the end of the main corridor and manned by Nolan Dalla, the WSOP media director. Nolan, a husky Texan with a red beard, wore a dapper suit and shiny shoes. His distinctive booming voice could be heard over a hundred yards away. The former sports handicapper had recently published *One of a Kind*, a book on the life of legendary poker pro Stu Ungar which he co-wrote with Peter Alson. Nolan handed me his glossy business card with a royal flush on the front. Classy. I handed him one of my cheap business cards that I had purchased before moving to Las Vegas – 500 for $4.99.

10

Amy Calistri was one of the many reporters who set up camp in the media room. She was always clad in a funky black cowboy hat, the same one that she compulsively wore in every single photo of her that I had seen. Amy, a well-known industry figure who wrote a gossip column for Bluff Magazine, somehow found out everyone's dirty secrets. If you wanted gossip on a pro, you asked Amy. Who's on the sauce? Ask Amy. Who's getting a divorce? Ask Amy. Who's fucking who? Ask Amy.

Aside from starting up the first series of blogs for Poker Pages, Amy also shot video interviews and daily recaps of the WSOP. The crew at Poker Pages published some of the best poker coverage in cyberspace including a comprehensive tournament database. Their team of reporters shared a mansion out in the suburbs where most of them sat around the living room playing online poker during their off hours.

Amy was kind enough to let me follow her around on my first day of work. We hung out in the hallway and she included me in her conversations with random pros as they smoked cigarettes on their breaks. I felt like the new kid being shown around by the most popular girl in school. We bumped into Lou Krieger, a pro and author from California who penned *Hold'em Excellence* and *More Hold'em Excellence*. He laughed when I called him "Mr. Krieger" after Amy introduced us.

"What's with the Mr. shit? Call me Lou," he said as we shook hands.

We didn't get to talk for very long before Lou's break in the Omaha 8 event ended. Amy used our brief meeting as the perfect illustration of the benefits of roaming the hallway. With the constant ebb and flow of people you never knew who you might see, which made it the perfect place to network, score gossip, and secure interviews.

I wandered back inside the media room and found Jen Leo, a writer from California who edited a series of award-winning women's travel books called *Sand in My Bra*. She had secured a blogging gig covering the WSOP for a new gambling site created by start-up entrepreneur Jason Calacanis. The always feisty Leo was up for anything including spending time at the craps tables and playing low-limit poker.

"Yo, Michalski, do you have any weed?"

To this day Dan Michalski insists that this is one of the first things I ever said to him at the WSOP. He's wrong. What I really said to him was, "Do you have any nugs? Because I have the sickest hook up, this Korean kid who thinks he's black."

Michalski created Pokerati.com, a website focusing on the Dallas poker scene. He ran weekly tournaments at the Lodge, the hottest strip club in Dallas. When he wasn't trying to bang strippers, he'd teach them how to deal poker. He hired them to work his weekly tournament and by the end of the night they were dealing naked after shedding all of their clothes for extra tips. Like most freelance journalists, Michalski made very little money. He was forced to crash at his grandmother's house in the suburbs in order to cut expenses.

Rounding out the media room were Steve "Foiled Coup" Hall and Oliver Tse. Foiled Coup, a British expat, had lived in America for the last couple of decades. Like John Caldwell, he once earned his living in the music industry in the 1990s before switching to the gambling world. Foiled Coup had a fetish for young Asian women, often pulling me aside to show me stealth photos he'd taken of random poker pros such as Evelyn Ng and Liz Lieu. He titled his photo galleries with "hot Asian chick of the day" and the "tit shot of the day."

Oliver Tse, an Asian-American business writer and sports journalist from the Bay Area, did everything by the book. He was an encyclopedia of poker information, rattling off statistics and obscure facts like he was Rain Man. Sporting coke-bottle glasses and dressing like a pall bearer, Tse was easily one of the more eccentric members of the poker media, yet he had no illusions about our job.

"We are entertainment-writer hacks," Tse explained, "We're the bottom of the food chain."

Chapter 3

June 2005.

I wasn't happy with the overall security of my ground-floor unit. Anyone could turn off Tropicana and roll into the ungated complex at any time. Animals roamed around outside in the 105 degree heat. Scrawny dogs, feral cats, and small shoeless sun-burned children ran around the parking lot. A roving band of miscreants terrorized the complex, pissing in the stairways and banging on doors at all hours. When someone answered, they scattered like cockroaches. I wanted to provide photographic evidence of this daily plight, but I knew I'd make myself a target if my neighbors caught me snapping pictures. I feared that the local authorities would find me with my throat slashed and my laptop would have been traded for a hand job from one of the crack whores strolling Tropicana.

I never had to set an alarm clock because the folks next door were kind enough to shout at each other at the top of their lungs. I was never sure whether their drugs were kicking in or wearing off, but I couldn't have asked for a more dependable wake-up call. In a sleepless city where clocks are rarely needed, Las Vegas destroyed my biological clock and any concept of time. I could never tell what day of the week it was. There was no distinction between a weekday and a weekend. Every day had a Saturday mentality. Just when I thought I had been living in Las Vegas for only a couple of days, I discovered it had been almost two weeks.

I covered the WSOP at the Rio with Flipchip until 5 a.m., and then returned to my apartment to write for a couple of hours. I usually passed out around 8 a.m. after an exhausting shift and by 11 a.m. it was "Redneck Family Hour" which came complete with drunken arguments, slap fights, and no less than a dozen malnourished children running rampant outside my window. Trying to fall back asleep while rowdy banshees re-enacted the Battle of Antietam in the parking lot, complete with a fireworks display and an accompanying soundtrack by Lynyrd Skynyrd brought frustration to a whole new level.

Flipchip knocked on my door and when I answered, I spotted a couple of my neighbors sitting on lawn chairs with inquisitive looks. One of the disheveled jackals spoke with a slight drawl.

"Are you one of them dealers on the World Poker Tour?" the fattest of the bunch barked.

He had a valid question. Flipchip and I looked like we could have been poker dealers, wearing all-black clothing with I.D. badges dangling around our necks. My neighbor's keen observational skills impressed me.

Note to self: *Never underestimate the intelligence of people with less than nine teeth.*

Ah, who the hell am I kidding? He was a shirtless inbred nitwit who drank Mike's Hard Lemonade for breakfast. His beer gut hung over his waistband by three and a half inches and he happily sported a "Fuck Osamma" tattoo on his left arm. I wanted to point out the spelling error but I was in a rush. I took all of my valuables to work with me, including my poker bankroll. I only left my clothes behind. If a speed freak wanted to steal my t-shirts and limited wardrobe for $50 worth of crank, then so be it.

Thinking back on it, I should have made an effort to get to know the delinquents who lived in my building. After all, they were simply misguided souls with unhappy childhoods. Besides, you never knew when you might need to score some OxyContin from Julio two buildings down.

I befriended a poker dealer at the Rio who looked like Stiffler from the *American Pie* movies. During one of the dinner breaks, he stopped me in the hallway and took note of my black Grateful Dead hat with a *Steal Your Face* logo. It turned out that he was also a Deadhead and we struck up a conversation. I eventually told him where I lived and a grim look came over his face.

"I hope you have a weapon," he said.

He told me that he had also experienced life at my apartment complex for two years while he dealt poker at a casino on The Strip.

"Don't leave anything lying around, especially cash," he explained. "My roommate was robbed twice. Most of the robberies in Vegas are inside jobs. You need to be careful especially if someone decides that you have something worth stealing."

Stiffler suggested that I pick up a weapon and even recommended a gun store. He wrote down the address and then asked to buy some of my pot before heading back to the tables.

The next morning, I called Joo-Chan. A photographer friend of mine in Brooklyn had met Joo during a previous trip to Las Vegas and referred me to him for my ganja needs. Joo was not your ordinary 21-year-old college student. He looked like he had walked off the set of a hip-hop video with his baggy pants, LeBron James basketball jersey, sideways hat, and enough neck bling to choke a horse. Joo's family had migrated from South Korea to Southern California when he was a baby.

14

He had moved to Las Vegas with his parents a few years before I met him. His mother owned two Subway franchises near UNLV and he worked for her as the assistant manager. Because he was upgrading his car to "pimp" status, a project that required a lot of cash, Joo sold pot to fund his expensive hobby.

Joo agreed to meet me before work. When he rolled up in his car, he handed me a bag of Subway cookies and then played me some of "his music." An aspiring hip-hop artist, he spent his free time honing his rhymes. I sat and listened for two minutes.

"What do you think, Doc?"

"It has potential. You have a lot of energy and passion in your music. The lyrics are deep. 'Bitch suck my fuckin' cock/or I'll shoot yo momma with my glock' is pure gold. You're speaking from the heart and that's what matters the most. Keep it up."

We bumped fists twice and he turned up his song.

"Doc, do you have a gun?" he asked. "Do you have any kind of weapon?"

I raised my right hand and clenched my fist. He didn't laugh.

"You got some crazy-ass motherfuckers living here. Sketchy, yo. New York crazy is one thing. But this is Las Vegas crazy, yo. These stupid motherfuckers don't know any better. As soon as they find out you don't have a gun, they'll rob your ass."

"I got nothing to rob."

"They don't know that shit! All they know is that you're a punk-ass bitch without a piece and they are gonna bust in and take all your shit. If you don't got anything they're gonna beat your ass down."

I sat in silence pondering Joo's advice. Hell, maybe I should get a gun. A big one. Something that will blow out chunks of flesh the size of a manhole cover.

"I know a real gun dealer with a store and shooting range. If you buy a gun there, you get to use his range for free for a month. It's not cheap, but they give you free fuckin' bullets to use at the range. Think about it, Doc. You got some crazy-ass motherfuckers living at your place."

Joo grabbed a small bag out of the back seat of his car. He dug around for a few seconds before he pulled out a hunting knife and handed it to me.

"It's not much, but I'd carry that fucker around with you at night," he suggested. "I'm surprised that you're living in that ghetto crib. Here's the number of the gun dealer. Call him tomorrow."

I thanked him for looking out for me. Within 24 hours, two locals had told me to buy a gun. They must have known something I didn't.

* * * * *

The left-handed Las Vegas Metro police officer had horrible handwriting. He scribbled a couple of things that I told him about the early morning shouting sessions and slap fights from the trouble-makers next door.

"Does this have anything to do with the shooting yesterday?" I asked.

He ignored my question. I had heard rumors that someone had been shot in an adjacent unit. Supposedly, it was a drug deal gone bad and a trigger-happy speed freak shot up the place. His getaway vehicle was a stolen bicycle. At least that's what old lady Agnes in the wheelchair told me. She lived at the end of the hall and constantly spit sunflower seeds out her window. Despite her one glass eye, she was the building's version of the *National Enquirer*. She had been pumping me for information since I moved in, but I told her nothing. The less anyone knew about me, the better.

On my walk over to grab a double cheeseburger and a chocolate shake at In-N-Out Burger, I spotted Agnes and told her about my morning wake-up call from the police. That's when she spilled the beans. The thug next door to me beat the shit out of one of his girlfriend's kids. When the girlfriend confronted him, he wigged out and broke her jaw, then stole her car and took off.

On my way back from lunch, I spotted two maids and the manager cleaning out the room. While they hauled out jumbo trash bags, the manager held her nose as she wiped the blood-splattered walls.

Sprinkled among the bizarre inhabitants, some "normal" people also lived there. Casino workers sporting their uniforms and costumes walked to their cars at odd hours headed to their shifts. Construction workers with out of state license plates from Utah, California, and Arizona parked or drove off in their pickup trucks to work on projects around Las Vegas, a city constantly under development. Although the construction workers were relatively quiet during the weekdays, weekends were a completely different story, especially on payday weekend. Then they raged hard in random rooms around the complex attracting dealers and working girls.

Where there's money, there's sex, and Las Vegas overflows with both at the crossroads of some of the largest sex trafficking enterprises in North America. The problems were already spinning out of control when aptly named Mayor Oscar Goodman attempted to legalize prostitution in Las Vegas in late 2003. Although prostitution is legal in Nevada, it is outlawed within the Las Vegas city limits, so the closest legal brothels are a couple of hours away.

Although prostitution is illegal within city limits, private escort services cater to the needs of tourists. These services blatantly advertise in free adult magazines and they hire "porn slappers" on The Strip to get your attention. Porn slappers are mostly illegal immigrants who hand out business cards and brochures for the various escort services. By law they are not allowed to talk to you, so they have to make snapping and slapping noises with the cards to get your attention. These porn slappers are a Las Vegas institution that any visitor has experienced.

In addition to supporting private escort services, the Las Vegas Valley hosts massage parlors that specialize in rub-and-tugs by Asian sex slaves. Freelance working girls frequent the bars at Strip casinos and will fuck your brains out in your hotel room for a few hundred bucks. Many of the casinos look the other way; others are paid off by the pimps or the girls themselves.

Probably the most dangerous level on the prostitute food chain is the lowly street walker. Jack the Ripper allegedly killed almost a dozen of them in London. The majority of the Green River serial killer's 48 victims were streetwalkers. Las Vegas hookers disappear every day, but does anyone really care? The local streetwalkers mostly congregate on Tropicana Avenue around where I lived, extending past The Orleans casino a mile or so away.

The Wild Wild West offered up cheap rooms for as little as $19.99 a night, making it a popular housing option among both the Trop hookers and weary truck drivers stopping for the night in Las Vegas before driving on with their cargoes. The Trop hookers prey on the truckers at the bar inside the Wild Wild West or they hang out in bus shelters (to appear less suspicious to any vice cops out on patrol) and wait for drive-ups. They lure johns to their rooms, do the nasty, and then return to Trop to repeat the process until sunrise when they disappear like vampires evading the first rays of sun.

My transient apartment complex seemed to attract every unsavory character who had fallen through the cracks of society only to end up in Las Vegas seeking that one big score. These unfortunate ones, whether in love or in life, always think their luck will change in Las Vegas. It rarely does, so they end up renting a place in between tweakers cooking a fresh batch of Nazi crank and a team of strung-out cokehead prostitutes who roll drunken tourists to feed their $200-a-day addiction.

A dealer lived down the hall to my left. Coke? Smack? Ice? Probably all of the above. Every twenty minutes, cars drove up and customers sprinted to the door, anxiously knocked, completed the transaction, and drove off.

Whenever I left for work, I always worried that someone's meth lab in an adjacent building would blow up and destroy the possessions that I did not take with me on my daily rounds. Upon my return home every day I tried to mentally prepare myself for a fight upon stepping out of Flipchip's car. I also always expected to find my apartment broken into, so I'd make sure I searched the place thoroughly for signs of theft. Once I completed my inspections and deemed it safe, I continued my nightly routine. I'd shower, read my notes, smoke a joint, brainstorm, and complete my writing assignments.

One early morning, a few minutes past sunrise, I had just emailed my daily recap to the Prof when I heard a car pull up. I peeked out of the blinds and saw two girls wearing slutty outfits stumbling out of a taxi while screaming at one another.

"Why didn't you fucking wait for me?" snapped a buxom blonde hauling an oversized gym bag.

"I didn't know you wanted me to!" shot back a tiny tattooed redhead carrying a leopard-skin purse.

"Stupid bitch! I told you when we were in the bathroom."

"No you didn't. You're fucked up!"

"Fuck you, bitch."

"Coke slut. You always get fucked up and think you said things when you didn't!"

"Shut the fuck up bitch or I'll beat your ass down."

"Try it cunt face!"

The two scuffled in front of my door. They swung their bags at each other before they graduated to hair pulling. Both screeched like raccoons in a rumble, but it wasn't even a close fight. The blonde whaled on the smaller redhead, who absorbed two punches to the face before she fell down. The blonde grabbed both bags and sprinted up the stairs into the apartment. The redhead unleashed a trail of obscenities and ran after her friend. She banged on the door and her friend refused to let her in. Locked out, she caused a ruckus for about forty minutes shouting, "I'm gonna call Rocco! He's gonna fuck you up and carve out your implants!"

Welcome to the Redneck Riviera.

Chapter 4

June 2005.

The morning sun sizzled 111 degrees while a roach the size of a poodle scurried underneath my front door. The parking lot was littered with tiny empty frayed baggies and the condom wrappers in the stairwell told of the usual slovenly events of the night before.

I had hacked up a piece of lung the size of Paris Hilton's dog. Flipchip referred to this as "The Cough," a common ailment among most non-Nevadans during their first few weeks in the desert. I had a feeling it was going to linger.

Voices coming from outside the door were clear enough to make me peek through the blinds. Then I sat and watched with morbid curiosity as a chubby hooker and an old white guy exchanged money in the stairwell. The hooker dropped her jean skirt and he banged her from behind. After the first thirty seconds she asked if he was done yet. After four and a half minutes I could tell she was getting exasperated.

"Jesus, mercy me! Are you done yet?"

You know you've hired a bad hooker when after a few seconds she's asking if you're done. Those disturbing visions danced in my head when I fought the blazing heat and walked across the street to the coffee shop at Wild Wild West. Mrs. Flipchip said they had good breakfast specials and suggested I try one. I only ate two meals a day, so after a week of Wendy's, In-N-Out Burger, and Subway it was time to expand my breakfast palate. I felt like that dude from *Super Size Me* when my kidneys began throbbing from all the recycled grease.

I devoured French toast, bacon, hash browns, and drank an iced tea with lemon while reading a copy of USA Today. Discovering an inexpensive place to eat only a few minutes from the Redneck Riviera was a godsend. The only problem was the deplorable service. Well, that and the casino freaked me out. The Wild Wild West was a low budget casino, a side of Las Vegas missing from guidebooks and travel magazines. Now I understood why. It was like walking into a time machine and zapping yourself back to 1981. The clientele at the Wild Wild West were older than Bob Hope and sat at the bar in silence while drinking $1.49 draft beer specials and chasing keno jackpots. Geriatric ladies shoved pennies into slot machines in between huffs on bulky oxygen tanks attached to the backs of their wheelchairs. It was a hospice with slots, and the owners were more than happy to accept the remnants of Social Security checks.

A pregnant teenager who looked a bit like Scarlett Johansson with smaller tits served me. I stared at the large silver crucifix dangling around her neck and wondered what it must be like to carry around a bowling ball all day.

"What's your name?" asked the Jesus freak waitress.

"Paul," I said. "My friends call me Pauly."

"I like Paul. It's a good Christian name."

I felt guilty for getting annoyed with her slow-as-shit service. She worked at quite possibly the worst restaurant in Vegas and I knew she was getting stiffed by all the broke gamblers who showed up to eat the $1.99 cheeseburger special because they were down to their last $2. We made small-talk and I found out that she also lived at the Redneck Riviera, a couple of buildings down from me. I made a crack about all the pot-bellied kids with mullets that lived in the pool, and when she didn't laugh I spent the rest of the meal wondering if she was offended because the rugrats were hers.

I did my good deed for the day; I left $5 on a $9 check.

* * * * *

The Rio's hallways were a zoo during breaks, congested with spectators and players smoking tough. Thick clouds of second-hand smoke hovered a few inches above my head. A group of girls wearing fishnet stockings, hooker boots, and short black skirts worked the Havana Honeys cigar booth in the hallway. I could always count on at least one of the vixens to tempt me with a cigar when I walked past. I overheard one girl say she was too tired from dancing (on the pole) the night before. Flipchip snapped a few photos of the girls and showed me a couple of his shots, when Dan Michalski wandered over and interrupted my ogling.

"I gotta say Doc, I'm disappointed about the lack of liquor in the media room," he said. "Hunter Thompson would be sorely disappointed. I'm gonna bring in a bottle of hooch one of these afternoons and then we can do some drunken live-blogging. So, are you holding?"

We went outside to the parking lot and I rolled us a joint of Joo's weed. We sat inside a Ford Taurus, a loaner from Grandma Michalski, who had knitted a dainty pink steering wheel cover with little flowers on it to keep the blistering desert sun from overheating the wheel. We smoked up and chatted as Michalski drove around in circles.

On my way back into the convention area, I bumped into Mrs. Flipchip. She told me that a wasted guy had just wandered up to her in the hallway and offered to sell her some ecstasy. My immediate stoned response was, "How much?" and I quickly followed up with, "Did you score me any?"

Sadly, the answer was "no." Instead, she dug into her purse and pulled out two $100 bills. She had hit a big score for a couple of grand at the slot machines and wanted to share the wealth.

"Here you go, Sweetie," she said. "You're working so hard and we're hardly paying you anything. Please take this. If you don't take it, then I'll piss it back away at those terrible evil slots."

* * * * *

Once again, I had only been asleep for a couple of hours when a series of large crashing and thumping sounds woke me up. I glanced at my clock: 9:04 a.m. Two people screamed and a loud bang followed. Just another altercation in the parking lot.

Fuckin' hell, there's shooting right outside my door and I'm rolling over and trying to go back to sleep. What have I become?

I brushed off the unkempt skater kids who routinely knocked on my front door and asked me to sell them rock. The urine-soaked pants of the homeless drunk passed out in my stairwell left a stench that had become all too common. I constantly worried about all the tweakers, gang bangers, cops, politicians, hustlers, hookers, suits, and everyone else of dubious moral value. In a city full of losers, thieves, and drug fiends, who could you trust? But none of them scared me more than I scared myself. I doubted my ability to survive another day.

After forty minutes of self-loathing in bed, I gave up and walked across the street to Wild Wild West. I was hungry and hoping to see my new favorite girl. As I waited for an open table, the pregnant waitress lumbered past. She remembered my name and quickly hustled me over to her section. I called her Suzy a couple of times and she politely corrected me. Her real name was Elizabeth.

"I started working here last week," she said. "And they didn't have a name tag for me so I had to wear an old one."

"You could always cross it out with a marker and write your name by hand," I suggested.

"I could have, but I never liked my name too much. Suzy sounds better, don't ya think?"

"Yeah. It works for me. Suzy."

I sensed that she wanted to stay and chat, but a customer was always trying to get her attention, and I didn't want to hold up her already slow service. When the meal was over, Suzy handed me the check and refilled my iced tea.

"So what is a nice person like you doing here?" she asked.

"I was about to ask you the same thing," I said. "I'm a writer on an assignment covering the World Series of Poker at the Rio. And how do you know I'm nice?"

"I can see the good in people."

"Like auras?"

"Something like that. It's more like some people are brighter than others. They shine. You know, they give off light. They stand out from the rest because mostly everyone else is dim. They're fuzzy. Does that make any sense?"

I wasn't sure how to answer that one.

"Oh, I'm sorry, never mind," she said as she touched my arm. "I'm just babbling. I didn't mean to freak you out or anything like that."

"You're not freaking me out. And, I believe you. People have energy fields and give off vibes. I just think that you're way off with your assessment of me."

"Well, maybe I was stretching the truth a bit with you. Honest to Jessup, I see a lot of brightness, but with a few dark spots here and there."

"That I believe. So, now that we've talked about the spots on my soul, you have to tell me how you ended up here."

Suzy never answered. A portly trucker at an adjacent table was demanding her services. I left another exorbitant tip and skipped out without saying goodbye.

* * * * *

I took a well-deserved half-day off, which meant that Flipchip and I worked eight hours that day instead of eighteen. I was itching for action at the poker tables and decided to play in the late morning tournament at the Aladdin. There wasn't much time to spare before play began so I tried to be efficient by calling for a cab before I jumped in the shower. The dispatcher said ten to fifteen minutes, which usually means thirty. In New York City, all I had to do was step off a curb and raise my arm. In Vegas, if you weren't at a taxi stand, you had to call and wait. And wait I did. After forty-five minutes I called the dispatcher who assured me that a cab was on the way. I waited twenty more minutes and called back angrily. The dispatcher told me, "Fifteen minutes."

"You said that to me over an hour ago!"

I finally gave up after waiting outside for an hour sweating my ass off waiting for a cab that would never show. The Redneck Riviera was a no-fly zone, even during the day. I couldn't really blame them.

I gazed at the skyline of the faux New York City in the distance. The collective fakeness of The Strip's carbon copy of NYC made me even more homesick. I finally trudged back inside to log onto Party Poker. If you ever want to feel like a degenerate loser, play online poker in Las Vegas on a dial-up connection. Sylvia Plath level depression began sinking in as I missed another flush draw and realized I was smoking my last bit of ganja. I considered turning on the oven and sealing my windows to escape my misery.

I brushed off the sudden suicidal thoughts by searching for something productive to do. Laundry quickly came to mind since my last clean underwear had just soaked through while I waited for the no-show cab. I gathered my dirty clothes and headed down to the vending machine in the laundry room in search of detergent. No such luck. I was obviously running bad. The manager at the front desk told me to try the gas station, and so, with my laundry over my shoulder, I walked three blocks in the stifling heat only to find out that the cashier at the gas station did not speak English and had no clue what I was talking about. I searched the aisles and found nothing. During the walk back I nurtured the faint hope that I would find a friendly neighbor in a giving mood. Instead, I found an obese woman smoking a menthol cigarette while folding oversized panties as she watched Oprah on the TV attached to the wall. I told her my sad story and she offered to sell me a cup of liquid Tide for $20.

"Piss off," I barked. "$20? Come on, I could get a crappy handjob from one of the crack whores in the building next door for $20. I'll wear dirty boxers for one more day."

No cab. No live poker. No detergent. No clean underwear. I couldn't catch a break until I bumped into Suzy wearing a flowery summer dress. It was the first time I'd seen her out of her drab waitress uniform.

"So you never finished your story about how you ended up here," I pressed.

"Well, if you really want to know," she said, rubbing her stomach, "I'll tell you the short version. I kinda got pregnant. Obviously. My loser boyfriend dumped me. I left St. George and I moved in with my sister who lives here. But her husband had a bad gambling problem and he lost all their money and couldn't afford to pay the mortgage, so the bank foreclosed on the house. That loser skipped town and we had to move. So it's me, my sister, and her two kids living here while we wait to find a new place. The first night here, we went across the street to eat at the Wild Wild West, and I saw the Help Wanted sign. I really needed the money and got the job the next day."

She quizzed me some more about my line of work while randy thoughts infested my brain.

"I forgot to tell you that I've been watching poker on the TV," Suzy said. "It seems exciting. Do you play too?"

"Of course," I said, as I stared at a bead of sweat running down the side of her face. I'd never had sex with a pregnant woman before, but the sundress and the sweat had me thinking about it. "By the way, sorry to change the subject, but I have this thing tomorrow night. Umm... it's an opening of some art show, along with a book signing downtown. Umm, if you wanted to go..."

"I'd like to but I can't," she said rather quickly. "My sister works the swing shift, so I have to watch her kids."

Rejected by a pregnant Jesus freak waitress. My ego reeled. On the walk back I tried to shrug it off by telling myself it was fate reminding me to stay away from troubled girls, but I knew that was bullshit. Then again, maybe I frightened her and she thought I was a potential serial killer who would strangle her and sell her unborn fetus on the black market to the highest bidder. White babies fetched a nifty price in Sin City.

Utterly humiliated, I returned to my apartment where I hopped in the shower and masturbated furiously.

Chapter 5

June 2005.

Flipchip handed me an envelope with my first official payment of the WSOP. We hopped in his car and drove to Smith's, the local grocery store chain that, like every other grocery store in Las Vegas, housed a bank of slot machines conveniently located near the exit. In New Orleans, you can buy hard liquor in supermarkets, but in Las Vegas, you can buy hard liquor and then piss away the rest of your grocery money at some of the loosest machines in all of Nevada. Picking up milk and eggs was an impossible task with gambling demons molesting you with their temptations.

I purchased laundry detergent, a new notebook, and a plunger. The plumbing in my apartment was terrible and the toilet was constantly clogged. I had to leave a $10 deposit and my driver's license at the main office every time I wanted to borrow a plunger – which at that point was occurring every other night. The previous hooker tenants clogged up the pipes with soiled condoms.

The brutal schedule was kicking me in the junk every few hours. I was constantly fatigued but my dour mood softened when Otis arrived (albeit a couple of weeks late) from Greenville, South Carolina. He was an award-winning television reporter turned poker writer and an integral part of a website called Up for Poker that covered the underground poker scene in South Carolina. Otis was the first blogger I knew who had landed a full-time job in the poker industry. He got his start heading up the PokerStars official blog and flew all over the world covering the PokerStars Caribbean Adventure in the Bahamas and the newly formed European Poker Tour.

Otis noticed that the long hours and lack of sleep were taking a toll on my physical state. I may have looked like a zombie, but I never missed a deadline. On some regretful nights, however, I rushed my assignments and turned in sloppy copy, cranked out at the end of an eighteen-hour shift. As long as the recaps came in on time and weren't full of shit I was golden.

"Slow down, man."

Otis' advice was a clear reflection of the fact that I really had no plan for how to cover the WSOP. At the end of each night (more like around 6 or 7 a.m. every morning), I emailed my daily recaps to the Prof and Flipchip would then upload a couple of his photos for the article. The sole reason I was in Las Vegas in the first place was to cover the final tables and write daily recaps for LasVegasVegas.com, but I soon picked up gigs with Poker Player Newspaper and FoxSports.com. If the suits at Fox Sports liked what they read, they would add it to the front page of the poker section. I guess that the long hours were paying off, because inside of a few short weeks, I had gone from crashing on my brother's couch to writing a feature story on Fox Sports.

At least one final table is scheduled for every day during the WSOP, and on some days two or three tournaments ran simultaneously when players busted out at a slower rate than anticipated. Regardless, it was hell for a single media person trying to keep up.

I used my poker blog, Tao of Poker, as an electronic notepad for jotting down hands and thoughts about the action and trying to squeeze in updates on the general happenings in the Amazon Ballroom when I could. The immediate gratification of live blogging updates became more popular than the end-of-day recaps, with increasing numbers of friends and readers constantly refreshing my blog. Tao of Poker was one of the few websites providing updates in real-time. While many poker and gambling websites were inaccessible thanks to proliferating nanny state directives, I thanked the poker gods that somehow Tao of Poker continued to circumvent anti-gaming firewalls.

Adaptation to my new desert surroundings came slowly as I consumed bottled water at a staggering rate trying to hold the constant threat of dehydration at bay. In frequent trips to the toilet I was always amazed how at any given time I'd find myself right next to one of the world's premier poker players. "The Last 5 Pros I Pissed Next To" was born and became a popular segment on Tao of Poker. It was a complete joke, sort of like a throw-away sketch on *Saturday Night Live* (e.g. "Wayne's World") that somehow became an instant hit.

During my time playing online over the previous year I had befriended a former AOL executive turned semi-pro from Golden Valley, Arizona named Felicia Lee. She and her husband relocated to the desert from Virginia because of her ailing health. In a short time Felicia had become one of the top seven-card stud players in the area. She had also done a brief stint as a tournament reporter and knew firsthand the negative aspects of the job, including the random difficulties that unexpectedly arose every day.

"You're a writer, so write, dumbass!" she said. "I don't care about who busted with aces or who's the chip leader. Tell us what's really going on. If someone kicks a chair, then write about it. If someone is trash-talking, tell us what he's saying."

I heeded Felicia's judicious advice and every day more new readers tuned in. Wil Wheaton linked up Tao of Poker's WSOP updates on his blog, wilwheaton.net (or WWdN for short). The star of the film *Stand By Me* and a cast member of *Star Trek: The Next Generation* had moved away from acting and made a successful transition into freelance writing. His cult-following fans, thousands of them, checked his site every day to find out what was going on in his life. Wil caught the poker bug and read every possible book on the subject, and though we had never met, we exchanged several emails and played against one another in different online tournaments.

Earlier that year, Wil appeared on an episode of the World Poker Tour's Hollywood Home Game (the *Star Trek* edition) and played in the WPT Championships. He almost made the money until Annie Duke cracked his pocket kings and knocked him out. Wil's solid play and his fervent online following drew the attention of PokerStars. That garnered an invitation for him to join Team PokerStars, a small group of pros and celebrities who represented PokerStars in both online tournaments and live events. Other members of Team PokerStars included 2003 World Champion Chris Moneymaker, 2004 World Champion Greg Raymer, and French-Canadian hottie Isabelle Mercier.

I hit the wall three weeks into the WSOP and was about to crack when I received an uplifting email from Wil. He cheered me up when he mentioned that he religiously followed updates on Tao of Poker and loved reading about my apartment complex. One line stood out in his email... *"Remember to take care of you, or the Redneck Riviera will suck your soul right out of your body and feed it to a crack baby."*

Wil understood some of my struggles and equated my rough acclimation to living on a film set for months at a time. He suggested that I stop working through my dinner breaks and use that time to relax. His bits of positive feedback kept me going on days when I felt I was wasting my time screaming into the void of the internet.

* * * * *

Given the choice, I preferred covering no-limit hold'em over other variations of tournament poker. No cap on betting means that players can find themselves eliminated at any given time, as opposed to limit or split-pot events like Omaha high/low in which a player's journey to the bottom of their chip stack typically takes much longer. The Razz final table, for example, lasted past sunrise. Because the event was not televised and played out away from the TV set, the floor staff allowed an exhausted Amy Calistri to take a seat at the end of the final table during the never ending heads-up play.

Covering the typically faster-paced (with a few exceptions) no-limit structure meant that I stood a decent chance of getting more than two hours of sleep. During lulls at final tables, I worked on various freelance assignments while Poker Wire Jen shopped online for shoes and purses and still managed to somehow maintain her chip count duties. Other media reps fed their inner action-junkies by playing online poker. During slow periods, Flipchip drove home to upload pictures. He'd keep an eye on Tao of Poker and when the action got down to three players he'd jump in his car and return to the Rio to snap shots of the winner posing with a bracelet and a newly acquired mountain of cash. Some players excitedly held up their winning cards while others just stood there looking too exhausted to care. The winner's photo exists to preserve a poker player's hard-won moment of triumph and Flipchip never missed one.

On slow nights, I pestered Flipchip for stories about his time in Vietnam. He was a decorated vet, and like most who were there, he didn't relish the idea of talking about it after the fact. Still, he opened up on a few sleep-deprived nights. To my surprise, he told me that it was "in country" where he picked up a camera for the first time.

"I was supposed to be a machine gunner," Flipchip said. "One morning I was standing next to my CO and a Major stopped by carrying a camera. He needed someone to take photos of dead VC a couple of clicks away. He handed the camera to the CO, who handed it to me, so I hiked to the spot and took the photos. That's how I got my start, taking photos of dead bodies. I took photos the rest of my tour."

Flipchip told me that while growing up in East Texas he'd been bit of a square who had some big adjustments to make during his first weeks in the jungle.

"A couple of the black guys in my unit kept giving me shit. They said that I was too jumpy and that I needed to smoke some pot or I was going to end up getting everyone killed. I had no idea what pot was at that time. I knew that the hippies smoked it, but I couldn't have told you what it looked like or where to get it, especially in a foreign country. One of them said, 'Bro, just look around. It's growing everywhere!' while the other walked over to a stalk and grabbed a fistful of leaves and rolled it up for me. Man, what a buzz. Coping was a lot easier with it than without it, that's for sure."

Some of the stories were hysterical, like hearing about their vernacular for the local prostitutes, LBFMs, or "Little Brown Fucking Machines." But some of his stories were downright dark and confusing, like the Thanksgiving turkey drop.

Flipchip had been in the jungle with his unit for weeks. On Thanksgiving morning, they were told that a batch of fresh provisions, including a turkey meal, were to be dropped off later that day. They worked all morning and afternoon clearing a landing zone by hand, using machetes to take out trees and bamboo and whatever else was in their way. They waited and waited and as soon as the first helicopters arrived with their Thanksgiving dinner, a couple of soldiers in his unit sprayed the helicopter with gun fire.

"They took it out. It crashed before they could drop us off our dinner."

"What? Why would grunts work all day to clear a landing zone for a helicopter flying in a much-anticipated turkey dinner, and then shoot it down when it approached?"

"That's the thing about Nam," Flipchip said. "We were kids and there was no logic there. Nothing made sense and there were no rules. Unless you were there, you have no idea how absurd it was."

Chapter 6

June 2005.

Jason "Spaceman" Kirk, a friend of mine from Ashland City, Tennessee, authored a Nashville Predators hockey blog. Spaceman sent me an email containing bad news about his best friend, Charlie Tuttle, who had been diagnosed with terminal cancer. Charlie was rushed to the hospital because a series of tumors had pressed up against his lungs resulting in serious breathing problems.

Although I had never met Charlie, we had played a lot of online poker together. In one tournament, I knocked him out on a vicious bad beat when I moved all-in with the Hammer (7-2 offsuit) against Charlie's pocket kings. We were in a three-way pot where a third player was all-in with pocket aces. I caught a miracle and flopped trip sevens. It held up. I won the pot and busted both players. Charlie sent me a Nashville Predators hockey puck as a bounty for busting him. I felt bad about cracking his kings, so I sent him a Phish bootleg.

Charlie's favorite pro was the flamboyant and entertaining Marcel Luske from Holland. Marcel sported finely tailored suits at the table, wore his sunglasses upside down, and despite his thick Dutch accent, was known to spontaneously break into song. Spaceman asked me to convince Marcel to call Charlie in the hospital, but the Amazon Ballroom was enormous and I didn't know if I could find him. I recruited Flipchip to help me and he kept an eye out for Marcel in the congested hallways.

We got lucky that afternoon when Flipchip bumped into Marcel who agreed to call Charlie. I contacted Charlie's mother and we spoke for a minute before she handed the phone to Charlie in his hospital bed. That was the first and only time we spoke.

"Thanks for calling," Charlie struggled to say between troubled gasps for air.

"I wish we could talk longer, but there's someone I want you to talk to."

I handed the phone to Marcel. He and Charlie spoke for ten minutes while I returned to work. Spaceman later told me that he was in the room when Marcel called. He said that Charlie laughed for the first time in ages. Marcel Luske gained all of our respect for doing something special for someone he didn't even know. Marcel made a tremendous effort to help ease Charlie's pain and even sang to him.

"What I really remember the most about that time is that so many people reached out to Charlie, and they made him smile while he still had enough energy to do that," explained Spaceman about the impact of the poker community's goodwill.

The entire situation sunk in when Marcel returned my cell phone. I was overcome by an unexpected wave of sadness and walked outside to collect myself. Charlie was bedridden and on his last breaths while I hung out with poker pros in Las Vegas. It didn't seem fair.

When I returned to media row, Max Pescatori was waiting for me and offered to buy me coffee. The Italian Pirate was one of my favorite professional players and the mainstream poker media had no clue about him. Max was originally from Milan, Italy but had been living in Vegas for several years trying to make it as a pro. Max sent Charlie a care package that included a copy of *Doyle Brunson's Super System 2* autographed by Todd Brunson, Jennifer Harman, and the legendary Doyle Brunson himself. Max had also called Charlie after Felicia Lee had rallied pros such as Barry Greenstein, John Juanda, and Ted Forrest to phone Charlie at home. They didn't do it for publicity; they did it because they cared. Despite being sharks at the tables, the hearts of some of the biggest names in poker were filled with compassion.

Later that evening, I bumped into Marcel Luske in the hallway. He had busted out of his event and didn't want to talk about poker. Instead, he asked about Charlie. Although Marcel had never met Charlie, there was an intense concern on his face as though Charlie was a family member.

"Life is incredibly precious and we need to enjoy every day," Marcel said.

Filpchip and I had a rough Monday ahead of us with three tournaments to cover, including the final table of Event #19 $1,500 Pot-Limit Omaha which included Chris "Jesus" Ferguson and Barry Greenstein in the hunt for a bracelet. The final table was held on ESPN's set but was not being taped. Despite a couple of popular big-named players at the table, the grandstand was mostly empty.

During one of the breaks, Barry Greenstein sat in the empty bleachers and ate a cheeseburger. Greenstein played in the highest-stakes cash games in the world including the "Big Game" with Doyle Brunson and Chip Reese at the Bellagio. Greenstein is known as the "Robin Hood of Poker" because he donates a percentage of his tournament winnings to various charities including Children, Inc.

I wandered over and thanked him for calling Charlie. Between bites, Greenstein told me that he was going to dedicate the win to Charlie when he won the event. He specifically did not say "if" he won; he said "when" he won. That was a bold prediction but Greenstein was confident in his abilities. When I thanked him again, he said something that I'll never forget.

"It's easy to do a good deed."

Although we're supposed to be impartial as members of the media, I rooted for Greenstein. He mounted an amazing comeback and won two big pots off Toto Leonidas to get back into contention. Greenstein found himself heads-up with an amateur player named Paul Vinci and quickly finished him off. Greenstein won the tournament and collected his second career bracelet.

"This is for you, Charlie Tuttle," Greenstein said to the audience. He couldn't really speak much more because he had to rush over to the pot-limit hold'em tournament and play in that event. I thanked him again as we walked over to his table. Along the way, Greenstein fought back tears. One of the coolest and calmest poker players in the world was overwhelmed with a plethora of emotions.

I escaped to the hallway and found a corner where I lost it. Otis wandered over. He was visibly upset too. After a quick interview with Nolan Dalla about Charlie, I headed to the bar by myself and downed a few double shots of Southern Comfort to dull the emotions so I could get back to work.

I stayed up until sunrise writing an article called "A Guy Named Charlie" for Poker Player Newspaper. The publisher, Stan Sludikoff, ran it as the feature story under the title "Barry Greenstein Dedicates Bracelet." It was my first cover story for Poker Player Newspaper. Fox Sports also ran the article on its website.

Charlie Tuttle died at his home in Clarksville, Tennessee less than 24 hours after Barry Greenstein dedicated a bracelet victory to him. Charlie was only 26 years old.

But the story did not end there. Greenstein had sent the very first copy of his book *Ace on the River* to Charlie. Although Charlie never got a chance to read the book, it was among the many items placed on the memento table at his funeral.

"Barry Greenstein dedicating his bracelet to Charlie was a very gracious thing to do and is indicative of why he's a step above so many others in the game in terms of class," Spaceman explained. "I just think that for those of us here in Tennessee, because of the timing, Barry's gestures *after* Charlie's death were really more impressive and meant a lot more than the bracelet dedication. The following January at the World Poker Open in Tunica, he met up with Charlie's parents, spent the day with them, and then took them out to a really nice dinner. I know he has also sought them out on return trips to Tunica. Anyone can dedicate a bracelet, and it's really cool to do so, but to stay involved after the fact is much more impressive."

Sometimes life can be as fragile as a house of cards and the littlest movement or vibration can make it all tumble over. But sometimes, a good deed can zip through the cosmos and illuminate our desolate universe. Anyone who has spent an inordinate amount of time on the circuit knows that tournament poker is a cutthroat business. The word "friend" is often tossed around half-heartedly because after all, there are no friends at the poker tables.

Las Vegas is a city built on greed and poker is a game that often attracts some of the lowest forms of life. Amid all the darkness and debauchery, I caught a few glimpses of humanity's bright side. Although all the goodwill in the world could not prevent Charlie from dying, those good deeds reminded everyone involved that there is more to life than poker.

Chapter 7

June 2005.

The food on the banquet tables in the Rio hallways disgusted me. The crust on the greasy pizza tasted like cardboard. The burgers were boiled and I wondered about the origin of the animals that they ground up in the burger meat. Kangaroos? Horses? Dogs? All three? The unseasoned chicken sandwiches were dry and barely edible, and after a week I couldn't choke down another. The Rio's buffet was always crowded at dinner break, so Otis suggested that we consume a liquid dinner instead. We left the convention center and sat down at the closest bar we could find. We both inserted $20 into the video poker machines, which got us a free round of Coronas.

"I hit quads on these machines four times already," Otis said. "And last night, this bar was crawling with hookers."

I frequently wrote about "The Hooker Bar" on Tao of Poker and it became a popular topic of conversation. By definition, a hooker bar is any bar where working girls congregate. These bars are found all over Las Vegas and in major cities across the world. The Rio had a Hooker Bar that became our hideout because it was the last place someone would come looking for us.

We heeded Wil Wheaton's advice about using the dinner break for personal time, which was spent binge drinking and discussing life outside of poker. Otis and I had one rule: No Poker Talk. We swapped stories about our formative years growing up in The Bronx and Missouri respectively. Although we were roughly the same age and held similar jobs, Otis was a true family man and it was easy to see he was conflicted by his presence in Las Vegas. On the one hand, as a journalist and a poker player he was eager to witness history as we sat on the sidelines of the WSOP. On the other hand, though, he desperately missed his wife, his son, his home and his dog. He loathed being a prisoner inside the Rio Casino. He rarely left the property aside from a couple of minutes every day when he would step outside to smoke a cigarette, usually with a grimace.

"Murderers and rapists get more time outdoors than us," Otis pontificated.

"Well, then. I propose a toast," I said and raised my beer. "To St. Otis, the patron saint of hookers and other sex workers in the state of Nevada."

"And… to the Hooker Bar!" Otis said as we clinked beer bottles.

My first ever run-in with a local harlot had occurred during a trip to Las Vegas many years earlier. I was sitting at the bar in the Bellagio sports book watching the NBA playoffs. She "accidentally" nudged my elbow reaching for an ashtray.

"Do you have a light?" she asked.

I fumbled inside my pocket and found a lighter. I casually lit her American Spirit cigarette and she seductively glanced at me as the flame flickered between her eyes. Her firm breasts bulged out of a sleek olive green dinner dress, detracting from the elegant string of pearls around her neck. Her nails and blonde hair looked too perfect. Her lips glistened in the low light.

"How did you do tonight?"

"Huh?" I mumbled, with one eye on the basketball game and the other on her cleavage.

She motioned over to the poker room.

"Oh, I did pretty good, but I've been getting my ass kicked all week."

"I saw you in there with a lot of chips, so I guess you're a good player. I was playing low limit, you know, because I'm still learning. How long have you been playing?"

"Since college. But playing seriously for a year or so."

"You playing in the World Poker Tour Championships tomorrow?"

"Yeah." One-word lies are always the easiest.

"Cool. Best of luck. Winner is gonna get almost $2 million."

I nodded and winked. She slid closer to me and gently touched my arm.

"So, are you staying here?"

"No, at the Excalibur."

"You know, it's super crowded here. Do you want to go back to your place and party?"

C'mon now, you foul wench. I didn't just fall off of a turnip truck from Georgia.

"I'm Crystal," she said before I cut her off.

"And I'm in the middle of watching this game here," I said, pointing up to the multiple TV screens. "I've got big bucks on Denver. I really don't have time to haggle with hookers. How much will it cost me?"

"$1,000 for an hour."

"And how much for just a blow job?"

"$500."

"How much will you charge to do my laundry?"

"Fuck off!"

She smashed her cigarette into the ashtray and left in a hurry. The bartender poured me another drink and I watched the game for a few more minutes before I felt someone slithering into the empty seat where Crystal had just been. A few seconds later, a new girl nudged my elbow as she grabbed for the ashtray.

Beneath the bright lights of Vegas it's not always easy to spot hookers. I have a quick rule of thumb – if a single woman approaches me in a casino any time after midnight, then odds are she's a hooker. Working girls flood The Strip nightly, seducing johns at random watering holes in the middle of the casinos while playing cat-and-mouse with the local vice cops.

The Hooker Bar at the Rio is a popular spot for working girls because of its strategic location. It's the first bar in the casino on your way to the convention center housing the WSOP. If you want to head back to your room or go to the taxi stand, you have to walk past the Hooker Bar. These bankroll hunter-killers sit and wait for pissed-off amateurs who just busted out of their first major tournament.

"Nothing shakes off a bad beat better than hate fucking a hooker," an elderly local once told me at a poker table.

I couldn't tell if he was serious or joking, but it made sense. There's a running joke in poker that when someone tells you a bad beat story, they have to pay you $1 for wasting your time. Somewhere in Las Vegas, right at this very moment, a sloppy, smelly, sweaty poker player is complaining about his aces getting cracked while a disinterested working girl unzips his pants.

Inside the city limits, sex for money is technically illegal, though you would hardly know it. Many working girls actively seek out their customers inside casinos. They prey on the desperate, the lonely, and the down-and-out. I fell right into their target demographic, but all that Catholic guilt in my loins kept me from even considering hiring the services of a working girl, not to mention the morbid fear that I'd catch a horrendous venereal disease and my penis would shrivel up and fall off.

Savvy pimps figured out that the biggest poker tournament in the world was also an untapped source of customers flush with cash and adolescent sexual frustrations. Like Mormons blanketing a suburban neighborhood with bible-carrying missionaries, pimps sent forth a wave of invading strumpets into the WSOP. They wandered the hallways in front of the Amazon Ballroom in search of potential clients. Let's face it, the average poker player looks like the type of guy who would pay for sex. For the pros playing high-stakes cash games, what's $400 for a romp in the sack when the price of a hummer costs the equivalent of one big bet? The skin game is also a numbers game. The girls have a quota to fill, and the faster they get there, the faster they can go home.

The shelf life for any individual hooker is short-lived because of the dangers and hazards associated with the job. However, when one group of prostitutes was impregnated, incarcerated, or completely strung out, then a new batch of eager-beavers quickly replaced them. Many of them were illegal immigrants and minors who were caught up in the lucrative sex trade industry. Flipchip wasn't kidding when he said the hookers got bused in from all over the country.

Only a small percentage of the working girls were freelancers and independent contractors – part-time hussies from Hollywood and New York City with model looks. Shit, most of them *are* models who fuck for greenbacks on the side to cover luxurious shopping sprees, pay their Beverly Hills plastic surgeon, finance extended holidays in Provence, or fund their exorbitant cocaine habits. I often heard whispers of some high-end call girls who make $20,000 for a weekend of work in Vegas.

Instead of settling on stripping or shooting porn movies as a source of income, an elite collection of working girls arrive in Las Vegas every day with one goal – to catch a whale. You had to lavish them with gifts and fine dining before they even considered going up to your hotel room. And it had to be a suite because they were not the type of girls who were going to let you bang them doggie-style in your $99 cheapo hotel room overlooking the parking garage. These girls were the Monets of the sex industry. It cost at least $5,000 for a three-hour romp. Double the price if you wanted to fuck them without a condom.

Indeed, it's true – the better-looking hookers were able to charge more per trick. The working girls at the Redneck Riviera who patrolled Trop were the bottom of the barrel. They were strung out, overweight, and outright nasty – basically catnip for serial killers.

Street pimps don't have a chance with the premier girls who are quickly snatched up by the organized ethnic criminal element controlling the majority of Las Vegas escort services. Prostitution in Las Vegas is like calling up a pizza delivery service. You simply dial one of the numbers in the back of a sex magazine that the porn slappers hand out on The Strip. Someone from the agency calls you back in your hotel room to verify that you're a guest in that hotel (and not a vice cop or someone pulling a prank), and in less than an hour an authentic working girl of your specific tastes shows up at your door. Of course, you're playing hooker roulette when you call an escort service. Even though you requested a busty blonde or a petite Asian girl, your first choice might not show up and you'll be stuck with a pregnant tweaker with bad acne or an Oprah look-a-like spilling out of her miniskirt.

Luckily at the Hooker Bar, what you see is what you get.

Chapter 8

June 2005.

Flipchip circled the upper parking lot twice. With the annual researchers' convention in town, the Rio was flooded with BlackBerry-obsessed dorks and the parking lot had no open spaces. I spotted Doyle Brunson in his trademark white Stetson sputtering along in his motorized scooter. Brunson had a bad hip and walked around with the help of a crutch.

It just didn't seem right that the Godfather of Poker (and arguably one of the greatest gamblers who ever lived) had to park in the boondocks like the rest of the masses. Flipchip parked a few spaces down from Brunson's Cadillac. I watched the aging legend get out of his scooter with the help of his crutch. The words "Texas Dolly" were stitched in gold lettering on the black leather handle.

"Hot enough for you?" Brunson joked.

Flipchip and Brunson launched into "old fogey" banter as they commiserated about having to park so far away from the entrance to the Rio's convention center. Brunson mentioned his request for heavily armed security guards to roam the parking lot as a deterrent for any potential robberies.

I wondered how many $25,000 Bellagio chips he had in his front pocket, but decided to ask him a question about his son, Todd. The previous night, Todd had won his first bracelet in the $2,500 Omaha Hi-Lo tournament after he bested Allen "Chainsaw" Kessler in a ninety-minute slugfest.

"I couldn't be more proud of Todd," Brunson said. Even though Brunson played in a different tournament, he frequently hobbled over to the final table to check on his son's progress.

Todd's victory had historic implications because the Brunsons now held the honor of being the first and only father-son duo with WSOP bracelets. Doyle had won nine bracelets, which tied him with Phil Hellmuth and Johnny Chan for the player with the most WSOP bracelets. No one had ten bracelets yet, but that's what everyone was gunning for. In baseball terms, it was like the pursuit of Roger Maris' single-season home run record.

Number 10. Doyle Brunson had his eyes on becoming the first player to achieve that historic milestone.

I'll never forget June 26, 2005. It was a Sunday and one of busiest days at the 2005 WSOP with three final tables scheduled and four tournaments to keep tabs on including the special Ladies Event.

Poker tournaments are overwhelmingly filled with men and women typically comprise less than 3 percent of the field. On a normal day, the majority of the women inside the Amazon Ballroom were spectators, media, staff members, and the occasional enterprising working girl who made the trek to the tournament area. During the Ladies Event, however, the Amazon Ballroom was filled with women in pursuit of a WSOP bracelet.

I slicked back what little hair I had left, splashed on some cologne, wore my cleanest clothes, and brought my camera to snap pictures of my favorite women in action. In 2005, Harrah's changed the Ladies Event to a no-limit tournament instead of limit hold'em as it had been in previous years. The new format attracted an astonishing 601 players, up from 201 the year before. The event was originally scheduled to be a one-day event but with so many entrants, I knew it was going to be a late night.

Despite the increasing popularity of the tournament, a few professionals like Annie Duke, did not play in Ladies-only events. Felicia Lee also frowned on these gender-specific events.

"They're totally demeaning to women," Felicia explained. "Besides, who wants to play with other women? They're the most annoying poker players on the planet."

A barrage of sexist jokes from chauvinists filled media row. "Can we get a cock check at Seat 3 on Table 6?" was my favorite. Contrary to what you read on internet forums, not all of the participants in the Ladies Event were lesbians. I had a few uncomfortable moments, however, when I walked the floor and felt daggers shooting out from the eyes of some of the players. A few men-hating feminazis were visibly pissed that I only photographed hot chicks. I quickly snapped photos of my friend Shirley Rosario from PokerBabes.com, along with Jen from Poker Wire and Liz Lieu, then got the hell out of that section before one of the bull dykes tackled me, sat on my chest, and choked me to death with her "You Don't Want to Know Where I Hide My Bankroll" t-shirt.

I wisely focused on the other tournaments.

ESPN filmed the final table of Event #24 $2,500 No-Limit Hold'em on the stage, but it lacked star potential. The majority of the media migrated to the floor to sweat Event #25 $2,500 Pot-Limit Hold'em. Johnny Chan, Humberto Brenes and Phil "The Unabomber" Laak had advanced to the final table and the producers at 441 Productions and ESPN were wishing they had scheduled that event for filming. More TV viewers played no-limit hold'em than pot-limit hold'em, so ESPN opted to film Event #24 instead of #25. A table of unfamiliar faces sat under the bright lights on the stage, while Johnny Chan chased his tenth WSOP bracelet away from the cameras.

Not wanting to miss a historic moment, ESPN sent out its second unit to film the action at Chan's final table. Unfortunately, poker is not a timed sporting event. The producers, Matt Maranz and Dave Swartz, were essentially leaving it up to the fickle poker gods to determine whether they would get a chance to record Chan's run for the bracelet with a full film crew including the hole-card cameras. Obviously, two things had to happen: players in Event #24 had to bust out at a much faster pace, and Chan had to avoid elimination in Event #25, staying alive long enough for the producers to move his table.

To make a crazy day even more hectic, a roast for John Bonetti had been scheduled that evening across the hallway. Dinner breaks for all of the tournaments were extended so the players and media could attend the roast. Brooklyn-born Bonetti was an illustrious character in the poker world with a foul mouth and a vicious attitude. This pro was one tough son-of-a-bitch having beaten prostate and spinal cancer a decade earlier. He had over $2 million in career WSOP earnings, collected three bracelets, cashed over 25 times, and advanced to over 20 final tables.

Before the roast began, I went outside and smoked a joint in the parking lot. Until then, I'd been a very good boy and only drank on the job. Joo scored me premium California-grown kind bud and I had a low tolerance. Nothing beats the first high of the day. It's the unattainable perfection that you chase until you fall sleep. After I smoked up, I floated back inside nearly a foot off the ground.

I was roasted and toasted and a lit fuckin' monkey when I encountered Phil Hellmuth in the hallway. He was easily one of the hardest interviews to secure and rarely available for any one-on-one time. I mustered my herbal courage and seized the rare opportunity.

"Hey Phil, how about an interview with Fox Sports?"

Hellmuth grumbled and avoided eye contact, even though he wore sunglasses. He seemed uninterested and walked away. He claims he can peek into your soul and read your mind. I sensed he knew that I was chemically imbalanced.

"It's just a single question interview, Phil. What's on your iPod?"

He stopped in his tracks and perked up.

"My iPod?" he said. "My 15-year-old son uploaded a lot of rap and hip-hop onto my iPod. I like 1980s music and all the new stuff. I like some of the rap. I'm a guy who's into new music. A lot of old and a lot of new."

I thought he was fucking with me but he insisted that he really dug hip-hop. He showed me his iPod and I saw songs from Jay-Z, 50 Cent, Linkin Park, Nirvana, and Styx.

Bonetti's roast began and the munchies kicked in. I raided the buffet with Greenspan and Michalski and devoured Swedish meatballs, bacon-wrapped scallops, and crab-stuffed mushrooms – or what I called the best meal I had eaten in weeks. We listened to Mike Sexton razz Bonetti pretty good before Dan Goldman from PokerStars told a funny story about Bonetti shouting obscenities at a video poker machine.

Clonie Gowen, one of the pros under the Full Tilt umbrella, drew a significant amount of attention in the media because she was a MILF. In a poker room full of fat guys, she sticks out like a daisy in a pile of cow shit. Michalski knew Clonie from the underground games in Dallas, and she walked over to bum a cigarette. They had an odd relationship that reminded me of something out of high school, with Clonie as the popular cheerleader that used geeks like Michalski to do her homework assignments.

After Bonetti's roast ended, word had spread about Chan's run and more fans gathered around his outer table than were seated in the bleachers on the stage. Phil "The Unabomber" Laak looked like the figure in the sketch drawings of the alleged Unabomber on the FBI's "Wanted" poster. A few years earlier, Laak had too much to drink the night before a tournament and woke up hung over, so he wore sunglasses to hide his eyes from the bright lights and pulled the hood tight over his head. Thus, the trademark was born.

The fun and effervescent Laak relished the spotlight and always garnered plenty of camera time, saying the weirdest things, playing without his shoes, and occasionally breaking into calisthenics during the action.

After Laak won an uncontested pot, he offered to show his cards for $4. Johnny Chan agreed. Laak flipped over A-K and then pestered Chan for the money.

"Come on! You're Johnny Chan, I know you have $4. You're Johnny Chan!"

"My smallest bill is a $5."

"I always got change for Johnny Chan," he said, tossing a rolled up $1 bill across the table.

Laak garnered even more media attention when word got out that he and Oscar-nominated actress Jennifer Tilly were an item. Tilly was a regular player in high-stakes home games in Hollywood and Laak was tutoring her in tournament poker. His advice was working because she was amassing chips in the Ladies Event on the other side of the room.

Laak won another uncontested hand and again offered to show his cards for $4, however, no one was interested. He turned around and extended the offer to the spectators on the rail. Jon Eaton (a fellow tournament reporter) and I both chipped in $2 and Laak quickly snatched the money out of our hands. He waved us over and showed us Ac-Jc.

Phil Hellmuth and Doyle Brunson, both tied with Chan for nine bracelets, constantly stopped by the rail to check on Chan's progress. Hellmuth knew that Chan was well within reach of a tenth bracelet and tried to tilt Chan by talking some passive-aggressive smack. Laak objected and rushed to Chan's rescue and snapped, "If it weren't for luck you'd win every time, right Phil?"

The rail burst out with laughter and Hellmuth sheepishly walked away. The crowd grew bigger and bigger hovering shoulder to shoulder because everyone wanted to say they witnessed Johnny Chan win his tenth bracelet. Michalski stood up on a chair so he could snap a few photos and was quickly scolded by one of the producers.

Some nights everything goes your way. After Richard Harroch's A-J outflopped Chan's pocket fours, Chan caught running cards for a straight to win the pot. Harroch exited in seventh place. With six players to go on Chan's table, the producers sent them on an extended break and hoped that Event #24 would end quickly. However, when Chan's table reconvened at midnight, #24 was only down to two players. Lars Bonding and Freddy Bonyadi were about to begin a grueling two-hour heads-up match that went virtually unnoticed (with the exception of the film crew) because everyone inside the Amazon Ballroom flocked to Chan's final table. Despite the lack of space, I had secured a ringside seat just five feet away from Chan.

Chan quickly found himself in a horrible spot – all-in with pocket queens against Frank Kassela's pocket aces. Chan seemed destined to win the entire tournament when the dealer fanned out a flop and a queen appeared on cue. Chan won the hand and his railbirds exploded with applause. Kassela finished in sixth place as Chan raced toward the chip lead.

Laak eventually caught a bit of luck. He raised pre-flop and Richard Osbourne reraised all-in. Laak took forever to make his decision, running the math over and over out loud as he verbalized his internal dialogue for the crowd. Laak eventually called with K-10. He trailed Osbourne's weak ace. When a ten spiked, a batch of Unabomber fans on the rail went berserk and began chanting his nickname. Laak caught one of the six cards in the deck that could help him win, and quickly fell on the floor while a stunned Osbourne busted out in third place. The crowd parted and Jen Tilly ran over to the rail and smothered Laak with a big wet kiss.

At that point, ESPN's producers had no other choice but to halt heads-up play between Chan and Laak. The two went on an indefinite break, and neither player minded. Laak was an admitted TV whore who welcomed the publicity, while Chan, a savvy businessman himself, knew the benefits of waiting until the other final table was complete.

At 2:01 a.m., Event #24 crowned a champion and Freddy Bonyadi won his third bracelet. He must have had the quickest bracelet ceremony at the 2005 WSOP as photographers and reporters were rushed off the stage to set up the heads-up match between Chan and Laak. Talk about two contrasting personalities. Chan was quiet, calm, and serene at the table while Laak could not sit still and talked constantly. The guy is a poster child for adult ADD.

With my notebook and pen in hand, I sat in the front row only a few seats from Doyle Brunson. I wanted to soak up every second of the impending historic moment. The bleachers, empty just moments earlier, had filled up with fans and curious pros, including Chan's son who sat nearby.

Laak was outchipped going into heads-up play with the crowd mostly rooting on Chan. It only took sixteen hands to determine a winner. On the final hand, Laak and Chan were all in preflop. Laak flipped over K-J and Chan showed Q-Q. Although Laak flopped a jack, his hand did not improve and he was eliminated in second place. Laak left the stage and went to check up on Tilly's progress, while Chan hugged his son.

Tilly made a deep run in the Ladies Event and ESPN wanted to capitalize on the rare opportunity when a celebrity advanced to a final table. ESPN had already filmed two final tables, and the exhausted crew couldn't handle shooting any more poker. The producers spoke to the remaining players in the Ladies Event and gave them the option of playing through as scheduled or quitting for the night and returning the next day. A few players were against the delay and play continued. At 4 a.m., the remaining four players agreed to stop the tournament and resume the next day. The postponement allowed ESPN to film a bit of the Ladies Event final table featuring Jen Tilly and also including Cecilia Mortensen from Spain, the wife of former WSOP Champion Carlos Mortensen.

I went home to the Redneck Riviera to write and passed out for a couple of hours before Flipchip swung by to pick me up. We rushed back to the Rio to watch the remainder of the Ladies Event. The final table went quick and Jen Tilly easily won her first WSOP bracelet.

"This is better than an Oscar," Tilly said during her beaming acceptance speech. She happily showed off her bracelet to the media and the large crowd that had gathered.

When asked about her future, Tilly responded, "I'm hooked on poker. I'm not going to stop playing until I lose all my money."

* * * * *

Less than a week after Johnny Chan broke the bracelet record, Doyle Brunson equaled the feat when he won his tenth bracelet in Event #31 $5,000 Short-Handed No-Limit Hold'em. Brunson's bracelets include two that he collected after he won the Main Event in 1976 and 1977. He also won bracelets in H.O.R.S.E, deuce-to-seven draw, no-limit hold'em, seven-card stud, seven-card stud hi/lo, and mixed doubles.

When tournament director Johnny Grooms announced the final table players in Event #31 (including Scotty Nguyen, Minh Ly, Layne Flack, Jason Lester, and Ayaz Mahmood), Brunson received a raucous standing ovation from the audience. The final table lasted several hours with Brunson playing hands of Chinese Poker with Layne Flack during the numerous crew breaks.

Brunson finally found himself heads-up with Vietnamese pro Minh Ly, whom he frequently played with in the Big Game at the Bellagio. Brunson held the chip lead over Ly, but at 71-years-young, Brunson visibly fought fatigue with cans of Red Bull. On the final hand, Ly limped and Brunson pushed all-in. Ly quickly called with K-Q and Brunson flipped over 10-3. Although Ly thought he trapped him, Brunson flopped a three to take the lead. Ly's hand did not improve and he busted out in second place. It wasn't quite 10-2 offsuit (Brunson's signature hand – he won both WSOP Main Event titles in consecutive years while holding 10-2 offsuit), but damned if it wasn't close enough.

46

Brunson collected $367,800 for first place. The money was an afterthought because the bracelet meant everything. Chan's record only stood for four days when Brunson tied it by beating out one of the toughest final tables at the 2005 WSOP. Brunson proved once again that age didn't matter at the poker tables.

"It's hard to substitute for experience. And let's just face it, nobody has more experience than me. Nobody is as old as I am either," Brunson quipped.

Chapter 9

July 2005.

The smoky hallway made it difficult to see more than a few feet in front of you. In a groggy hungover haze, I nearly trampled a couple of tiny preteen girls who had converged on the Rio for a national dance competition. It was the Jon-Benet Ramsey look-a-like version of the ultra-erotic Kirsten Dunst vehicle *Bring It On*. Spray-tanned stage mothers in Juicy sweat suits splattered hooker makeup all over their daughters' faces and barked out orders like drill sergeants. A couple of cheerleaders practiced their routines on the carpet, tumbling and twisting all the way down the corridor. Las Vegas was no place for these innocent porcelain dolls. Deviants on three-day benders were stumbling through the corridors clutching watered-down glasses of scotch. Grizzled gamblers chomping on stogies older than the little dolls gawked like depraved animals. The place was an Amber Alert waiting to happen.

Benny Binion would have shit an egg roll if he had walked into the Horseshoe and caught a glimpse of little girls in tights doing backflips in front of the World Series of Poker. "Post-modern Corporate Vegas" is very different from the halcyon days of "Old Vegas." The casinos rake in mountains of cash from the convention culture because Las Vegas is an attractive location for a wide variety of groups and professions who want to party on site during their annual gatherings and retreats. Trekkies, in full costume and talking to each other in Klingon, flock to Vegas for Star Trek conventions. Even the sex industry hosts an annual Adult Entertainment Expo in January when porn stars and sex freaks invade The Strip like clockwork.

The WSOP is a seven-week-long convention. Wars have been won and lost in less time. As we got closer and closer to the Main Event, the hallways at the Rio swelled with poker addicts and wild-eyed tourists excited about seeing their favorite pros. Many were respectful and treated the Amazon Ballroom like it was a tour of the Sistine Chapel while annoying drunkards showed little respect for the players, treating them more like Shamu at Sea World than the world's top professionals. The Fourth of July holiday especially brought a slew of idiots to Vegas. One yokel walked up to Doyle Brunson while he was in the middle of a hand and begged for an autograph and a picture. I'd like to see one try and walk up to Derek Jeter while he's in the middle of an at-bat and ask to take a photo.

Navigating through the hordes of cheerleaders and poker fans became a chore like trying to endure a standstill jam on a Los Angeles freeway. With low visibility, I shuffled my way to the gift shop near the business center. I purchased a 24 oz. can of Miller Genuine Draft for $4 and noticed a young Nubian princess wearing a skirt so short that you could almost see the Black Forest. She stood in line in front of me holding hands with a middle-aged tourist. The guy with a beer gut and a cheap watch held a three-pack of condoms. I shuddered.

Like an amnesia-riddled character out of a Philip K. Dick short story, I waded through the cheesy sea of cheerleaders and elbowed a few slow-walking tourists in my path. I finally made it to media row and split the tallboy with Otis. We poured the MGD in paper coffee cups. Breakfast of Champions.

Despite our work area being blocked off by ropes, it didn't prevent tourists from running through trying to catch a piece of the action at the final table. One soused dickhead tripped over my power cord and knocked over my laptop. The situation clearly called for coping aids. And fast.

I walked across the hall to the Full Tilt Poker hospitality suite. The back area was roped off and designated for players only. This is where Phil Ivey and Jesus Ferguson hung out on their breaks. The front part of the suite contained a minibar, two banquet tables stocked with food, and merchandising tables full of free Full Tilt Poker branded t-shirts, hats and posters. Foiled Coup spent a significant amount of the day inside the suite devouring chips and salsa in the corner.

"Have you seen all the hot tail running around the Rio today?" he asked. "With all of the little girls roaming the hallways, you should be having a field day."

"Me? You better be careful before Homeland Security carts you away to a prison camp in Gitmo. In this country, they lock up British pedophiles with the Islamic fundamentalists."

I grabbed a Full Tilt chocolate bar and ordered two Coronas. I tipped the bartender $5 and safely returned to media row without spilling the beers. Otis and I refilled our coffee cups and soldiered on with our final table coverage.

* * * * *

With the Main Event only days away, the highly anticipated WSOP party season began. PokerStars and Full Tilt had scheduled their soirees for the same time, and I heard a rumor that Nicky Hilton was confirmed to appear at Doyle Brunson's party. I made sure that I was on that guest list. My goal was to get Flipchip to stealthily snap a photo of Nicky Hilton giving me a hand job while I smoked a joint.

My friends in the media were excited about the parties. Drinking gallons of free booze is always the best way to let loose some steam after being away from home for over a month and working shitty hours inside a casino. The night was so special that Amy Calistri shaved her legs for the Full Tilt party. Even the Poker Prof ventured out of his bunker to attend the gala event. I didn't give a shit about the opportunity to schmooze the big dogs in the gaming industry or get a chance to hang out with all of the famous pros. I was only there for the free booze. I know I already said that, but seriously… GALLONS OF FREE BOOZE.

Full Tilt hosted the party at La Bete, the hippest new club in Las Vegas, located in the Wynn casino at the base of a waterfall. Three tuxedo-wearing thugs the size of NFL linemen carefully guarded the ropes. The lady with the list out front had to clear us before we were let through. The invite specifically suggested we dress "L.A. Chic" but I didn't know what that meant. I called up my ex-girlfriend and quizzed her about the term. She told me not to show up in a Hawaiian shirt and jeans. Failing to comply with the dress code ensured that I would not gain entry. I decided to dress identical to the Prof. All black. Shit, I looked like Johnny Cash, but that was my best attempt at L.A. Chic.

The lady with the list spoke softly into a headset as she looked us over. She slightly nodded in approval and we got the green light. She led us down a stairwell into a square room with marble floors. We walked through two small hallways draped in red Italian silk, with muffled break beats growing louder and louder as we finally entered the club.

I made a beeline for the open bar and ordered two drinks. I found Shirley Rosario, my friend and ticket to excessive insobriety for the rest of the night. Bartenders make it a point to serve hot chicks first even in the most crowded of clubs. Shirley fetched me no less than seven double SoCos. Without her, I'd have been lucky to even get one or two.

La Bete was packed with dozens of the pros I had covered during the previous five weeks. The Full Tilt pros shed their hockey jerseys and cargo shorts for proper cocktail attire. Everyone at the party engaged in binge drinking and enjoyed one last night out before the Main Event began.

I spent most of the party outside near the waterfall, where Michalski and I did our best to stealthily smoke a joint in the corner avoiding suspicious security guards and the eye in the sky. I bumped into two friends from Ireland, Tom Murphy and Mike "Lucky Blind" Lacey, who owned and operated Antesup.com. They were among the many members of the European press who had just arrived in town to cover the Main Event.

The night always takes on an extra level of rowdiness when you party with thirsty Irishmen under "open bar" circumstances. The gallons of free booze were the most I drank all summer. For Lacey and Murphy, that was the most they drank – since breakfast. My memory got a little fuzzy after the third Jager Bomb. The next thing I knew, we missed last call, the lights were on and the thick-neck security guards were pushing us toward the exit. The Prof, two Irish guys, Daniel Negreanu (doing a perfect Scotty Nguyen imitation), and I were the last to stumble out of the club. Sounds like the punch line to a bad joke.

Chapter 10

July 2005.

I marked July 7 on my internal calendar from the moment the Prof hired me. The WSOP's $10,000 buy-in championship began on July 7. The Main Event. The Big Cheese. The Super Bowl of Poker. When most people think about the WSOP, it's the Main Event that comes to mind. The WSOP itself is a wondrous spectacle, but the Main Event was the pinnacle of the seven week-long festival of poker. As long as you have $10,000 for the buy-in, you have a chance to win. The WSOP is the epitome of the American Dream. Everyone loves a good old-fashioned Horatio Alger rags to riches story. Go west, young man and win the richest prize in all of poker. Whoever won would become a multi-millionaire, an instant celebrity, and the biggest swinging dick in poker.

In the 1970s, very few mainstream journalists had ever seen a poker tournament, let alone covered one. On the eve of the WSOP Main Event, Benny Binion gave the media a chance to see what it's like to play poker at his downtown Las Vegas casino. The always publicity-seeking Binion created a media freeroll tournament as a no-limit Texas Hold'em tutorial for out-of-town media. Celebrities were soon invited to add a bit of glamour to the event.

The WSOP Media/Celebrity event gave me a chance to play poker with some of my friends. Harrah's donated the final table prize money to the charity of your choice. The winner would have $10,000 donated in his or her name. I knew that Harrah's would flag "Pauly's Save a Stripper Foundation" as my pick, so I opted to play in memory of Charlie Tuttle. I caught a lot of cards and somehow finished in sixth place. I missed a shot at the big money but won a couple hundred dollars towards cancer research at the Vanderbilt-Ingram Cancer Clinic in Nashville, Tennessee.

I stayed out late to celebrate my final table appearance with Otis and our buddy, AlCantHang. The day of reckoning, the start of the Main Event, had finally arrived; yet, I held everything together by the thinnest of threads – sluggish, beat down, drained, fried, not to mention hung over to all hell. That's what happens when you attempt to hang with AlCantHang, a professional party animal from the Philadelphia suburbs who looks like a roadie from a 1980s hair band. One of our friends aptly described AlCantHang as a walking party. Imagine trying to attempt the Running of the Bulls in Pamplona with your hands tied behind your back and hopping on one leg; gaping wounds and bloodshed ensue with a hysterical Spanish woman crying in the corner. Now you know the equivalent of a night of drinking in Las Vegas with AlCantHang.

Al had crashed on my couch and was already awake when I stumbled into the bathroom to throw up.

"They bombed the London subways," he said as he lit up a Marlboro and pointed to the TV.

CNN flashed various images of the carnage in London. We were glued to the TV all morning and I was haunted by flashbacks. I lived in New York City during 9/11 and the London bombings brought back unwanted memories of confusion, anxiety, and the nauseating stink of death.

When you hear tragic news in Las Vegas, it doesn't affect you in the same way as hearing it in your hometown. Once you set foot inside a casino, you tune out the rest of the world, and any tragic events that happen to occur generally fail to anchor roots into your sentimental side. It isn't uncommon for Las Vegas visitors to ignore CNN, the internet or newspapers for days or even weeks. Current events become secondary to feeding other addictions.

Most of the people I spoke to that morning had no idea that a terrorist attack rocked London. They could tell you which baseball teams won the night before but had no clue about the bombings. They really didn't care.

Kids starving in Africa? Hit me.

Another I.E.D. killed two marines and maimed three others in Iraq? I'm all-in.

Earthquake topples a town in China? Let it ride!

Jen Mason, a waif-like former poker dealer turned poker reporter, nervously chain-smoked cigarettes in the hallway. The visibly rattled London native told me her tube stop was one of the bomb sites. Her WSOP experience was already strained after she discovered that her credentials for BlondePoker.com were not approved. The British are most known for their resolve during difficult situations, and Jen set up camp in the hallway on a bench anxiously awaiting the start of the Main Event to keep her mind off the terrorist attack.

I arrived at the Rio a few hours early to avoid the crowds. A couple of media friends stopped by to chat, but no one mentioned the London bombings. All they wanted to talk about was how I knocked Shannon Elizabeth out of the Media/Celebrity tournament on a vicious suckout. The buzz had made its way around the Rio, and I quickly became "that guy who laid a beat on the *American Pie* chick."

The Amazon Ballroom had a 2,000 player capacity (or 200 poker tables) and as a result, the opening day of the Main Event was split into three flights to accommodate 5,619 players. They forked over $10,000 each, creating a record-setting prize pool worth over $52 million. First place paid out $7.5 million, loosely translated as "fuck you" money.

I wandered through the sea of poker tables and found Wil Wheaton. PokerStars paid for his entry into the Main Event, one of the perks of being a sponsored player. Like many first timers, he couldn't believe he was about to play in the most prestigious tournament in the world.

"I'm a little nervous, but ready," Wil said.

"Don't play like a pussy today," I said.

Pros confidently walked into the Amazon Ballroom and took their seats. It was just another day at the office for former world champions Johnny Chan, Scotty Nguyen, and defending champion Greg Raymer. But the majority of players in the room were at a fantasy camp. Thousands of amateurs, who won their $10,000 buy-ins through online satellites, were about to play in the Main Event for the first time. Many had never ever played in a live tournament, let alone one of such supreme significance. You could taste the fear and see the morbid confusion in the glazed eyes of the amateurs. They were lambs being led to the slaughter.

Every seat at every table inside the Amazon Ballroom was full, including the tables set aside for cash games and satellites. An eerie silence pierced the normally raging circus. A tense mood lingered. No one wanted to be the first to bust out. The distant clatter of shuffling chips slowly increased. Everyone was on edge. It took only 11 minutes before the first elimination – and then everyone unleashed a collective sigh of relief.

The media room reminded me of a refugee center with hundreds of writers, photographers, and video crews cramped together. Steve Rosenbloom, the renowned sportswriter from the Chicago Tribune, set up his space in the hallway on a bench next to Jen Mason. He chomped down on a cigar as he pecked away at his laptop. Rosenbloom followed Michael Jordan and the Chicago Bulls during their dominant championship runs, as well as covering the Olympics, the Super Bowl, and the Stanley Cup Finals. His presence at the WSOP was an indication that poker had officially hit the big time among the sporting literati.

The hallways had reached maximum capacity. A dense fog of cigarette smoke hovered everywhere. The line to the men's room was so long that many took a whiz in the ladies room. The frantic scene reminded me of a cross between Mardi Gras and halftime at a football game.

While waiting in line to piss, I caught bits of hundreds of conversations.

"I'm the best player at my table and I'm getting killed," said one guy in a PartyPoker.com shirt.

"As long as I outlast my ex-wife's new husband, that's all that matters. She married a fuckin' fish," said another guy in jean shorts and a muscle shirt.

"Pocket aces have already been cracked three times at my table. It's just like Party Poker," said a young kid in a Peyton Manning jersey.

"I got Gus Hansen at my table. I almost pissed myself," said a guy in a Hawaiian shirt as he rushed by me, hung up his phone, and shoved a slice of pizza in his mouth.

Day 1A progressed rapidly with nonstop eliminations, something I didn't think would happen at a $10,000 buy-in tournament. I expected much tighter play, but the field was packed with amateurs making costly mistakes. It was impossible for one person to monitor all of the action, so luckily everyone in media row shared notes. Plus, the European media clued me in on the progress of their top players. Jen Mason closely followed the British players, while Murphy and Lacey told me everything I needed to know about the Irish.

"Andy Black is going all the way," Murphy said. "He disappeared from the circuit for several years while he studied Buddhism in a monastery. But now he's back. This is his year."

By the time Flipchip and I left the Rio, we had been there for almost 19 hours. I wrote until sunrise and slept for an hour before I woke up and made one last deadline.

* * * * *

On Day 1B, Otis took his seat in media row and revealed a startling fact: 1,116 players of the 5,619 who entered the Main Event had qualified via satellites at PokerStars. Sweet Jesus, that was nearly 20 percent of the field and that figure represented only one online poker site.

The previous two world champions (2003 winner Chris Moneymaker and 2004 winner Greg Raymer) had both won their Main Event seats through PokerStars satellites, and 1,116 players hoped that they would also follow in Moneymaker's and Raymer's footsteps.

The most exciting moment on Day 1B occurred on the first hand at the TV table between Las Vegas pro Sammy Farha and actor Oliver Hudson (Kate Hudson's brother and Goldie Hawn's son). Farha, decked out in a luminous tangerine shirt, raised in early position with A-10. Hudson reraised with 10-10 and Farha called. The flop was A-A-10. Talk about a fuckin' cooler. Farha won the pot and Hudson went busto. He ran over to Tobey Maguire's table next to media row.

"I'm out," Hudson said.

"You're kidding, right?" Maguire said.

"I wish. Farha busted me on the first hand."

Everyone knew Tobey Maguire for his role as Spider-Man, and Spider-Man refused to be photographed at the poker table. The Hollywood actor often covered his face or looked the other way whenever a photographer stopped by his table. Maguire's unwillingness to cooperate with the poker media made Flipchip even more determined to get a shot, so he snuck up to the security platform overlooking the entire Amazon Ballroom. Maguire sat several tables away and had no idea that Flipchip pointed a camera with a lens the size of a pitbull at him.

"You should be a hitman," I told Flipchip after he showed me the stealth photos. "Or go to Hollywood and make a fortune in the paparazzi snapping snatch shots of starlets."

"I'll consider it. Definitely beats taking pictures of these stiffs," he said.

During dinner break, Otis and I skipped the Hooker Bar for the first time since the routine began. We were both too busy. I completed a deadline for Fox Sports and then checked out Doyle Brunson's party down the hallway. I slammed four beers in fifteen minutes and returned to media row to watch the TV table featuring Phil Hellmuth. A known media whore, Hellmuth notoriously arrived late for the Main Event. He stood at least six foot six and was an imposing physical presence at the table. He could implode at any moment, treating everyone to a classic Hellmuthian meltdown. The self-professed "Poker Brat" was entertaining, if nothing else.

Hellmuth's demise began after he made a huge laydown with A-K. Even though he flopped trips on a board of A-A-4, he folded when his opponent shoved over the top of him. How Hellmuth knew that his opponent had him beat, well, no one knows except him.

"Honey, I should have gone broke on that hand!" Hellmuth shouted over to his wife (ironically she's a psychiatrist) seated in the stands. He stood up and pointed at his opponent. "I betcha didn't know, but I can dodge bullets, baby!"

BJ Nemeth and I burst into an uncontrollable laughing fit.

"How cool is this," said BJ, "Hellmuth is going to have a mental breakdown right here and we have a front-row seat."

The implosion continued when one amateur player shoved all-in with K-J against Hellmuth's A-K. Hellmuth was ahead until his opponent caught a miracle jack on the river to double up. It was a terrible beat, but most pros would have shrugged it off and kept playing. Not a livid Hellmuth. He sprinted over to his wife and said, "These fucking guys don't even know how to spell the game they are playing. P-O-K-E-R. Unbelievable! And hold'em has six letters including an abbreviation."

"Actually, hold'em is a contraction, not an abbreviation," BJ corrected.

Hellmuth sat down and played one hand but continued to simmer. He returned to the stands and his wife unsuccessfully tried to calm him down. He decided to walk off his tilt instead, circling media row like a pissed-off vulture. He stopped and leaned in between BJ and myself.

"What are you guys writing about me?"

"The blow-by-blow recap of your meltdown," I said.

Hellmuth inspected BJ's work and said, "Make sure you say how that fucking idiot shoved 17,000 into the pot with king-fucking-jack!"

Hellmuth wandered off into the crowd with ESPN cameras in pursuit before eventually cooling off and returning to his table. Everything seemed normal until former backgammon pro Paul Magriel joined the TV table. Hellmuth and Magriel had a tumultuous history and the two jawed back and forth. Magriel got the last laugh when he knocked out Hellmuth. His pocket sevens held up against Hellmuth's A-Q.

Hellmuth stormed off the TV set screaming: "That's the worst hour of poker I have ever seen in my life! What a fucking joke! These guys don't even know how to fucking spell poker!"

* * * * *

Friday night festivities at my apartment complex included binge drinking and Redneck Karaoke. The wastoids were out in force howling along to *Sweet Home Alabama*, while in the shadows, the working girls hobbled around with their infamous inflamed crotch gait.

Or maybe was I still at work? It was hard to tell as Day 1C rolled around like a scene from *Groundhog Day*. I wandered into the Rio around two hours early like a stoned zombie.

Five minutes before the scheduled start time of Day 1C, Doyle Brunson entered the ballroom and slowly made his way to his seat. Every person in the room rose to their feet and unleashed a thunderous round of applause that gave me goose bumps.

Mike "The Mouth" Matusow started a ruckus twenty minutes into the start of the third and final flight. The former Las Vegas poker dealer turned poker pro had just finished serving a stint in jail for selling cocaine to an undercover officer. To this day, Matusow claims that he was set up. At any rate, he was a free man but completely broke. A big score in the Main Event was exactly what he needed to get back on his feet.

Matusow jawed with his tablemates and even though he was sitting in the middle of the Amazon Ballroom, his shrill voice still managed to rise above the clattering of chips. His garrulous musings were keeping us amused on media row when he suddenly erupted, calling one of his opponents a "fucking moron." The tournament director assessed Matusow a ten-minute penalty requiring him to leave the table and post/fold his blinds. Matusow was not pleased and let another F-bomb slip out. He received another penalty. Matusow harbored a disdain for authority figures and wasn't going to take shit lying down. He unleashed another F-bomb. The tournament director gave him a third penalty. Matusow vehemently protested with still another F-bomb and picked up penalty number four. He had racked up a total of 40 minutes in penalty time and went berserk as he headed to the rail to sit out his multiple infractions. Matusow was one of the saltiest characters in poker and you never knew what he was going to say.

"Tournament poker is a fucking joke," Matusow screamed as he left the tournament area. "Whoever gets the most lucky is the next superstar."

* * * * *

I woke up to the sounds of things breaking. The meth heads who lived on the second floor were involved in another domestic dispute. The skinny guy with bad tattoos stood outside while his girlfriend threw all his stuff off the balcony and shouted obscenities. The remains of a VCR were scattered on the walkway while he dodged the heavier items. His clothes were spread out in the parking lot. The screaming halted when a Las Vegas Metro Police cruiser arrived. I expected to see a *COPS* camera crew jump out of a production van.

Day 2 of the Main Event was technically the fourth day of action. For the first time, the remaining players from the opening three flights were all seated together. Otis was swamped trying to cover over a thousand PokerStars qualifiers for the PokerStars Blog with Mad Harper, a British ex-pat living in Spain. She followed European PokerStars qualifiers and relayed the info to Otis. Mad was appalled at our unhealthy diet and the infrequency of our meals. She fetched us fruit salads while Otis and I poked fun at the hate mail that trolls sent us.

I inspected all of the interesting card cappers (something a player uses to protect their cards). Greg "Fossilman" Raymer acquired his nickname because he used fossils to protect his cards. Poker players, being a superstitious breed, used an assortment of card cappers to bring them luck. Some used specialty poker chips from their home game or local casino. Joe "The Show" O'Neill from Ireland exhibited his wry sense of humor with a pile of fake dog shit. Other odd card cappers included a blue Matchbox car, a dreidel, a small pyramid, a tin of Copenhagen, a framed photo of grandchildren, and a Rubik's Cube. My favorite? The guy with the sixteen-inch bowling trophy.

One superstitious British player insisted on wearing his lucky football jersey in the Main Event. He refused to wash the jersey because he feared it would lose its powers. The jersey emitted a horrendous stench that lingered in the Amazon Ballroom. Many of his opponents refused to continue until the he changed his shirt. Action was halted until "Mr. Smells Like Ass" finally acquiesced. The Gutshot poker club out of London gave him one of their logoed shirts hoping to catch some free publicity. He busted out twenty minutes later. They let him keep the shirt.

* * * * *

A group of five hippie kids moved into the adjacent building. Two white guys (with dreadlocks longer than Bob Marley's) and their girlfriends (with armpit hair that put mine to shame) unloaded a psychedelic-painted mini school bus. If there was a more "probable cause" vehicle on the road, I still have yet to see it. The girls had the usual hippie names like Astral and Jupiter and mentioned that they were en route to a couple of summer music festivals. I traded a small bag of Joo's weed for a handful of magic mushrooms. I considered brewing up a batch of shroom tea for the media room. That mind-bending state of consciousness would allow us to better cope with the remainder of the Main Event.

At the beginning of Day 3, Michalski and I watched Sammy Farha and Shawn Sheikhan engage each other in high-stakes prop bets as the money bubble approached and action slowed during hand-for-hand play. It was simple, as props should be. Each would pull a card out of the scramble and the person with the highest card won $1,000. They played it for a few minutes before being busted by the tournament director and forced to quit. Action-junkies being action-junkies, they flipped coins instead. Heads or tails for a grand. Farha went on a cold streak and lost $25,000. Once the money bubble burst, Farha settled his debt by tossing a $25,000 Bellagio chip over to Sheikhan.

"$25,000? We barely earn that much in a year," Michalski said.

On Day 4, Phil Ivey's table attracted fervent fans who stood ten deep on the rail in an attempt to snap a photo of the "Tiger Woods of Poker." I was living in an epileptic's nightmare as flashes went off every few seconds. I sweated Ivey's table with Jay Greenspan for a bit. One railbird leaned over and pushed both of us out of the way in a frenzied state trying to see the action.

"I can't see. You're standing in my way," the audacious railbird said.

"Don't fucking touch me again," I warned. "Do you want me to call the goons? They'll drag you into the back room and anally rape you with your Yard-o-Margarita."

Tensions were spiraling out of control because of the rail jackals. Their boldness increased the more that they drank. For whatever reason, drunks seemed to especially enjoy needling Andy Black. The savages were instinctively trying to break the Buddhist for simple sport. Black never backed down, and security had to be called in a couple of times.

Greg Raymer, defending champion and former patent attorney, also found himself jawing with a spectator after he pestered Raymer's wife, who tried to quietly watch the action from the rail. The complete stranger kept querying about Raymer's daughter. That'll draw anyone's ire,

60

and fast. An extremely serious Raymer stood up and pointed his finger at the guy.

"If you fuck with my daughter, you're dead," he barked.

Raymer spoke loud enough that everyone heard him in media row. The floor staff called for security, but the guy bolted before they arrived. He picked the wrong guy to mess with. Although Raymer seemed laid back at the tables, word on the street was, "Don't fuck with Raymer." Several months earlier, two guys jumped him on the way back to his room at the Bellagio. The assailants had guns and Raymer didn't. Standing almost six feet tall and weighing more than 300 pounds, Raymer took on both gunmen and thwarted the robbery attempt by sheer force.

On Day 5, the temperature inside the Amazon Ballroom reached the hottest it had been all summer, and it actually felt like we were in the Amazon jungle. It's not until the air-conditioning goes out that you remember Las Vegas was built up from scratch in the middle of the desert. Temperatures consistently soared past 110 degrees in July and I cursed the suit at Harrah's who decided to move the WSOP to the middle of the summer.

The ravenous railbirds returned and a dozen frat boys dressed up like nuns posed for photos with Andy Black in the hallway. A confident Mike Matusow walked over to media row and announced, "I'm playing the best poker of my life right now, boys! I can't help it. I play so good that the chips just come to me."

The bleachers at the TV table were packed as Matusow took center stage. The Mouth did not disappoint. He put on a show for the spectators and especially for ESPN's cameras. During one of the craziest hands at the Main Event, Matusow seized the chip lead after he bluffed Freddy Bonyadi with absolutely nothing. Never one not to rub it in, Matusow showed his cards which riled up the crowd.

Day 5 ended with 27 players remaining, officially marking the last day of the WSOP at the Rio Casino. The final two days were to be played out downtown at its traditional home, Binion's Horseshoe. I looked forward to shifting locales to downtown Las Vegas. After working in the same dreary place for six weeks straight, I finally said goodbye to the Rio.

Chapter 11

July 2005.

"Every May, you knew that the Horseshoe was the place to go for the World Series of Poker," Flipchip said. "It's going to take a while to get used to that change."

The WSOP and Binion's Horseshoe were such powerful brands that you never thought one would be able to exist without the other. But this is exactly what happened when Becky Behnen, the daughter of founder Benny Binion, allowed the Horseshoe to fall deeply into debt and the IRS closed its doors in early 2004. Harrah's Entertainment purchased the bankrupt Binion's and acquired the rights to the WSOP brand. Harrah's sold Binion's to the MTR Gaming Group, which took control of the casino itself and renamed it Binion's Gambling Hall and Hotel. The doors reopened in April of 2004.

Harrah's continued the tradition of the greatest poker tournament in the world, but it required a change of venue. By 2004 the WSOP had become so popular that Binion's had a tough time handling the influx of rabid poker fans and the lack of tournament space, prompting the move to the Rio. With respect for the historical significance of the WSOP, Harrah's executives agreed to play the final two days of the Main Event downtown in Benny's Bullpen at Binion's one last time.

In less-sanitized terms, Binion's turned into a piece of shit after Becky ran her deceased father's casino into the ground. What Binion's lacked in class, it made up in character. The lighting was intentionally poor in order to shield your eyes from the dismal plight of its inhabitants. Depending on where you stood the schizophrenic air-conditioning would either freeze your tits solid or leave you sweating your ass off. If you dropped money on the floor, you were better off letting it rot than risk contracting some form of flesh-eating bacteria trying to pick it up. The waitresses were hot pieces of ass – during the Cuban Missile Crisis. Binion's perpetually smelled of Ben-Gay, stale cigars, and a truck stop urinal. Downtown's dinginess made it a perfect backdrop for the Main Event. When you have to step over people lying in puddles of their own urine on Fremont Street in order to walk into the Horseshoe, it's a harsh reminder that you're only one bad beat away from lying face down in the gutter yourself.

The Strip became the hip place in town to stay and downtown couldn't hold onto its former luster. Nothing had been updated in a decade or more transforming the area into a dump. While you still had a steady flow of tourists seeking cheap rooms and food, the majority of the local clientele tended more and more to represent some of the lowest form of gambling scum in the Las Vegas Valley. The 99-cent shrimp cocktail specials don't exactly attract a jet-setting crowd. The ambiance and atmosphere were just as Al Alvarez described in *The Biggest Game in Town*. At one moment you could expect to see a high roller jump out of a limousine with a bag full of cash and the next you were worried about getting shanked in the parking lot by a tweaker. You might catch a glimpse of Johnny Chan signing autographs and then bash your shins on an old lady's wheelchair while she stuffs the last of her monthly annuity check into the penny slots. Downtown encapsulated the pinnacle of Western Civilization and its immediate downfall.

Flipchip parked in a desolate garage across the street from Binion's. He pointed to an unmarked door and I followed him. We walked up a flight of stairs, crossed the street on a pedestrian foot bridge, wandered down a long corridor, hopped on an escalator, and then magically appeared inside Binion's.

Binion's closed its Chinese restaurant and transformed the space into a makeshift media room with reporters sitting in big round booths with their laptops on the table. You could access Benny's Bullpen via a secret passageway in the kitchen. We used the shortcut to avoid the congestion of fans and media in the narrow hallway. As Flipchip showed me the way, I felt like I was part of a tracking shot in the Copacabana scene from *Goodfellas*.

A chill ran up my spine when I stepped into the room. I was inundated by a nostalgic feeling similar to my first visit to Yankee Stadium when I looked out onto the field where the ghosts of Babe Ruth and Joe DiMaggio held court. Benny's Bullpen was a post-modern version of the Roman Coliseum where gladiators fought to the death. Johnny Moss. Doyle Brunson. Stu Ungar. Johnny Chan. They all shared the same stale air as me. No wonder Benny's Bullpen was such an intimidating place. Players not only had to slug it out with the best in the world, they also had to survive the taunts and teases from the ghosts of the gambling greats.

Benny's Bullpen was poorly lit and smaller than I imagined. The media area was in the far back, tucked away in a corner, and I sat there with the rest of the peanut gallery – Greenspan, Otis, Mike Paulle, the Irish guys Murphy and Lacey, and Jen and Heather from Poker Wire. We couldn't view the tables from media row and had no other place to go since Benny's Bullpen was standing room only.

"You have no idea what it used to be like," said Mike Paulle, a former media director of the WSOP. "They never used to give internet guys badges. Five years ago, they never would have let you in."

The shoddy wi-fi inside Benny's Bullpen posed a threat to those producing live updates. The router had to be recycled once an hour, and even then the connection was often nonexistent. With no other options, everyone did their best to work with it. Flipchip wisely bought me an air card and that purchase saved the day.

With 27 players remaining, the big story was Greg Raymer's attempt to win the Main Event in consecutive years. I was rooting for Phil Ivey after I made a $100 bet with a Costa Rican sports book a few weeks earlier that Ivey would win it all at 300-1 odds. He was among the chip leaders and the bookmakers had him listed as the current 3-1 favorite. Raymer was the second favorite at 5-1. Mike Matusow was listed at 6-1 and Andy Black at 10-1. An amateur player and former chiropractor from Australia, Joe Hachem, was one of the long shots listed at 15-1.

Everyone in the room focused on Matusow, the most volatile and entertaining player left in the tournament. Everyone loves "rags to riches to jail" stories and Matusow fit the description perfectly. It took only ten minutes of action before he acquired his first F-bomb penalty of the day. I lost a prop bet to Otis because I incorrectly predicted the exact time that Matusow would get flagged for foul language.

Over the first couple of hours of play, the ESPN film crew frequently paused the action to record bust-out interviews. During one of the breaks, I went to the gift shop and bought my brother a deck of Binion's cards for his collection. I wandered out to the parking deck and found a secluded spot to smoke a joint. When I returned to Benny's Bullpen, one of the Irish guys asked me if I wanted a beer, and a round of Coronas ensued. They spent the rest of the night drinking Coronas and celebrating Andy Black's deep run. It seemed as though every poker enthusiast in Ireland was glued to their website awaiting updates on Black.

Greg Raymer suffered an ugly beat and lost most of his stack, busting out shortly afterwards in 25th place. He received a raucous standing ovation as he left Benny's Bullpen. Raymer collected a payday of $304,680 and ended a sensational two-year run in the Main Event.

With Raymer's elimination, Andy Black made some noise in a hand with Tim Phan. Although Black was way behind, the luck of the Irish prevailed as Black caught running queens to knock out Phan. I peeked down media row and saw Murphy and Lacey jumping up and down like little kids. Just as Black was attempting to pull away, however, he lost a chunk of his chips to Joe Hachem. That was the first time we heard the catchy chant from a contingency of Australians in the crowd.

"Aussie, Aussie, Aussie! Oi, oi, oi!" they screamed in unison after Hachem won the pot.

Phil Ivey busted out in 20th place and I didn't win my bet. With Ivey's departure, it came down to the two most experienced players left in Benny's Bullpen; Mike Matusow and Andy Black. By Midnight, Andy Black had taken over the chip lead with 11 players to go. The Irish guys could not contain their excitement. We're supposed to be impartial as members of the media, but Irish Pride trumped that unspoken rule. Murphy and Lacey did their best to celebrate as quietly as possible, but sometimes they exploded in jubilation.

When ten players remained, the Main Event reached the final table bubble. Only nine players advanced to the final table and we'd soon forget about the poor sap who busted in 10th place. An unusually quiet Mike Matusow lingered in the middle of the pack during the uneventful first hour of the bubble. By the second hour it appeared that fatigue was setting in for everyone including ESPN's second unit, which had been taping the facial expressions of the players' loved ones looking for a shot of pure joy or utter disappointment. The crowd lost their rowdy enthusiasm and was being lulled to sleep by the lack of action. With millions of dollars on the line, no one wanted to make a foolish mistake. The Aussies screamed "Oi, oi, oi!" every time Joe Hachem won a pot, but even the exuberance of their chant was slipping. By 3 a.m., the final table bubble finally burst. Nine players remained, and both Matusow and Black had advanced with a shot at becoming the next world champion.

* * * * *

Although the final table was scheduled for 4 p.m., Flipchip and I arrived at Binion's two hours early to get into position. The stands were packed with friends and family of the final table players – Joe Hachem, Andy Black, Tex Barch, Daniel Bergsdorf, Mike Matusow, Aaron Kanter, Brad Kondracki, Steve Dannenmann, and Scott Lazar. Railbirds were already lining up just to watch the last final table ever to be held at Binion's. The line wrapped around the buffet, down the narrow hall, and backed up all the way to the media room. Everyone who couldn't get inside Benny's Bullpen watched the action on big screens inside the buffet or downstairs at the sports book. 1973 WSOP champion Puggy Pearson made an appearance at the final table and even sang a song he wrote specifically for the occasion.

Noel Furlong was the only Irishman to win the Main Event. All Irish eyes hoped that native son Andy Black could bring the championship back to the Emerald Isle for the first time since 1999. Within minutes of setting up shop in media row, Murphy and Lacey were on their second round of Coronas.

Greg Raymer started things off as he announced, "Shuffle up and deal." Less than eight minutes later, Matusow moved all-in with pocket kings and found himself trailing Scott Lazar's aces. Matusow flopped a set of kings to take the lead, but Lazar caught running hearts to make a flush. Lazar doubled up and the anti-Matusow fans in the crowd went ballistic while Matusow looked devastated, furiously rubbing his temples.

During the first break, I walked into the bathroom and waited for an open spot. Phil Hellmuth peed with his sunglasses on as he chatted with Raymer about the final table players. Raymer was kind enough to sign a few autographs in the men's room – after washing his hands. Matusow suddenly burst into the bathroom on tilt and steaming.

"Hang in there, Mike," Hellmuth said. "You have plenty of chips. Just play smart."

"I told myself I wasn't going to play any big pots early. And I played three. Fuck!" Matusow lamented.

"Tough spot there. It's hard to lay down kings pre-flop like that," said Hellmuth sympathizing with Matusow.

"The guy next to me said he folded two hearts too. Can't believe it. I flopped a set too. Fuck!" Matusow shouted.

By the end of the first break, Matusow was in trouble with a short stack and looked like Patrick Ewing during a free throw as a river of sweat ran down his face. Alas, Matusow's comeback came to a screeching halt when he became the first player eliminated at the final table, winning $1,000,000 for ninth place.

With Matusow's departure, Andy Black was the most skilled player remaining and he quickly applied pressure with a barrage of raises, increasing his stack and taking the lead. With six players to go, Hachem doubled his short stack and the Aussies unleashed their chant. His cheering section had been silent for most of the final table until they finally had a chance to go nuts and frantically wave the Aussie flag.

Black coughed up the chip lead after losing two decisive pots and went from being the hunter to the hunted. He busted out in fifth place after losing a race against Steve Dannenmann. Black won $1,750,000 for his efforts, but looked like he was going to cry. Hellmuth rushed to Black and offered up some encouraging words as the crowd gave him the loudest send-off of the final table.

"He deserved better," Murphy said. "He played his heart out."

With Black's departure, the Irish guys packed up their gear and left. Their last post said something like "Going to celebrate with Andy. For updates on the rest of the tournament, go read Pauly's blog."

With four players remaining the action slowed considerably. By 3:15 a.m., the crowd at Benny's Bullpen had thinned. On every break, I snuck through the secret passageway in the kitchen and smoked a joint on the desolate parking deck.

Around 5 a.m., Aaron Kanter was eliminated in fourth place and Hachem took over the chip lead. With three players left, ESPN halted production for the money presentation. Two thugs with shotguns followed a procession of suits carrying boxes full of money. They dumped bricks of cash on the table and placed the winner's bracelet on top of the pile. Security guards kept the swarm of photographers away from the table.

"Unless you have a shotgun, you need to step away from the money," tournament director Johnny Grooms said over the PA.

In typical Vegas fashion, it's all for show. The shotguns are empty. The pyramid of money on the table is not really millions of dollars. The bricks are $1 bills with $100 bills wrapped around the outside to give the illusion of a monstrous mountain of cash.

The action dragged for another hour until Tex Barch busted out in third place. When heads-up play finally began, the world championship came down to two amateurs; an Australian chiropractor, Hachem, and an accountant and financial advisor from Maryland, Steve Dannenmann. After a half-hour of heads-up play and at 6:40 a.m. local time, Hachem flopped a straight with 7-3 off-suit becoming the new world champion. He won $7.5 million and outlasted 5,618 players (at the time, the largest field at the Main Event) at the longest final table in the history of the WSOP, clocking in at over 14 hours.

Like most major events, the climax was uneventful because everyone involved was dogtired. After patiently waiting to snap a winner's photo, we left Binion's at around 8 a.m. and said goodbye to Benny's Bullpen for the last time.

"The WSOP might go on forever," Flipchip mentioned. "But as long as the final table is not played in Benny's Bullpen, it will never be the same."

Chapter 12

July 2005.

"I accidentally smuggled a hit of ecstasy past customs," she said. "Do you want half?"

She had forgotten about the pill. It must have been at least a year old. She stashed it with her vitamins and needed to get rid of it before she was grilled by airport security. It was her last night in Las Vegas before flying back to Europe. I snapped the familiar pill in half and washed mine down with a swig of Southern Comfort. She popped her half and disappeared into the crowd of gamblers at the Mirage.

I sat in the lounge near the sports book with Otis and some of his work colleagues. We were done with our assignments and ready to celebrate. It was Otis' last night in Las Vegas; he rebooked his flight for a couple of days earlier because he missed his family. Las Vegas was a tough assignment for scribes without any attachments, let alone someone with them. I wanted to leave as well, but I was stuck in the 120 degree heat for a couple of more weeks.

After getting cold-decked at the video poker machines, we ended up in the pits at an empty craps table. I kept the betting simple; Pass Line bets and odds behind the line. We each rolled once and I didn't hit any points. On the second go-around, we made a run while Jesus, a friend of a friend from California, stood at the other end of the table ready to roll.

Nothing is more magical than a sizzling craps table in Las Vegas, where loud and rowdy behavior is encouraged. The ruckus induces more action. You want to gamble more when you see other people win large sums of money right in front of you with a simple toss of the dice.

Jesus from California was on a hot rush and I relinquished my roll, so Jesus shot again. Everyone else at the table did the same and passed their rolls to Jesus. I drooled at the collection of green $25 chips that had accumulated after a series of successful come bets. Jesus hit three points in a row and the volume at our table grew louder and louder as a crowd of curious spectators gathered.

Every time Jesus from California hit a point, I screamed out in the most obnoxious crooked preacher voice I could muster, "Thank you, Jesus!"

Greed seeped into my brain and I deviated from my simple betting strategy. Everything was happening so fast. I spread money all over the table and even bet a green chip on a hard eight for the boys. I never saw a stick man happier than when he acknowledged my bet.

I should have walked when I was up. How many other losers say the same thing? But we were on a sick rush. Jesus was untouchable. Life seemed too perfect until a slick L.A. douche bag in a $500 blazer joined the table. I immediately picked up a bad vibe from the guy when he threw his money down on the felt like a mush. My gut told me to flee, like when a smelly bum plops down next to me on the subway. Yet, I stuck around and lost the majority of my profit during his roll. Even Jesus succumbed to the dark veil of the hipster's bad luck when the dice danced on the felt like a nimble ballerina, only to fall onto the side of desperation. We all looked at each other in a communal moment of clarity and finally walked away. I wanted to give that ass-clown the beat-down of his life and steal his expensive jacket as fair compensation for being a cooler.

I retreated to the sports book bar with Otis to shake off L.A. douche bag tilt. A championship dog obstacle course race was airing on ESPN2, and I turned to Otis and nodded. It was time to recklessly gamble on heads-up canine obstacle races. Otis picked a scrappy dog named Quick. I picked Splendor. After a slow start, my pooch closed the gap. For the next two minutes, we were two drunken idiots cursing at the TV monitor and cheering on the dogs as they navigated the course.

"Come on, Quick!" Otis screamed.

"Get yer ass in gear, Splendor!" I shouted.

The gambling gods were on my side. My dog won the first race and Otis tossed me cash. A chubby tourist in flip-flops waddled over, "Are you guys betting on those dogs?"

"Fuck yeah," I responded. "$100 a pop. You want in, tough guy?"

The tourist declined and waddled away while Otis and I prepped for the next race.

* * * * *

After seven tedious weeks of work, I finally had time to myself and developed a routine. I spent most of my days writing at the Redneck Riviera and hung out with Grubby at night. It was during those nights that I really got to know Las Vegas through the eyes of a local.

Nine months earlier, Grubby had quit his job at a magazine in Washington D.C. and moved to Las Vegas to play poker for a living. A short Asian guy in his thirties, Grubby looked like a college student and was constantly carded all around town by dealers, bartenders, and security guards. Grubby adored buffets, developed an addiction to slot machines, and absolutely loved strip clubs.

Grubby lived in a condo in Henderson and played slots all around town. He accumulated a ton of food comps at different casinos and he treated me to a couple of free meals every week courtesy of his staggering slot losses. For Grubby, a buffet is both an art and a science. He exhibited a voracious appetite for a small guy. As a connoisseur, he was highly critical of my food choices, scolding me for filling up on too many pastas and starches.

"Why get the pizza, when there's prime rib or sushi on the menu?" Grubby asked. "To properly destroy a Las Vegas buffet, eat little to nothing on your buffet day. If you gamble, ask for a comp or line pass; besides drinks, it's the cheapest thing for casinos to give away. Arrive at the tail end of the lunch session so you can stay and enjoy the dinner spread at a cheaper price. Go to the serving stations first to put in your order, then load up your plate with the expensive food. Seize the opportunity to sample what you don't normally eat. Then return and claim your custom food on a different plate."

The philosophy is simple. Devour the high-end items at the buffet, such as Alaskan king crab or Kobe beef. Grubby also recommended saving more room for the delicious desserts, but he primarily judged a buffet on two things: corn on the cob and peeled shrimp. If a buffet had both items, then it had a chance to receive his highest rating.

After visiting many buffets with Grubby, I've devised a method of buffet feasting more suited to my tastes. Instead of waiting until the end of the meal for dessert, I ate a round of sweets in the middle. My first trip includes a plate of high-end specialty items per Grubby's suggestion. On the second trip, I pile up a bunch of pies, cakes, pastries, homemade cookies, and gelato. After my sugar rush subsides, I return to the main buffet and eat a couple of those items that Grubby thinks are a waste of space.

Grubby and I maximized our buffet experiences and spent at least two hours in every buffet that we hit, sometimes more. Between rounds of eating, we engaged in lengthy discussions about poker, usually about a hand we played the night before. I asked a lot of questions about Grubby's gambling and he was brutally honest about his losses. Poker was the only game he won at, yet he pissed his bankroll away at the slots or playing online blackjack.

"If I don't start winning soon, I'll have to get a regular job," he said.

On rare instances, we talked about writing since Grubby was also a former playwright. When he originally moved to Las Vegas, he thought that he'd write a couple of hours a day and work on a screenplay. Instead, he found himself spending those hours wasting away at a Mr. Cashman slot machine or trying to win a share of the bad-beat jackpot at one of the Station Casinos.

"Someday, I'm gonna hit that jackpot," he said.

* * * * *

Señor looked like Vince Vaughn, but he barreled through life with the spirit of John Belushi. We went to college together in Atlanta and rushed the same fraternity. We frequented the local strip clubs on nights when I should have been preparing for my film studies exam or writing a paper on Huey Long for my Southern Politics class. Instead, I spent many a hazy, fuzzy, bourbon-drenched night at Tops N' Tails sitting in the front row of its biggest attraction – hot oil wrestling. What can I say? I was a horny teenager and sexually repressed after attending Catholic school for thirteen years.

After our roaring twenties, Señor settled down and started a family. He worked in the financial industry while I continued to live on the fringe. Once he found out I was moving to Las Vegas for work, he booked a trip after my assignment was over so we could hang out. I offered to let him crash at the Redneck Riviera but he read about the plight on my blog and opted to stay at the Luxor. He bribed the front desk clerk with a $20 bill and a sly smile and she upgraded him to a suite.

After getting our asses handed to us at the sports book, Señor, Grubby, and I needed stripper therapy to get our minds off the losses. We stumbled into Sin, one of the newer establishments in town. Señor bought the first round. The waitress fumbled with our overpriced drinks and I stared out at the main stage. A young lady in a fluorescent orange thong with manufactured breasts the size of cantaloupes jiggled upside down on a pole as the last few lines of a vaguely familiar Motley Crüe song blasted over the speakers.

Grubby ordered an imported beer; I asked for a Stoli and tonic, and Señor aptly grabbed a Corona and a shot of tequila. The man cannot under any circumstances remain sober and fully enjoy himself inside a strip club.

Rebekka, a former XFL cheerleader, wandered over to me. The striking 23-year-old black woman was working her first shift after being hired the day before. She had quit Spearmint Rhino after a dispute with the manager. Grubby told me that if the girls don't like working for a particular club, it usually meant that they were sick of performing sexual favors on their sleazy managers.

"What's your name?" she asked.

"Charlie." Love those easy one-word lies.

"What do you do for a living?"

"I work on Wall Street."

That was only a partial lie. I was retired. Rebekka sat on my lap and immediately invited me into the VIP room, the biggest hustle in town where the strippers try to get the rest of the cash left in your pockets. Although comedian Chris Rock once said, "There's no sex in the Champagne Room," that does not necessarily apply to Las Vegas. However, if you want to get laid, you have to shell out big bucks. This one thought I was a rich guy from Wall Street and was going in for the kill early. I didn't like the hard sell and sent her away.

Grubby and Señor were in the middle of simultaneous lap dances while I sipped on a warm Corona and stared at the acrobatic stripper spinning around the pole on the main stage. My mind raced back and forth between different topics. I thought about philosophers like Kierkegaard, Heidegger, and Sartre and how the face of 20th Century philosophy might have changed if they had frequented Las Vegas. How could you maintain a meaningless and bleak existence when your face was buried in the chest of a tweaking former homecoming queen who used your nose as her personal ass-battering ram?

I made eye contact with Jessinna and she honed in on me. She wore a pink Victoria's Secret bathing suit and I became enamored with the Jessica Alba look-alike. I debated whether or not God created the perfect stripper. She lived in the moment and focused all of her attention on me. She purchased her own Coronas and wasn't there to suck every dollar out of my pocket.

"You having a good time tonight?" she asked.

"The possible ranks higher than the actual."

"You didn't just make that shit up?" she screamed into my ear over the blaring music. "You don't think I'm that fuckin' stupid where you can pass off a second-rate quote from an out-dated philosopher like Heidegger? He's a Nazi, you know."

My bluff had been called. There's something very sexy, yet surreal, when a naked woman debates Heidegger with you while you attempt to drown out the Britney Spears song blasting in the background. Jessinna sat down on my lap and we discussed the origins of all her tattoos, including the Taz inked on her ass, which was a long and convoluted story that took about four songs for her to explain. The aroma of her light brown hair aroused me. I had doubts and kept badgering her about it. She insisted that Jessinna was her real name and that her father back in El Paso, Texas had picked it off a Mexican soap opera.

The first few notes of *Enter Sandman* boomed over the sound system and Jessinna jumped to her feet. She took off her top and gyrated and grinded and I sniffed her hair as it dangled over me. I felt the warmth of her blowing into my ear.

Normally, I equated *Enter Sandman* with the New York Yankees relief pitcher, Mariano Rivera. That Metallica song played whenever he entered the game. Since the late 1990s, Mo has been the most dominant closer in all of baseball. As soon as you heard *Enter Sandman* on Yankee Stadium's PA system, Mo would sprint out of the bullpen toward the pitcher's mound and Yankees fans went apeshit. The game would be over in a matter of minutes because Mo was untouchable.

"I fuckin' love this song!" Jessinna cooed.

Mo who?

Chapter 13

December 2004.

The Excalibur. My friends condescendingly called it "The Castle" because that's what it was – a big white fucking castle across from the MGM and nestled next to the Luxor. The cheesy medieval-themed casino offered inexpensive rooms that attracted vacationing families and budget travelers. The Excalibur's poker room catered to beginners and tourists. They used kitschy promotions to snare locals, offering free food (the "best boiled" hotdogs in Vegas) and cash bonuses if you had your pocket aces cracked.

The Castle is where I took my brother Derek to pop his Las Vegas poker cherry. We played at the same table with a drunken conventioneer, who continuously passed out between hands. I knew my brother had the killer instinct to play poker when he had no qualms about fleecing the shitfaced guy for every last dollar in his pocket. Despite it only being his first Las Vegas session, I was impressed with my brother's tenacious survival instincts. Show no mercy at the poker tables.

The following year, we visited Las Vegas with a group of twenty or so poker bloggers and capped off the amazing weekend with a visit to the Excalibur poker room. Grubby, Derek, and I were seated at different low-limit tables. I found a spot in the first seat, to the left of the dealer. An extremely drunk chubby girl, looking like Drew Barrymore's trailer-park cousin, sat next to me in Seat 2. She slurped a pink drink through a straw and giggled uncontrollably. Her breasts trembled like the ground near Kilauea volcano every time she laughed. As I watched her spill out of her white Juicy Couture halter top, I actually wrote down in my notebook, *"She had tits the size of a microwave."*

She played any two cards to the river and roared through her rack of chips with questionable calls while pounding drinks like Judy Garland. She bombarded me with questions.

"Where are you from?"

"Rhode Island," I answered.

"What do you do?"

"Aquarium salesman at Fish R' Us. Do you want my card?"

"Why are you here?"

"The rodeo. My probation ended and I was finally free to leave the state."

When I asked her what she did for a living she giggled and threw me a seductive glance. Her voice lowered, "I make men happy."

I waited for the punch line, or at least an explanation. Nothing. She let my mind wander. How could she make men happy? She's a kick-ass mechanic? An amazing cook? Cocaine dealer? A call girl?

She ordered another vodka-cran and begged the cocktail waitress to go heavy on the vodka.

I shuffled my chips a couple of times. Nothing fancy, just a basic chip trick that somehow caught her attention.

"That's coooooool! Can you teach me how to do that?"

I gave her a thirty-second tutorial on how to shuffle a stack of chips. The drunk girl gave it a try. Chips flew all over the table and fell on the floor. She giggled.

"I can't do that. But I can do this trick!"

She touched her nose with her tongue. Twice, just in case I missed it the first time.

"My," as I paused for dramatic effect, "That's impressive."

"I can do it again!" she squealed.

She was the perfect Vegas fish – soused and without a clue, evidenced by the pot I won against her with bottom pair. Whenever she'd lose all of her chips, she sprinted over to a table on the other side of the room where her "friend" was seated. Her friend was a silver-haired gentleman who was old enough to be her grandfather. She asked him for more chips and always returned to my table with $25 or so, then proceeded to lose it all on one hand. She repeated this process seven more times.

My rush was just beginning to get its legs when a new guy in a blue Boeing baseball hat sat down in seat 5.

> *Seat 1: Your hero*
>
> *Seat 2: Chatty chubby hooker with huge tits*
>
> *Seat 5: New guy*
>
> *Seat 7: Drunk married woman*
>
> *Seat 8: Husband of drunk married woman*

A new dealer sat down and I asked how her night was going.

"I just started my shift. Ask again in a little bit," she said.

On the first hand, I got dealt Qs-9s on the button. I limped into a seven-way pot. The flop contained the ace of spades and a baby spade. Someone bet out and everyone called. The turn was a blank. Someone bet again and I raised with my flush draw. Everyone folded except the new guy in Seat 5 and the drunk married woman in Seat 7. The king of spades fell on the river and filled in my nut flush. Apparently, I spaced out for a few seconds, most likely distracted by the hooker with big tits next to me. The dealer reminded me that everyone checked and it was my turn to act. I came to, cursing the distractive power of Microwave Tits. I paused for a couple of seconds and reached for my chips. Drunk married woman thought that I also checked the river. She exposed her cards.

"Wait, I had not acted yet. I was going to bet," I said.

"Ma'am, it's still his turn. Please turn your cards back over," the dealer said.

"What the fuck? He checked!" the drunk woman screamed.

"No, ma'am. It's still his turn to act," the dealer said.

Drunk woman threw up her arms and cursed again under her breath.

"Please watch your language, ma'am."

I bet $6. The new guy in seat 5 check-raised me to $12. The married woman folded and obnoxiously threw her cards towards the center of the table.

"Asshole," she blurted out giving me the evil eye.

"Way to go you dumb shit," the new guy said.

"Go fuck yourself!" the drunk woman yelled.

"It won't be as good as fucking you," the new guy said.

I picked up chips and was about to announce a raise when the husband in seat 8 jumped up to defend his wife's honor. He ran towards the new guy, who stood up to confront the bull charge. The husband threw him onto an adjacent poker table. Chips flew everywhere as the two scuffled.

"Security! Security!" one of the dealers screamed.

"Protect your chips, motherfuckers!" I hollered to the rest of the players at my table. I slammed my hand down on my hole cards to protect my winning hand and positioned my left arm over my stack just in case someone decided to use the fight as an opportunity for a grab-and-run.

White $1 chips were scattered across the floor. The entire room buzzed with excitement. Players on other tables stood up on chairs to watch. The fracas continued until a swarm of security guards rushed into the poker room and pried the two apart. The drunk wife attempted to sneak out but got nabbed a few steps outside of the poker room. Three innocent bystanders, including an elderly woman, suffered minor injuries when the melee spilled over to their table.

Despite being interrupted by the fight, the hand was still live. I had the stone-cold nuts and I wanted to get paid off. The floor supervisor walked over to the table to discuss the situation with the dealer. A Las Vegas Metro Police officer escorted the guy back to the table. His right eye was swollen and his bottom lip puffed out. He had a welt the size of a golf ball protruding from his forehead. Tourists usually buy souvenirs to remind them of their trip to Las Vegas, but this chump got his face rearranged.

The officer and the floor supervisor hovered over our table as we were signaled to complete the hand. I should have reraised him, but I felt bad that he got his ass kicked, and I just wanted to get the hand over. I only called and won the pot with the nut flush. I tipped the dealer $10.

* * * * *

August 2005.

I sat next to an attractive woman with long brown hair and a Hollywood starlet smile. We struck up an hour-long conversation during a late-night session of poker at the Excalibur. She was in town for some sort of architecture convention. With an early morning flight to San Diego scheduled, she decided to stay up all night. After she lost her stack on an ugly beat, she'd had enough poker.

"I'm going to grab a drink at the bar," she said and I accepted her invite.

After covering the top professional gamblers in the world, I got pretty good at reading amateur poker players and civilians. She gave off all of the obvious signs (subtle glances, flipping her hair, smiling whenever I spoke, touching my elbow) that she was interested in more than just a drink. Of course, that was part of the game.

We walked to the Mandalay Bay and I wondered if she was a working girl. We knocked back a few drinks at the Center Isle Bar and after some amateur detective work, I crossed prostitute off the list. Maybe she could be the rare exception to my "single women talking to me after midnight are hookers" rule, but I was still suspicious. Did I accidentally stumble upon a sophisticated ring of Chinese organ thieves and she was the bait? Perhaps she was duping me and preyed on lonely single men in the poker room? I could see her luring them back to her room where she'd drug them with roofies, steal their cash and credit cards, and pilfer organs with wild abandon. The poor schlep would regain consciousness many hours later in a bathtub full of ice with a poorly stitched scar on his torso.

I had been in Vegas for two months and hadn't gotten laid once. I was willing to take my chances, organ thieves or not, and followed her up to her room at the Mandalay Bay. The future was looking bright for my free-range penis when she pulled a piece of wadded-up paper out of her purse.

"We have to do all of this before my flight in a couple of hours," she said as she cut up a couple of lines.

P.J. O'Rourke wrote an article in Rolling Stone back in the 1980s about cocaine etiquette. He said that it was standard that if a man gave a woman coke, then she was obliged to have sex with him. And if a woman gave a man coke, then he was obliged to snort as much as he could before he came up with a believable excuse to leave – but not before he snorted a line for the road.

One rail. Then another. And another. The bathroom overflowed with cocaine gibberish. Another line. Then another. And yet another. I couldn't remember her name as we exchanged sloppy kisses. I scrambled to recall but my brain was fried. She told me. Twice. I forgot both times.

Missy? Sadie? Amy? I couldn't enjoy the blow job. What was her fuckin' name? Amanda? Megan? Nicole? The voyeur in me preferred the reflection in the mirror. However, the Buddhist in me wanted to enjoy the moment. I looked down. Rachel? Lindsey? Cindy?

Neither of us had any condoms. I pulled up my pants, tucked my erection into my waistband, and awkwardly rushed through the casino in search of prophylactics at the crack of dawn like a vampire running way behind schedule.

I rode the elevator clutching condoms as an evil wave of cocaine-induced paranoia set in. I convinced myself that I was being set up by a secret agent for the Chinese. But, what if she wasn't and was simply another harmless coke slut from Orange County? I was horny and didn't want to miss out on a sure thing. What was her name? Anita? Nina? Melanie?

I walked down the hallway calculating my odds. 29 percent chance she's trying to steal my organs. 64 percent chance she's a coke slut. But wait, that math didn't add up. I reached the door and slightly hyperventilated. I was either going to get laid or have my kidneys ripped out. That's makes my odds 50-50. I can live with a coin flip. I knocked. She slowly opened the door and let me inside. I looked inside the bathroom. No Chinese organ thieves. I quickly checked under the bed which drew her suspicion.

"What are you looking for?"

"No Chinese organ thieves here, either," I muttered.

It was just the two of us. The blinds were open and the first speckles of sunlight began to peer over the mountains. As more morning light made its way into the valley, the gold tinted windows of Mandalay Bay made the room glow. What's her friggin' name? Layla? Maya? Kristen?

The sex was complicated. I was too jacked up and distracted. I couldn't remember her name and it was killing me. I grabbed her hair and yanked it back. She squealed and I screamed, "What's my name? Who owns this pussy?!"

She blurted out, "Paul... Pauly! Pauly... owns my pussy!"

"Who owns this pussy?"

"Pauly! Oh, God Pauly!"

"And whose pussy am I fucking?"

"Stacy," she screamed. "Stacy!"

"Stacy? That's right, Stacy!" I howled. "Finally! Jesus. Fuckin'. Christ. Stacy!"

Part II

"At any street corner the feeling of absurdity
can strike any man in the face."

– Albert Camus

Chapter 14

October 2005.

I had just completed a work assignment at the Bellagio covering the Doyle Brunson North American Poker Classic that ended a few days before Vegoose, a multi-day music festival featuring some of our favorite hippie and hipster bands. The Joker flew into Vegas to throw down for Vegoose weekend, which kicked off on Thursday evening with back-to-back concerts at the theatre inside the Aladdin Casino.

The Joker and I began following the band Phish across America together in 2004 when he was a part-time musician and grad student in Dallas. After completing his M.B.A. in finance, the Joker relocated to Boulder, Colorado and found work as a stockbroker. He often joked that he was the only person in Boulder who wore a tie. He put in long hours during the week and went skiing every weekend. The Joker and I had a similar philosophy in life: work hard and party harder.

We walked into the lobby of the Aladdin and an old hippie, who looked like bluegrass legend Dave Grisman, sold me a hunk of hash for $20. Five minutes later, I bought a bag of aromatic blueberry marijuana from a kid with dreadlocks who said he drove down from Humboldt County, California. We completed the transaction in the men's room because I was too afraid of the eye-in-the-sky surveillance cameras. The Joker scored molly (pure MDMA) from a jittery kid with a sideways hat who ducked behind a row of Wheel of Fortune slot machines next to a geriatric zombie in a wheelchair.

We had tickets to an early show featuring Dave Matthews with Tim Reynolds, followed by the Trey Anastasio Band (fronted by the guitar player from Phish) at Midnight. After Dave Matthews finished his set, we mingled outside with a bevy of custie sorority girls (mostly known in music circles for their ability to smoke enough dope to get an entire horn section of a reggae band stoned, yet they also care enough about their personal appearance to shave their arm pits and wear Victoria's Secret g-strings). The sidewalk in front of the Aladdin had transformed into a "Shakedown Street" or an impromptu market where various goods were being sold such as concert posters, home-made t-shirts, marijuana cookies, and psychedelics.

We were smoking a joint of the blueberry and marveling at the brilliant lights of The Strip when a high school kid offered to sell us LSD. He wore a tie-dyed String Cheese Incident t-shirt and held hands with his hot, jailbait girlfriend. The Cheese kid needed to move an entire sheet of acid, but was worried about all the undercover cops roaming around. Even though we told him we were FBI agents, he sold us a couple of strips anyway. The Joker couldn't figure out how someone that naïve could be a drug dealer and score a beautiful girlfriend at the same time. For a brief moment, I considered beating the piss out of the Cheese kid, stealing his drugs, and running away to San Francisco with his girlfriend. But alas, then I'd have an Amber Alert on my hands. The federales would lock me up and throw away the key for sure if they caught me with a 16-year-old and a glove compartment full of doses.

The Joker and I sat in the next to last row for the Trey Anastasio Band show. The sound was blah, but we smoked hash during the entire second set. Trey's show ended around 4 a.m. and the crowd rushed out the theatre exits. Las Vegas casinos are built with the specific purpose of keeping people inside, and the Aladdin was one of the most confusing casinos on The Strip with its mile of shops and labyrinth gaming area. Thousands of spun-out hippies, Phishkids, wookies, and other mutants flooded the Aladdin casino floor.

"They're letting the freaks out! Here come the freaks!" I screamed.

For the tourists who had no idea a music festival was going on, the sight was startling. Eyes grew wide as gangs of dirty hippies stumbled around in a jovial daze. The unleashed miscreants, however, did nothing to deter the degenerates from plugging away at the slot machines. They kept their heads down and kept on gambling, ignoring the bizarre scene right behind them.

"Here come the freaks!"

Despite the eye in the sky, kids conducted deals behind rows of slot machines while rolling hippie chicks watched the hypnotic blinking lights. Others headed toward the bar for post-show cocktails or continued to dance at the bar above the poker room.

Grubby was playing poker at the Aladdin during the concerts and felt free to comment: "The entire poker room reeked of pot. Were those hippies getting high inside the casino? The aroma was so pungent. Everyone at my table was joking around that they got a contact high. The highlight of the night was when the concert let out and all those braless hippie chicks got lost and wandered through the poker room."

The Joker and I finally navigated our way through the madness and found the exit. As we walked down Las Vegas Boulevard, the Joker asked me for tips on how to spot a hooker in Las Vegas. I gave him a quick tutorial, and he properly identified two hookers in front of

Fatburger – a tall, lanky black woman in a blue wig and a portly white girl wearing a short skirt with her beer belly slipping out of her top. The Joker was amazed at the openness of the local sex trade even though I tried explaining (in our condition) that it was simply another integral part of Las Vegas, like the all-you-can-eat shrimp buffet, except with more STDs.

A trip to Excalibur's food court helped us beat the late night munchies, and I lost $50 on prop bets trying to flick a McDonald's cup lid into a trash can. We capped off the night with a run to Krispy Kreme and were on our way downstairs with a bag full of donuts when a Nubian goddess with gold hoop earrings stopped us in front of the escalators.

"What did you buy me?" she said.

"Um, how about an apple fritter with two bite marks?" I said.

"Ewww, no thanks. So what are you guys up to? Are you looking to party?"

"Not tonight. We're locals and we're heading home."

Mentioning that you're a local is code for hookers. It means you know they're working and are not interested in their services. It's the polite way to blow them off.

* * * * *

On the second day of Vegoose, the Joker wore an authentic UPS uniform while carrying a bag full of packages and a clipboard. He intended to deliver them to random people who he thought were wearing the coolest costumes. Each package included candy, party snaps, ribbed condoms, Mardi Gras beads, glowsticks, and his business card. The Joker is a master of clever generosity.

I wore doctor's scrubs and instantly bonded with others wearing similar costumes. We quickly became part of the "doctors schmoozing with other doctors" crowd, and I found myself walking up to slutty nurses and "examining" them for lumps in their breasts without any hassles. For a brief moment, I had an idea what Frank Sinatra must have felt like being able to get away with such tawdry behavior.

After being perfect little sheep for 364 days a year, Halloween is the one night when adults can fly their freak flags high. Closeted queers can act like their flamboyant selves without anyone giving them guff. Women dress up in provocative outfits and no one judges them on their choice of skimpy clothing. Total acid freaks can walk around dosed out of their minds and no one says a word. I especially appreciated the girls who incorporated fishnet stockings and cleavage into their animal costumes. Vegoose was populated with what seemed like an inordinate amount of slutty cats, mice, and bunnies.

For one of the late night shows, I headed over to the House of Blues at Mandalay Bay to see whether I could scrounge up an extra ticket to the sold-out Galactic show. No such luck. The only people holding tickets were sketched-out locals trying to scalp them for triple the face value. I milled around in front of the venue doing some people-watching when I ran into an old friend, Eddie from Chino. I barely recognized him in his costume; Baumer from the *Royal Tenanbaums*, while his girlfriend dressed like Gwyneth Paltrow's character from the same flick. They also failed to score a ticket, so we retreated to Mandalay Bay's Hooker Bar for cocktails. We were fascinated by the various harlot flavors hawking pussy to soused wastoids from the music festival who hadn't slept in two or three days.

I glanced at my cell phone and realized that it was past 5 a.m. I thought of my brother back in New York on the subway heading to work on a cheerless Monday morning while I hung out with Eddie and his friends. One squirrelly looking guy named Dodger – I never got the explanation of his nickname – had enough acid to light up the entire state of Wisconsin. The deviant fucker bought drinks for two hookers and slipped them a dose of liquid sunshine in the form of sugar cubes. They hardly noticed the extra sweetness in their fruity cocktails. As one of the working girls put a glass to her lips, she glanced at me as she caught her last breath of sober air.

"See you on the other side," I said.

* * * * *

For me, Halloween 2005 continues to be the measuring stick against which all other benders are gauged. The irony, of course, is that I wasn't actively attempting to pursue the achievement when it happened. It just happened. Las Vegas lulls you into letting your guard down and strikes when you least expect it.

Widespread Panic, one of my favorite Southern rock bands, based out of Athens, Georgia, capped off the Vegoose event with a Halloween concert at the Thomas & Mack Center. I've never been able to put my finger on it, but there's something about that building that harnesses a fantastic vibe and energy. Some of the best concerts I've ever seen have taken place in that arena, including a sizzling Phish show on Halloween in 1998, when they covered the entire *Loaded* album by Velvet Underground.

The Joker and I arrived early, in costume, and wandered around the parking lot to mingle with the thousands of other dressed-up fans. As serial attendees, we appreciated the people who put time and effort into their outfits. One stand-out was a guy dressed as The Dude from *The Big Lebowski*. We shot the shit with him for a few minutes and discovered that he was also a dealer.

"I got your ninja molly right here!" he yelled and unleashed a few karate chops.

The Joker and I inspected the goods and purchased a couple of pills. We already had a decent collection of party favors; our goal was to take all of them before the night ended. We'd been pacing ourselves and the time had come to escalate the intensity of our bender to its zenith.

Widespread Panic's concert had general admission seating and we made our way down to what would be the equivalent of center court at an UNLV basketball game. We popped a couple of pills and ogled the hippie girls in slutty costumes. A guy in green hospital scrubs and wearing a surgical mask wandered through the crowd with a small brown paper bag. Because we were both dressed up as doctors, he stopped in front of me.

"Hello, Doctor," he said.

"Hello, Doctor," I said.

He offered me the contents of the bag, which I first thought were sunflower seeds. I snatched up a handful and shoved them into my mouth, but something was wrong because it didn't taste like sunflower seeds. I finally peeked into the bag and saw dozens of tiny cubensis mushrooms.

"Enjoy your show," he said and disappeared into the crowd.

The magic shrooms hit me like a ton of bricks during the first set. The visuals were intense and for the rest of the evening my surroundings had a purple hue. The Joker was so spun out that he couldn't remember the names of the songs that Widespread Panic played. Every time a song ended, the Joker tapped me on the shoulder and asked me the title. My brain was so fried that I did not know either.

I walked around with my stethoscope (a real one that I purchased from a medical supply store) and checked heartbeats on skanky-looking women. They didn't seem to mind, and I wondered what might happen if this new habit of mine spilled over into normal life.

Widespread Panic opened up their second set with a cover version of Stevie Wonder's *Superstition* that blasted me into orbit. I surrendered to the flow of the music for the rest of the set. The molly kicked in and my mind and body became a battle zone for two distinctly different drugs. In one corner, psilocybin alters my visuals and turns my world upside down. In the opposite corner, MDMA kills every ounce of negativity and produces a severely heightened, euphoric sense of reality as the high spreads over every inch of my body. As a result, I couldn't think straight, everything I saw was blurry, and I wanted to hug every adorable hippie girl that walked past me. And I did, because that's what happens when you're tripping balls.

After the show, we stumbled out into the parking lot and waited to sober up before making the journey back to The Strip. A guy in a gorilla suit pissed in between cars and one girl wearing butterfly wings puked into her hands. Two shady guys with a dozen nitrous oxide tanks in the back of a van sold balloons for $5 each. Wasted kids frantically lined up for the nitrous balloons, otherwise known as "hippie crack." Shakedown Street was hopping with a fire sale on all goods. Food prices were slashed in half and it was a buyers' market as dealers ditched the last of their inventory. We bumped into The Dude again and he cut me a sweet deal on the rest of his ninja molly stash.

I hid a couple of grams in Grubby's freezer for a rainy day. When things get a little too dark and dismal, a little sprinkle of molly will certainly brighten your world.

Chapter 15

April 2006.

Grubby couldn't catch a break and was stuck in the middle of an awful losing streak. His poker winnings paid his rent and bills, but it also covered his slot losses. He had slowly burned through his savings and his poker bankroll was dramatically decreasing after a frigid run of cards. With no cash coming in, Grubby decided to take a part-time job at a local radio station to supplement his income. I moved into his condo in Henderson to help reduce his expenses further. Besides, staying in the suburbs was certainly cheaper than booking a hotel every time I flew to Vegas. I slept on an air mattress in Grubby's spare bedroom, which had become a storage room for books and movies. Grubby was rarely around, which gave me plenty of alone time to write.

I hadn't been living in Grubby's condo for more than a week when I felt flu-like symptoms with a sore throat and high temperature. Nothing is worse than being sick in Las Vegas, plus trying to sleep off the flu is utter torture for an insomniac. Nyquil would knock me out for a bit, but I'd wake up an hour later drenched in sweat. My life turned into a bad episode of the *Twilight Zone*. I didn't even have the option of falling asleep in front of the TV watching ESPN because to trim expenses, Grubby had decided that cable was a luxury.

A sullen funk invaded my mind as I stared up at the ceiling and contemplated my impending death. I was doomed to die alone in the middle of the desert. I thought about all the things I hadn't done in my life and the list was crushing me. I wondered how the hell I'd made it to 33 years old. I walked fast. I drove fast. I wrote fast. I only live life in one gear. Fast.

I'd received a scathing email from an ex-girlfriend (a hippie turned Jesus freak in the post 9/11 insanity) chiding me for my aberrant behavior. The highlights included assertions that God caused my sickness as punishment for living in Sin City.

The assertion that God was punishing me for engaging in a life of wickedness was a crock of shit. The last thing God had to worry about was settling a personal vendetta against me. If there *is* a God, then He is responsible for bestowing man with the ability to make his own choices in life. The good choices are supposed to lead toward His salvation and glory, while the bad choices will eventually lead him to the depths of Hades. Why would God give man the option to make a choice and then punish him for making the wrong one? It didn't make sense to me.

I struggled with the Free Will vs. Determinism issue while curled up in the fetal position trying to fall asleep. I firmly believed that God was not trying to punish me with the flu but I'm also not one to ignore signs and symbols. The clichés all fit. I was burning the candles at both ends. My body was going through withdrawal from too many party favors, and I got swept up in a tornado of corruption and perversion because I couldn't say "no." It applied to my work, too, because I rarely turned down assignments. The amount of free time in my life had decreased drastically, and I was still trying to squeeze in a social life with new friends and acquaintances, some of whom were nothing more than enablers and leeches. I had a potential disaster on my hands. If I continued on the same path, I would become the worst kind of junkie on the planet – one who happily traded his integrity for a cheap high.

My personality flaws were liabilities that Las Vegas magnified and mercilessly exploited, and I had welcomed it. I had to tone down the partying, and dedicate more time to improving my craft. I formulated a plan to create a healthier balance in my life and manage my time in more productive ways. The first step was to improve my immediate health.

When the over-the-counter drugs failed, I tried lemon tea and home remedies to cure my sore throat. I frequently gargled with hot water and salt, but this didn't do a thing. I couldn't talk. Chicken broth became too painful to swallow. My entire neck was swollen and a quick glance at the Web suggested that I had strep throat. If I didn't seek treatment right away, the infection would get worse and my tonsils would have to be removed.

Grubby was pulling a double shift at the radio station, so I called a cab to take me to the emergency room. Unlike cabs at the Redneck Riviera, the local cab company in Henderson showed up right away and drove me to the UMC Quick Care located in front of the Sunset Station Casino.

I sat on a filthy gray folding chair, and morbid depression began setting in. I was among the sickest of the sick with a surplus of elderly people who looked like they were on death's doorstep. Young single mothers clutched their crying babies, and a construction worker sat next to me with his hand covered in gauze and blood caked all over his jeans. I wondered if the two tweakers in the corner were good enough actors to fool the doctor into hooking them up with any sort of pharmies.

I waited three hours to see a doctor for less than a minute. The doctor peeked inside my mouth for a second and instantly diagnosed me with strep throat. He prescribed antibiotics and steroids to reduce the swelling. After he told me not to talk for a few days, he spent the rest of our examination boasting about his $500,000 profit from day trading the previous year. I didn't have health insurance and paid my bill with a credit card.

The antibiotic and steroid cocktail worked within 24 hours, dramatically improving my condition and saving me from potential surgery. When I felt well enough to travel, I fled to California for a bit of soul searching and to spend time with my new girlfriend, Nicky.

A few months earlier, Grubby and I had taken a road trip from Las Vegas to Southern California to visit his sister. The three of us all played in my friend Henry Wasserman's famous Murderer's Row home game in West L.A. That's where I met Nicky, a blonde with a flirtatious smile, who was easily the best-dressed person at Murderer's Row. She arrived at the game straight from her job as a development executive for a major production company. She had gotten her start in show business as a child actor in the late 1980s, before moving on to musical theatre and eventually the motion picture industry. As an avid reader of my work, she freaked me out with all of her inquiries into the obscure personal stuff she had pieced together from my online ramblings.

An extremely talented writer herself, Nicky authored a blog titled *Pot Committed*. She penned blind items about the movie industry and chronicled her poker play, as well as her fondness for the finest marijuana in California. I have a penchant for blondes, especially potheads, and I could tell right away that she was not your stereotypical Hollywood scumbag. A few months after we met, I flew in to cover the L.A. Poker Classic. For the duration of my assignment, Nicky offered to let me crash at her apartment in the slums of Beverly Hills. One thing led to another and we quickly became romantically involved.

After the medical scare in Vegas, Nicky suggested a road trip to San Francisco. During the trip, I encountered a one-legged panhandler. He sat in a wheelchair on a corner holding up a piece of paper. One side read, "Hi!" The other said "Smile!" As I waited for the light to change, the brisk evening San Francisco air made me shiver as a wave of humility fell over me. Life could be totally random, and I was just one bad decision away from being that homeless guy in the wheelchair. That eternal philosophical question popped up, "Why am I me instead of that guy?"

Luck? Fate? I had no idea. All I did know was that in less than a year, Las Vegas had brought out the worst in me, magnifying my existing problems, inflaming my addictions, and intensifying my deviancy. That needed to stop. I was determined to take a more laid-back approach and to have more fun with the work. I also knew that I had to exhibit more self-control when I returned to Las Vegas to cover the WPT Championship at the Bellagio with Flipchip.

Michael Friedman, an intense writer from Bethlehem, Pennsylvania, moved to Las Vegas after being hired by Card Player. We knew each other from the Borgata Casino in Atlantic City and had many wishful discussions about starting a music magazine together. Friedman, a spiritual guy with a proclivity for herbal refreshments, loved the outdoors. Before my work day began, Friedman encouraged me to join him on morning trips to Red Rock Canyon, a national conservation area thirty-five minutes from The Strip. It cost $5 to visit and all the proceeds go to maintaining the area. The canyon was a serene compliment to the chaos of Las Vegas below. The harmony of Red Rock settled my mind and allowed me to center my creativity and churn out higher-quality copy. Sometimes, we'd skip the hiking and drive the 13-mile scenic route instead. We rolled down the windows, fired up a fatty, and cranked music as loud as we could.

The Bellagio's security guards stopped me and asked to look in my trunk before I entered the self-parking garage. I wondered what they expected to find. The security sweeps fostered the illusion of safety; they allowed fearful people to sleep at night and feel more comfortable losing at the "terrorist-free" Bellagio. The lower levels of the parking deck were filled to capacity, an indication that people were still eager to lose their money.

After covering many events at the Bellagio, I knew the layout fairly well. I took a shortcut from the parking garage to the Fontana Room, navigating the lobby filled with sunburned tourists snapping multiple photos of the aromatic flower conservatory and the psychedelic Dale Chihuly ceiling sculpture in the lobby.

A crowd of poker fans milled around the front of the Fontana Room like rabid jackals ready to devour a dying carcass. The gregarious Marcel Luske always accommodated picture requests even though there was a slight fear in his eyes that the surrounding mob could turn on him and tear his tailored suit to shreds. The Unabomber unwillingly posed for a dozen tourists. Jen Harman got mugged by fans who whipped out their cell phones to snap blurry photos.

"One more photo Jen, please! You're my favorite poker player!"

Moments after fan favorite Daniel Negreanu busted, he quickly left the Fontana Room with his bag of homemade vegan food from his Romanian mother.

"Daniel!" one lady shouted. She weighed about 350 pounds and the casino floor shook as she rumbled toward Negreanu like a charging rhinoceros. "You have to sign my hat!"

"Make it quick," Negreanu said.

Negreanu eyed the flock of vultures with their digital, disposable and cell phone cameras swarming his way. He signed the hat and bolted through a row of $1 slot machines trying to lose the autograph hounds following behind.

A WPT souvenir stand was placed right in front of the Fontana Room to maximize profits, but it made getting inside the tournament room almost impossible. I flashed my press badge to the phalanx of security guards in maroon blazers. They didn't blink. Steve Rosenbloom appeared out of the dense crowd.

"It's good to see you," said the famous sportswriter from the Chicago Tribune, as he shook my hand. "Nice of you to end your early retirement."

I had skipped a few stops on the WPT tour and the hiatus had turned into a rumor that I had called it quits. Poker media loves to gossip, especially about their own. It felt good to be missed by one of my favorite sportswriters. The rest of us media reps were two-bit shysters compared to Rosenbloom, who had recently published a poker book, *The Best Hand I Ever Played: 52 Winning Poker Lessons from the World's Greatest Players*. I asked him how he never went crazy in all the years he's covered sports under the biggest scrutiny and immense pressure of writing for a major newspaper.

"I love what I do and realize there are a thousand guys who would kill me to get my job," Rosenbloom said. "And poker is great because the players are much more interesting than professional athletes."

A couple of wedding parties slid past the poker tables as they crossed the Fontana Room to access the veranda overlooking the Bellagio fountains. The brides provided an amazingly angelic contrast gliding past the hundreds of overweight and unshaven poker players.

On my way home to Henderson, I passed the exit on I-15 where the Redneck Riviera was located and pulled off the highway. The blinking In-N-Out Burger sign made me feel like Pavlov's frothing dog. I thought about driving through the Redneck Riviera for old time's sake but I didn't want to get carjacked by a gangbanger with a tear-drop tattoo or get caught up in a drug sweep during a meth lab bust by Las Vegas SWAT.

* * * * *

Grubby's living room had become a graveyard for old issues of Poker Player Newspaper, film magazines, fast food coupons, and promotions for casino comps like a free room at Harrah's or free tickets to the Amazing Johnathan. Random casino gifts that Grubby had collected were stacked on his dining room table; a luggage set from the Palms, a crystal vase from the Monte Carlo, and jumper cables from Fiesta Station. He was not able to fit those items in his "prize closet," which was stacked from floor to ceiling with casino freebies such as soap dishes and ear hair tweezers.

I sat on Grubby's couch writing as a sizzling Miles Davis bootleg from Paris echoed throughout the dark apartment. To cut down on expenses, Grubby only used lights when absolutely necessary. I glanced at my cell phone when it did the vibrate dance on the table for a few moments. It was Grubby. I recognized the ambient casino sounds.

"I'm at Red Rock playing poker. Come by after you finish writing," he said, before he quickly hung up.

I always have the itching desire to play poker when I'm covering tournaments. I drove to the other side of town and felt like a junkie sweating out the shakes before scoring a few grams of black tar heroin. I hadn't been to the Red Rock Casino in Summerlin since it had opened its doors a week earlier. Part of the Station Casinos chain, Red Rock cost $925 million to build, which made it the most expensive and luxurious hotel and casino away from The Strip. The suits hoped to capitalize on local gamblers who lived in the area and to lure younger visitors to the property by providing luxury amenities like an acclaimed pool, trendy restaurants, and a hip club named Cherry. Back in 1946, mobster Bugsy Siegel spent $6 million on construction costs and bribes to build the Flamingo. At Red Rock, the pool alone probably cost twice that much.

I wandered into the casino and immediately got lost between rows and rows of slot machines. I had never seen so many slots! I eventually found the poker room just to the right of the state-of-the-art sports book. Red Rock had a remarkable twenty tables and an electronic queue system. I sat down at the table right next to Grubby's so I could lean back and turn around to talk with him between hands.

I also started up a conversation with the guy to my left who looked like Captain Stubing from the *Love Boat*. I'm usually friendly at the table, and old guys like talking, especially if they're lonely or their wives are driving them nuts. Within a few minutes, Capt. Stubing offered me

$100 to guess which one of his eyes was glass. I figured that I was being set up so I counter-offered $20 to lower my risk. He thought about it for a few hands before agreeing to lower his price.

Capt. Stubing stood up and I inspected both eyes in search of the fake. Left eye was my initial gut reaction. According to Malcolm Gladwell's book *Blink*, we usually make up our minds within the first few seconds and we should go with that gut feeling because more often than not it's usually correct. I inspected his right eye then his left once again.

"It's your left eye," I said.

"You sure?" he said offering me a chance to change my mind. The Captain was trying to mess with my head.

"I'm positive."

"O.K., let's go."

I followed him into the bathroom. Capt. Stubing washed his hands then nonchalantly pulled his right eye out of its socket. I dropped a $20 bill on the sink and walked out.

Chapter 16

June 2006.

Flipchip's health took a downturn before the WSOP kickoff. The consummate tough guy refused to tell me the cause of his ailment and although he gutted through everything, he admitted that it slowed him down a bit. The Prof and I were concerned about how the expanded WSOP schedule and Flipchip's new health development would affect our overall productivity. We finally decided to ease into the WSOP and train our focus on the second half of the series, which included the inaugural $50,000 buy-in H.O.R.S.E. Championship, in addition to the $10,000 Main Event. We were going to need every bit of our energy to prevail over an increased field of competition from a score of new media outlets.

I continued living with Grubby in Henderson. Despite being stuck in suburbia tucked behind a regurgitation of family-themed chain restaurants and strip malls, my digs were a substantial improvement over the Redneck Riviera. There wasn't one meth lab within a four-mile radius, and I was no longer forced to brush off the advances of $20 crack whores with open sores. Instead, I was brushing off the advances of Botox-riddled cougars with wrinkly back tattoos.

Grubby and I barely saw each other. When he wasn't at the Mr. Cashman slots or playing poker at Red Rock, he was working long hours at the radio station and writing sketches for the morning show. My posh surroundings were crime-free and included busty strippers tanning themselves poolside in the late afternoons when the temperatures dropped to the low 100s. Still, there was a downside. A major construction project across the street emitted insufferable noises, which made it difficult for a night worker to sleep during the day. Annoying interruptions from the landscaping crew constantly trimming the hedges and mowing the lawns in the complex was no help either.

Tao of Poker picked up a new sponsor for the WSOP after Amy Calistri introduced me to a marketing rep from Costa Rica. He worked for Paradise Poker, which wanted to buy a banner on my website. I retained creative control while all they cared about were the traffic numbers. Paradise Poker paid me up front and they also inked a similar deal with LasVegasVegas.com. The unexpected influx of income guaranteed that all of our WSOP expenses would be covered and that we'd walk away with a substantially higher payday than the year before.

Other online poker rooms also paid me ungodly amounts of advertising and affiliate money to promote their brands on Tao of Poker during the WSOP. The year before, I flew under the radar because nobody had heard of my blog, but the changes brought a new and heavy load of expectations. If that wasn't enough pressure, we experienced a massive setback when Harrah's prohibited live blogging updates. The new rules threatened to hinder our coverage.

Media is a ruthless business for any major event, and the WSOP is the Super Bowl, the Oscars, the Olympics, and Election Night all rolled into one. The lucrative financial incentives turned poker media maneuverings into something that would make even Machiavelli or Henry Kissinger cringe. Card Player had purchased the exclusive media rights and access to media row would only be granted to their people wearing the green badges. We were no longer allowed to use laptops at the final table. Access on the floor was also limited and those restrictions affected guys like Flipchip and Otis. As a media rep holding the dreaded red badge, I was not even allowed to sit in the stands and take notes on a final table. With the new limitations in place, tourists and railbirds now had a better chance to view the final table than the majority of the media.

I set up camp in the media room, located in a small space across the Amazon Ballroom. Ninety people shared the room designed for twenty. For six weeks, I was trapped in that tiny gulag with fellow prisoners Otis, John Caldwell, Amy Calistri, Dan Michalski, Foiled Coup, Jen Leo, and the gang at Wicked Chops Poker.

The top three online poker rooms (Party Poker, PokerStars, and Full Tilt Poker) constantly clashed against each other to achieve supremacy, while the lower-tiered online rooms struggled to get any bit of the spotlight they could. Full Tilt Poker gained a tremendous advantage via Poker Wire, which gained an exclusive partnership with Card Player by providing the official chip counts.

Party Poker paid Harrah's a large sum of money to have its logo featured on every poker table inside the ballroom. Party Poker also purchased the pokerblog.com domain to try and build up its web presence. I was forced to decline a generous job offer to head the project because my plate was already full with other commitments for Tao of Poker, Fox Sports, LasVegasVegas.com, and a few others. Michalski was next in line for the juicy position. The suits at Party Poker gave him an unlimited budget to hire the bloggers he wanted. He offered me a cut of the pie but I suggested that he talk to my girlfriend instead. Nicky had recently found herself out of work when her megalomaniac Hollywood boss flipped out and fired most of his development executives. After a five-minute conversation with Michalski at the Hooker Bar, he hired Nicky to write a WSOP fashion column. Although Jen Leo and Amy Calistri teamed up on a website called *Breakfast Club Poker*, they too jumped on board with Party Poker's blog. Michalski rounded out his lineup with Foiled Coup, Dr. Tim Lavalli (a.k.a. the Poker Shrink), April Kyle (a friend of ours from Austin, Texas), and John Kampis (a journalist from Tuscaloosa, Alabama).

When the head honchos at PokerStars heard about the Party Poker moves they launched a swift counterattack and funded a full-scale reporting team for the PokerStars Blog. Once Otis got the green light, we struck a deal and I agreed to write for PokerStars during the Main Event. In addition to adding me to his crew, Otis assembled a few all-stars including Wil Wheaton and two British journalists, Mad Harper and Howard Swains. Otis also added our buddies, CJ Hoyt and Craig Cunningham, to the mix along with veteran reporter, Max Shapiro, and Ali Lightman, an Australian journalist who worked with the BBC.

I was a true mercenary with zero allegiances aside from Flipchip and the Prof. I followed the money and wrote for over a dozen outlets in 2006. In the end, it didn't matter if you were Party Poker or PokerStars. Everyone had the same goal: tap into the mainstream and attract a wider audience. Online poker had become the crack cocaine of the internet. More people playing meant an increase in the revenues generated from the rake and tournament fees. With gambling being what it is, many customers will eventually go broke which means that online poker rooms need a constant stream of new players. That's why someone like me is paid ridiculous amounts of money to pimp specific online poker sites over others. Everything is in play, from pro sponsorships to the slutty chicks in the hallways wearing Bodog Poker t-shirts; from the clever poker commercials on TV to the affiliate banners on Tao of Poker.

* * * * *

Milwaukee's Best shelled out top dollar as the official sponsor of the WSOP and as a result, six foot-tall inflatable beer cans lined the corridors of the convention center. Roaming the hallways felt like the first day back at school after summer vacation. John Caldwell manned the Poker News booth, and I found Otis in front of the PokerStars booth. I ran into Max Pescatori, who told me he had translated two of my articles for his Italian poker site, which marked the first time any of my work had been translated into a different language. He also advised me to bet on Italy in the World Cup. I hollered over to Greenspan and asked him when he was going to get me a copy of *Hunting Fish*.

"In a few weeks," he said with an excited look in his eyes.

Michael Craig, author of *The Professor, the Banker, and the Suicide King* stood in front of me as we waited in line to pick up our media credentials. He showed me some of his notes on an upcoming book he was working on with a couple of Full Tilt Pros. It was beginning to seem like everyone was either writing a book or promoting one. Steve Rosenbloom had his new book out. I had contributed a couple of chapters to a strategy book titled *Pressure Poker*, written and edited by my friend Scott Gallant, but it wasn't the same. I wanted a book of my own.

Otis and I set up shop next to Nolan Dalla's desk in the front of the media room. When dinner break finally came, we fled to the Hooker Bar with Grubby. The bartender remembered us from the previous year and served me a Red Stripe and Otis a Corona without asking for our order.

Grubby treated me to a free meal in the Diamond Club Lounge, a private area at the Rio designated for gamblers who reach a supreme frequent player status at Harrah's properties. Grubby never revealed the exact amount of money he lost to become a Diamond Club member, but I estimated the figure was somewhere near $10,000.

We walked through the high-limit slots area until we stopped at a podium in front of a nondescript elevator well hidden from the public. A casino host checked Grubby's I.D. and swiped his Diamond card and we were granted access. The elevator opened up to a salon with TVs, couches, and internet stations. The food spread included turkey and cheese wraps, and Buffalo chicken wings. I also devoured a chocolate éclair and two cookies for dessert. And lest I forget to mention it, the Diamond Club Lounge served free booze, which always satisfies the soul.

On my way back to work, a pretty young thing caught my attention as she rushed down the corridor past the steady flow of players on their dinner break. She was well tanned with perfectly manicured nails. She wore a pink N.Y. Yankees cap and carried a purse that was worth twice as much as my bankroll.

"I cracked his pocket aces," she shouted into her cell phone in a thick Long Island accent. "I cracked fuckin' aces with my sixes, too. It was so freakin' cool. Just like on TV!"

I put the accent at somewhere near the Nassau/Suffolk County line as she concealed her eyes behind oversized designer sunglasses. Even Daddy's Little Princesses were infected with the euphoric effects of tournament poker. Many of them had put down their fashion magazines in favor of picking up a copy of *Super System*. They were in the fight and issuing out bad beats to pros faster than you could say Fendi.

If Benny Binion were around today, I'm sure that he'd be cashing in on the popularity of the WSOP as much as he could, but I'd also like to think he would be continuing his practice of sharing the wealth with the players and others who contribute to making the event what it is. Back in the day, Old Benny hooked up media reps with free rooms and food. His tiny tournament held in the smoke-filled Horseshoe had morphed into a full-fledged corporate affair. In the modern era, poker agents roamed the hallways of the Rio like pimps seeking out a new stable.

PokerStars, Ultimate Bet, Doyle's Room and Full Tilt all tried to one-up their competition with swank hospitality suites, spending an exorbitant amount of money on rental and catering fees in an attempt to attract potential online players to their virtual card rooms. Full Tilt also gave away a plethora of free merchandise. On the weekends and during other peak times, the hospitality suites were packed with tourists stuffing their faces with free food and snatching up a couple of Full Tilt t-shirts. By the time I left Las Vegas at the end of the WSOP, I had accumulated a collection of t-shirts, golf shirts, hats, windbreakers, Frisbees, golf tees, mugs, and card cappers.

The Full Tilt pros hung out in a roped-off area in the back of the suite. I went in a few times to try and get interviews or just chat with some of them on their breaks. One afternoon, I spotted Gavin Smith and John Juanda engaged in a $1,200 prop bet. Smith bet Juanda that he could not successfully throw an empty canister of Airborne (equivalent to the size of a roll of quarters) into a trash can against the back wall. Juanda took him up on the bet, carefully calculating the distance and even rehearsing the motion several times before he made his attempt. He nailed it.

"Juanda, you lucky fucker!" screamed Smith in his Canadian accent, before he unfurled a batch of $100 bills and threw them to the ground.

PokerStars also hosted a hospitality suite where their pros hung out on breaks. Barry Greenstein had recently joined Team PokerStars and was a regular in the suite along with former world champions Chris Moneymaker, Greg Raymer, and Joe Hachem. PokerStars sponsored many celebrities into different WSOP events and the suite became their green room. Wil Wheaton could often be found pecking away on his laptop on a couch in the corner while Norm MacDonald (of *Saturday Night Live* fame) sat around and cracked jokes.

I couldn't tell whether PokerStars was exhibiting maturity or making a fatal mistake by being the only site not hiring two-bit hussies to pimp its product. The poker-playing demographic is typically lonely, sex-starved males. Simply put, throw a hot chick in front of anything in view of this crowd and it suddenly becomes more interesting. Other online poker rooms hired models to stand in front of their hospitality suites. The stunningly attractive women wore skimpy outfits with the online poker room logos. Some of the girls who worked in the suites handed out free merchandise, food, and drinks. Other girls chatted up tourists and were encouraged to take photos with poker fans.

Foiled Coup spent more time in the hospitality suites than out on the tournament floor not only because the food was free, but because that's where all the hot women hung out. We often chatted about the differences in talent that the online poker rooms were hiring. One afternoon, we made it a point to visit every single one and then sit down to discuss our rounds.

"Who has the hottest women working the hospitality suites?"

"I think they're all 8s out of 10s," Foiled Coup said. "But if you like the tall slim ones, I'd say Ultimate Bet. It's a particular favorite of mine. If you like the continental ones, then visit Doyle's Room. They have Russians and a girl from Holland who's my favorite. Full Tilt has some good ones. They all do. They hired models who are taking summer vacation. There are no disappointments there. They're much better than the skanky Sapphire girls down on the corner."

"The Ultimate Bet girls are hot but they look like they're 16 or 17 years old."

"In England, well, that's O.K., as long as no one finds out or if they don't have big older brothers with guns or anything."

"Well, in America we're civilized. You go to jail for that kind of aberrant behavior. Now, the Doyle's Room girls wear short jean skirts, cowboy boots and tight white t-shirts that say 'Doyle's Room.' Do you think Doyle picked out the outfits or personally designed them?"

"He approved them. They're going for the cowgirl image. Most of those girls look like they've never been near a farm, unless they were having sex in a field late at night or something."

"You said that Doyle's Room has that continental look to them. Don't you think that's an interesting contrast against the cowgirl look?"

"It's the exotic cowgirl look. I think they're chosen for their legs. They all look good in those short skirts."

"I heard a rumor that you took ice cream out of the UB suite and brought it to the cowgirls inside the Doyle's Room suite."

"Yes," said Foiled Coup, admitting to his infraction. "I gave some to one of the girls in Doyle's Room. This one said she was a vegan who didn't drink milk. But she gobbles down an ice cream every afternoon."

"Maybe she doesn't know there's milk in ice cream? Or is it because it makes her nipples hard?"

"This one looks pretty smart."

"Have you seen any cat fights between any of the different chicks? Let's say the Full Tilt girls got into a slap fight with the girls from UB…"

"I wish. If I had any pictures, I would have put them up on my site already."

"What's up with the Milwaukee's Best chicks? They rate high on the Skank-o-Meter."

"They're like porn star hot. Not as nice looking as the girls from Doyle's Room. Maybe some of them used to live at the Redneck Riviera? Do you recognize any of them?"

"No, the Milwaukee's Beast girls have more teeth than the crack whores who lived in my building complex."

Chapter 17

July 2006.

The Hooker Bar used to be the place where Otis and I escaped from work, but as its popularity increased it became harder and harder for us to find a comfortable space to drink with our friends on dinner breaks. We were looking for an out-of-the-way establishment close by when Johnny Walker from Card Player introduced me to the Tilted Kilt, a Scottish pub located in the Rio. He invited me for a pint and like any self-respecting part-time self-medicater, I accepted.

The waitresses in short plaid skirts were much more attractive than the surly barkeeps at the Hooker Bar. The sultry vixens looked more like strippers dressed as Catholic high school girls than bar maids. If you tried hard enough, you could almost see bush. Naturally, I was in heaven. The Tilted Kilt included a small bar area with a couple of tall tables and a full dining area with an abundance of TV screens. If you didn't face the front door (which opened up into the casino) you could trick yourself into thinking that you were drinking in an actual bar. Since the Tilted Kilt also served food, I let Otis know that we had found our spot.

"We're drinking at the Tilted Kilt for the rest of the WSOP," I declared.

The TVs provided us constant opportunities for a quick gambling fix. During baseball games, Otis, Wil, and I gambled on what type of commercial would appear first on a break: fast food, cars, soft drinks, or a movie trailer.

One of my favorite things about Las Vegas (and probably one of the most dangerous things) is the opportunity to win money gambling on something you know little or nothing about. Take soccer, for example. I know very little about international teams, but I bet heavily on Italy in the World Cup matches. I originally got the Italy tip from Max Pescatori whose home country advanced to the finals against France. The same day as the World Cup championship match, Max was playing at the final table of the $2,500 no-limit hold'em event. The floor staff graciously paused the final table so everyone, especially Max, could watch the dramatic end of the game as the Italians came through in the clutch and defeated France in an overtime shoot out. Their victory over the French fired up Pescatori and he rode that wave of nationalistic pride en route to his first WSOP bracelet.

Nicky moved to Las Vegas for the summer to write for Party Poker's PokerBlog.com. The two of us spent a lot of time at the Gold

Coast, the dive bar of all casinos, catering to locals and low rollers. Located less than a five-minute walk away from the Rio, the Gold Coast provided a haven of R & R for members of the media looking to flee the front lines inside the Amazon Ballroom. The Gold Coast contained a bowling alley, a couple of bars with drink specials, and inexpensive eateries such as a greasy 24-hour café and Ping Pang Pong, one of the best dim sum restaurants in Las Vegas. Rooms at the Gold Coast were cheap and many members of the poker media stayed there instead of paying the Rio's inflated room prices. Most normal nine-to-fivers have a favorite happy hour watering hole where they can get bombed after a bad day at work. The Gold Coast was ours.

Our post-work playground was a full-service Las Vegas casino with the occasional working girl wandering aimlessly through the maze of geriatric zombies glued to the penny slots. When we were getting off work in the wee hours between 2 and 6 a.m. the Gold Coast was always there to greet us with $2 beers and $10 Pai Gow tables.

Wil thoroughly enjoyed writing at PokerStars Blog, but he was having a brutal time at the tables and didn't cash in any events. Despite more than 90 percent of the field failing to make the money in any WSOP event, Wil was not pleased with his results. Not only was he a highly competitive person, but he also felt the looming pressure that all sponsored players feel during a downswing. Wil wanted go deep and make a televised final table in one of the events in order to prove his worth to PokerStars.

Nicky bumped into Wil in the hallway and later she said he looked utterly demoralized after misplaying a hand and busting out early.

"I played like shit today," Wil said. "I may have even played the worst poker of my life."

Wil's tilt spilled over to the next day. He had not been away on a lengthy assignment in a long time and missed his wife and kids. He had hit the wall. Otis recognized the signs and told him to take the afternoon off and relax.

"Cheer Wil up," Otis said, as he sent me on a special assignment. "And make sure he has fun."

Unfortunately, Wil isn't a strippers and blow type of guy, so I scratched Plan A. I suggested a barhopping sojourn at every possible bar inside the Rio. Wil, the self-professed geek, wasn't a heavy drinker, but he knew that the barhopping would keep his mind off poker. We started out at the Milwaukee's Best Tent. Six very leggy and busty stripper-model types in tight jean shorts stood in front of the entrance and handed us a souvenir poker chip. I declined and made a bee-line for the bar. I bought a couple of cans of Milwaukee's Best Light and handed one to Wil.

"I can't drink this shit," Wil said.

"Suck it up and drink the Beast, you pussy ass bitch!" I yelled in my best frat boy voice.

The tent included a pool table and an electronic bowling game. Wil schooled me in heads-up bowling, and I had to buy the next round of drinks. He begged for anything other than cans of the Beast. I agreed and on our way to the Hooker Bar I explained the drinking rule that he had inspired: no talk about poker or work. The Greyhounds were a welcome respite from the panther piss we'd been drinking, and we chatted about our lives outside of poker. Otis joined us at dinner break and hit quads at video poker. Again.

"It's like we're getting paid to drink here," he said.

The Hooker Bar filled up fast with players, so we retreated to the Tilted Kilt. Our extremely flirtatious waitress, Kary, rubbed up against Wil a couple of times as he ordered a pint of Arrogant Bastard Ale. She gave Otis shit for ordering a beer that had a low percentage of alcohol.

"At least this one orders real beer," she said, still rubbing on Wil.

"But he ordered a Stella," Otis said as he pointed in my direction.

"Stella has more alcohol content than almost anything else we serve," she deadpanned.

Otis finally succumbed to the teasing and ordered an Arrogant Bastard as well. Conrad Brunner, one of my British colleagues at PokerStars, always gave me guff for drinking Stella. Apparently all of the soccer hooligans drank excessive amounts of Stella, which the Brits referred to as "wifebeater beer."

Michalski held a staff dinner in the corner with his crew from the Party Poker blog. Despite the fact that our bosses were at war with each other, making us enemies, I told Kary to bring their crew a round of Southern Comfort shots. Michalski acknowledged our generosity as he wandered by telling me that he was sending a round back our way on the Party Poker tab. Five minutes later, Kary showed up at our table with three White Zinfandels.

"What the hell is this pink shit?" Otis growled.

"I told her to bring you the three gayest drinks in the Tilted Kilt!" Michalski shouted across the bar.

"Motherfuckers," I said to Otis. "We dropped $50 on shots and they send us this weak-ass shit?"

We chugged the pink wine in one gulp and I slammed the empty glass down on our table. Here's another one to remember, kids: slamming down a glass of White Zinfandel does not do anything to soften the fact that you just drank the gayest thing in the bar.

* * * * *

"Coronas and White Russians!" Otis shouted to a cocktail waitress as she buzzed by our table. "And keep 'em coming."

We sat down at an empty $10 Pai Gow table at the Gold Coast and our group took up every seat. The pit boss recognized Wil from his days on *Star Trek: The Next Generation* and stopped by to say hello.

In Pai Gow, you're dealt seven cards and have to set two different poker hands (one has five cards, and the other, two cards) which you play against the dealer's two hands. If you beat the dealer on both, then you win your bet. If the dealer wins both, then of course, you lose. If each wins one, then you push. Everyone keeps his bet and the next hand is dealt. Unlike craps or blackjack, you're not going to win a lot of money in a short time because a push is what occurs most often. However, your money will usually last longer. You can theoretically spend endless hours at one table without jeopardizing your entire bankroll. Pai Gow is a very social form of gambling and the perfect game to play with five or six of your friends. Wil called it "Chinese Poker for Stupid People."

The first two hours ran smoothly. Wil and I sat next to each other and created a prop betting game called "Clown or Cowboy." Crowds of rodeo fans who were in town for the National Rodeo Finals were flocking to Gold Coast to get the commemorative chips being issued for the occasion. The red $5 chips contained faces of different rodeo champions and clowns. I picked one up from my stack and Wil had to decide whether the chip had a clown or cowboy. If he chose correctly, then he won the chip. If not, then he paid me one of his.

Enter five foot-tall Flora. She didn't crack a smile and her robotic moves convinced me that she was a Vietnamese Terminator sent back in time to prevent us from winning any money. She cold-decked the entire table, scooping away all of our profits without an ounce of remorse. If you had a straight with pocket kings up top, she burned you with a flush and pocket aces. Flora the Ultimate Cooler decimated our stacks. Otis and I reloaded our chips. I increased my bets from $10 to $25, while Otis

106

kicked his up to $100 a hand. He went broke again and dug into his pockets for a third rebuy. Flora swallowed them up looking ravenous and ready for more. Otis, now on mega-Pai Gow tilt, pulled eight $100 bills out of his poker bankroll and tossed them onto the felt.

Flora yelled out something to the pit boss and counted Otis' money. The pit boss took note of the $800 cash wager and stayed at the table to watch the action. The mood of the table went from jovial to dismal after Flora's arrival. Otis' bet had brought us from dismal to intense. Wil and I stopped playing Clown or Cowboy, and my asshole clenched up as I watched the dealer place the cash onto Otis' betting space. My lonely green chip wilted in comparison. Flora pushed a button on the automatic shuffling machine about to set Otis' fate. Silence fell over the table as she laid out hands one by one. Even though I was still in the hole, I didn't care to see whether I had won or not. I couldn't take my eyes off Otis. He picked up his hand and sighed heavily. I couldn't tell if that was a good sigh or bad.

The first hand was a tie, so Otis pushed his bet and did not lose any money. Same thing happened on the second. Flora dealt us the third round of hands and no one said a word. I glanced over his shoulder as he unfurled his cards. It looked like a winner to me, but with Flora beating us down like Russian dissidents, it was hard not to expect the worst. It wasn't even my money and my heart was practically bruising my ribcage as she flipped over her cards and fanned them out in front of us. My eyes scanned back and forth a couple of times. Her best hand was a low pair and a king-high up top. After two pushes, Otis had finally won.

"You beat the cooler!" I said.

"$800? Ship it!" Nicky screamed.

Otis cracked a grin as the dealer paid him his eight black chips. He took his cash off the table and shoved it into his pocket with the rest of his poker bankroll, then pulled the black chips off the betting circle and replaced them with a green chip.

"I'm still not close to being unstuck. Does that get me steak and eggs for all of my friends?" Otis asked the pit boss.

She nodded and scribbled down her signature on a $90 food comp for the café, and we played a couple of more hands before cashing out. Wil, Nicky, and I dropped about $100 each. Spaceman and April dropped $200 a piece. Poor Otis became Flora's bitch. He was stuck almost a grand. I felt like calling 911 to report the rape. Inside of an hour we had burned through our winnings and amassed a collective $1,700 in

Pai Gow losses, and the return was a paltry $90 food comp. Hustled by Las Vegas once again.

Otis led our caravan of soused losers to the café. As we were being seated, I spotted a couple of ratty old Keno crayons. I pulled four $100 bills out of my poker bankroll and tossed it on the table. I placed two Keno crayons on top of the bills.

"Four hundred bucks to eat two Keno crayons. No water until you're done," I announced.

Otis didn't even blink and bit into both crayons. Within seconds an infectious wave of laughter engulfed the table. I whipped out my camera. Spaceman grabbed his and we focused in on Otis' frowning, determined face.

"You're a dumb motherfucker," Wil said to me.

"This was a bad bet," I admitted.

A man depraved enough to bet $800 on a single hand of Pai Gow was not going to have any qualms about eating two Keno crayons for $400. I had clearly miscalculated in my drunken bravado.

"The beauty of this bet, is there's no time limit," slurred Otis who had chewed off the top half of both Keno crayons. "It will take me a bit of time, but I'll do it. For $400? I'll fuckin' do it."

I asked him to show me what chewed Keno crayons looked like. He opened up his mouth and thousands of tiny crayon shards sat on clumps all over his tongue and teeth.

"That's soooo disgusting!" April said.

"You're going to be sick tomorrow," Nicky said. "Do you know how many people touched those crayons?"

"Oh man, you got the bird flu now Otis," Wil said. "There's probably Lupus all over those crayons too."

"After losing a grand at Pai Gow, I gotta get even!" Otis said.

"What does it taste like?" I asked.

"Um... crayons," Otis answered.

Otis slid four Benajmins into his pocket and smirked. The waitress finally arrived and gave us the stink eye, as would anyone having to wait on six drunkards hootin' and hollerin' at 4 a.m. Otis happily ordered his $1,000 steak and eggs. With the few bucks left on the food comp, he also ordered a shrimp cocktail and a strawberry daiquiri.

Chapter 18

July 2006.

The biggest cash games in Las Vegas are a mixed game format. If you want to play with the likes of Doyle Brunson, Lyle Berman, Jen Harman, or Bobby Baldwin in Bobby's Room at the Bellagio, you need a bankroll fat enough to choke a Rhino and a deft knowledge of every possible variant of poker.

H.O.R.S.E. is a mixed-game that alternates rounds of hold'em, Omaha eight or better, razz, seven-card stud, and seven-card stud eight or better. Harrah's had decided to add an inaugural $50,000 buy-in H.O.R.S.E. tournament to the 2006 WSOP schedule. It quickly became known as "The Players Championship" among veterans since they tend to measure poker players by their all-around ability rather than their expertise in one particular game.

The no-limit hold'em events had become crapshoots because of the massive fields of entrants that were a consequence of poker's booming popularity. You might be a great player, but the high volume of amateurs and push-monkeys made the events a minefield that not even the most careful could successfully navigate. A mixed-game format like H.O.R.S.E. tests all of your skills, and many of the top pros in the world had been training for months, conscientiously working on their weaker games to prepare. Whoever won the bracelet would have to demonstrate excellence in all areas of poker.

"The public only knows the good no-limit tournament players but they are fundamentally weak in these limit games," Barry Greenstein explained.

A handful of pros took the opposite view of the $50,000 H.O.R.S.E. event. There were major flaws with the structure. One was that the tournament should have been scheduled to take place over four or five days instead of three. Flaw number two had a handful of pros decidedly opposed to the inaugural event. British pro Harry Demetriou called the event "elitist" and felt that it overshadowed the purity and egalitarian nature of the $10,000 buy-in Main Event. Players like Andy Bloch and Paul Phillips exposed another flaw through their displeasure with management's decision to use old decks containing potentially marked cards. At one point during one of the opening levels, Bloch received a ten-minute penalty from the floor for crumpling up one of the old cards when he asked for a new setup and was refused.

"For $2,000 in juice, you figured Harrah's would have used new decks," Phillips said.

$50,000 was the largest WSOP buy-in in history and 143 players answered the call. First place would be awarded $1.7 million. The stacked field was a who's who of poker including the biggest of the big dogs: Phil Ivey, Phil Hellmuth, Johnny Chan, Gus Hansen, and Daniel Negreanu.

Only 13 players busted out on the first day. At around 2 a.m. on the second day, thirty players remained. Chip Reese had emerged as the chip leader and stayed ahead of the pack for the rest of the morning. That's right, the morning. Day 2 began at 4 p.m. and ended the next day at 9:30 a.m.. At the end of the grueling 19-hour session, Robert Williamson III bubbled out in tenth place. Reese finished Day 2 with 1.5 million, retaining his chip lead. Doyle Brunson had sunk as low as 25,000 in chips at one point during the somnolent session, but old Texas Dolly went on the rush of a lifetime and finished the day with a million in chips. Brunson impressed everyone with his amazing stamina and when asked, he credited Red Bull energy drinks as his reason for being able to stay awake and focused for such an extended time.

"One of those suckers is better than a whole pot of coffee," Brunson said.

There was an interesting twist to the final table that bothered a lot of media purists including myself. After playing H.O.R.S.E. for the first two days, the remaining nine players at the final table abandoned the mixed game. No-limit hold'em was played at the final table through the conclusion. What's the point of having a $50,000 H.O.R.S.E. tournament when you play nothing but no-limit hold'em at the final table? It was a controversial decision but in 2006, "conventional wisdom" held that no-limit made for better TV coverage.

Although Reese was considered by many to be one of the best cash-game players in the world, he was not the best no-limit player at his table. That distinction went to either Brunson or Ivey. At the time, Brunson was seeking his 11th bracelet and Ivey was looking to add number six to his collection. T.J. Cloutier, arguably the best player from his era who had never won the Main Event championship, was certainly not out of contention. Jim Bechtel, a former farmer and a high-stakes cash-game player, was also a world champion, having won the Main Event in 1993. Andy Bloch, a graduate of both M.I.T. and Harvard Law, was known around the circuit as one of the most intelligent players in the game. David Singer, a former environmental attorney from New York, had been a successful player on the circuit. Just a few months earlier, he almost won a half of a million with a third-place finish at the

PokerStars.net Caribbean Adventure. Dewey Tomko, a three-time bracelet winner, came out of retirement shortly after the poker boom began and returned to the tumultuous world of tournament poker. Lastly, Patrik Antonius, the boy-toy from Finland, was the youngest player at the final table and considered by many to be the best all-around European player. The female members of the media swooned. I believe one direct quote was, "I'd drink his bathwater." Antonius, however, had next to zero chance of winning the H.O.R.S.E. bracelet because he began the final table with the shortest of short stacks.

The final nine of the inaugural $50,000 H.O.R.S.E. event will go down as one of the most distinguished final tables in the history of the WSOP. It represented several generations of poker anchored by the legendary Texas Dolly himself. I made a prop bet with Wil before the final table began. He picked Phil Ivey to win it all and I picked Chip Reese. At stake? If Reese won, Wil would sign over his quarterly residual checks from *Stand by Me* for one year. If Ivey won, I would give him Grubby's 1991 Geo Metro, which I had just acquired in the mother of all prop bets, but that's a story for another time. The blue book value of the car was the equivalent to Wil's last residual check from DVD sales and international airings in Bulgaria.

The championship would come down to an intense battle among the final three players – Phil Ivey, Chip Reese, and Andy Bloch. Reese held a slight lead with 3.2 million in chips when Bloch hit a flush and sent Ivey packing. When heads-up play began shortly after 2 a.m., the chip counts between Reese and Bloch were almost even.

Those few souls able to shrug off their fatigue witnessed poker history. The subsequent duel lasted an excruciating seven and a half hours, as the two traded blows back and forth like an epic fifteen-round heavyweight championship fight. In the first hour of heads-up play, Bloch gained an early edge but it took nearly two hours before Reese inched his way back into the lead. Bloch counterattacked shortly before dawn and regained a 2-1 edge over Reese. Each player found himself on the ropes at some point and on the verge of getting pummeled to death, but neither seemed to be able to deliver the fatal knockout.

Action had been paused while the film crew changed tapes, and I headed back to the media room for a five-minute catnap at my desk. Jen Mason from Blonde Poker found a more comfortable and less visible spot to nap by ducking underneath a table. As soon as I sat down, I fell into a deep slumber and began snoring. Snoopy, a British writer with a cheeky sense of humor, took a photo of me passed out and plastered it all over the internet. Jen Leo and the rest of my friends gathered around and jeered. Their raucous laughter finally woke me and I ran out of the media room under a cloud of humiliation.

The Amazon Ballroom was nearly empty save for a late-night cleaning crew who swept away all the crap that had accumulated underneath the 200 or so poker tables and a handful of cash games running in the corner. The few diehards remaining in the stands sipped energy drinks or coffee between yawns. I tried everything possible to stay awake: chocolate bars, Red Bull, No-Doz pills, and over-the-counter non-drowsy cold medication. I had been cocaine-free for months but at that point I would have ripped a line just to stay awake.

A short time after sunrise, Reese was facing elimination after Bloch flopped two pair with K-J against Reese's flush draw. However, Reese made his flush for a timely double up, and yet another knockout blow from Bloch missed its mark. One hour later, Reese pulled even in chips when he doubled up with pocket kings against Andy Bloch's 9-9. After he raked the pot, Reese walked over to his sons in the audience and jubilantly declared, "We're back in the game, boys!"

Reese regained the lead and lost it yet again as the see-saw battle continued. By that time, sleeping bodies had piled up in the media room and people were dozing on the bleachers at the TV table. During one of the breaks, I headed outside to the parking lot to walk around and get some fresh air. I went to my car and fired up a Maceo Parker CD while I smoked a joint hoping that the funk music would wake me up and invigorate my brain. Instead, the pot buzz lulled me to sleep. I woke up ten minutes later to my cell phone vibrating in my pocket. Jen Leo was calling to tell me that the tournament was over. Reese had finally beat Bloch at 9:30 a.m. in the morning, and I missed the final hand because I had slept right through it.

Chapter 19

July/August 2006.

Our apartment on Horizon Ridge in Henderson was one of the highest points in the area, surrounded by mountains and commanding a majestic view of the city below. On clear days, you could see Red Rock Canyon on the other side of the valley, causing me to despise the thick layer of pollution that was the norm. At night, however, The Strip glistened magnificently, highlighted by the single beam shooting out from the top of the Luxor, a beacon of light helping all lost gambling souls find their way back to the mother ship.

For a couple of hours every day, Nicky and I transformed into a happy suburban couple as we enjoyed the relative serenity of Henderson. We preferred a bleak existence of suburban drudgery to evading gang bangers. Nicky embraced her newfound profession as a poker writer and thoroughly enjoyed getting paid to make snarky remarks about the fashion disasters plaguing the Amazon Ballroom on a daily basis. She also bubbled with excitement as the party season approached.

In the days leading up to the Main Event, different online poker rooms sponsor parties at the hippest clubs in Las Vegas. During my first WSOP, I was excited for the party season solely because I'd been working for a month straight and desperately needed a few evenings off. But in 2006, I didn't care as much. I prefer dive bars with a good jukebox over a trendy nightclubs blasting Eurotrash DJ mashups any day of the week. Establishments with roped-off entrances being guarded by someone with a clipboard on a power trip does not appeal to me. I refuse to wait outside in line for an hour just so I can be granted the privilege of buying an overpriced drink. That being said, I was more than willing to suspend my anti-club convictions for one week a year to attend poker industry parties. Besides, Nicky was dying to go, so I dressed up and hit up the clubs for free cocktails.

I had secured multiple invites to Pure for Liz Lieu's birthday party and the Full Tilt gala, as well as an invite to Bodog's blowout at Tao nightclub. Nicky insisted on dragging me out to shop for a new outfit. It should go without saying that shopping malls and I do not mix well, but I enjoyed seeing Nicky in a state of nirvana as she shopped for shoes. I wandered into Bath and Body Works and three young women in green smocks immediately converged on me.

"Can I help you?" they said in unison.

"I play a lot of poker and handle a lot of grimy, hepatitis-infested poker chips. When I'm not doing that, all of my waking life in Las Vegas is spent in casinos sucking down pure oxygen and shaking hands with strangers. I need some anti-bacterial hand stuff."

"Right this way!"

The braless sales girl reminded me of actress Claire Danes circa 1999. She led me over to a ten-foot high shelf filled with anti-bacterial lotions. She showed me all the variations.

"These are three for $10. I absolutely love the Coconut Lime Verbena and Tropical Passion Fruit."

I was shocked that hand lotion was so cheap. All of them were too girly. I liked the Sun-Ripened Raspberry but it had too strong of an after-scent.

"I guess this one is for potheads?" I said as I picked up Crisp Citrus Herb and showed it to Claire Danes. "Crispy potheads."

She forced a laugh, obviously not a toker. I finally settled on Juniper Berry because it had the least pungent aroma. As I applied it, I thought, "Wow, my hands really feel smooth and germ-free."

"Buy two more for $10?" she pressed.

I flashed her a look. "Hell no. Ring me up before I'm spotted by someone I know."

The poker parties were growing more decadent with every passing year, and the Bodog party at Tao was looking to take top honors with an epic bash. I had a tough decision to make. Either watch Phil Hellmuth try to win his tenth bracelet or party it up at Tao with friends and business partners. The year before, I had witnessed Johnny Chan become the first player to win ten bracelets and then watched Doyle Brunson win his tenth a couple of days later. Hellmuth was much younger than both Brunson and Chan and there was no question that he was going to catch them. I figured Hellmuth was on pace to win 15 or 16 bracelets, so I decided to skip it. After all, Hellmuth already had his shot at a tenth bracelet a few weeks earlier and couldn't close the deal. There was no guarantee that he would win ten if I stayed, so I headed to Tao. In case you were wondering, Hellmuth did come through that night to win his tenth bracelet, tying Chan and Brunson for the record.

Nicky and I showed up fashionably late to Tao and walked right past the velvet ropes. A young woman in a black latex tube dress greeted us at the elevator. The doors opened in front of a huge wall resembling a Buddhist shrine with a champagne bar underneath. We wandered down a dim corridor where models in lingerie sat in birdcages, and we passed a hookah room playing hip-hop and featuring an ice cream sundae bar. We found our friends taking advantage of the free booze in the main room, and I hung out with the Costa Rican guys from Paradise Poker who had purchased the juicy ad on my blog.

The DJ pumped out late 70s disco and 80s pop music and a bevy of models in black and red Oriental-style dresses with Bodog branding flooded the dance floor. In one of the alcoves, a crowd was gathered around a pool table as Gavin Smith played Jeanette Lee, the Black Widow of Pool, in a heads-up match. I found myself in front of a tub on a platform mesmerized by an almost-naked woman in a bubble bath with rose petals pasted over her nipples and vagina. I saw some other weird shit that you'd only see in a club in Las Vegas, like the midget ninjas. They stealthily wandered around the party all evening and would sneak up behind someone to scare the shit out of them. Sometimes they swiped drinks off the bar when you weren't looking. They liked grabbing random asses and disappearing into the crowd.

Three of these little ninjas in black outfits stood in line in front of me at the bathroom. The trio of ninjas all ran into the same stall together. They were either queer or cokeheads. Or maybe both. I overheard snorting and sniffing noises before they all bolted out of the stall and made a beeline for the exit. The last midget ninja tossed a $20 bill in the direction of the bathroom attendant. An elderly black man in a tuxedo jacket bent over and picked up his tip, most likely the same bill that the midget ninjas used to rip lines.

* * * * *

I loathe the day before the Main Event. The reporters with dark circles around their eyes who had been at the Rio since the start of the WSOP were territorial about their space in the media room. Many of the vets arrived on Day 1A of the Main Event only to discover that what had been their permanent seat for five weeks straight had been taken over by someone they had never seen before. I was forced to sit in the hallway and write because of the resulting lack of power outlets in the media room.

I was outnumbered by dipshits. The new media reps were easy to spot versus the veterans who had been in the trenches for over a month with "Don't fuckin' talk to me!" written all over their faces. The newbies were fresh off of their flights to McCarran and had shiny new press badges. Nothing had changed; they rushed over the ropes to take photos of the "Hot Pro du Jour" and gawked at Erica Schoenberg, Lynette Chan, and Vanessa Rousso.

A short Asian woman stocked the media room with beverages and placed three huge party trays of freshly made sandwiches on one of the banquet tables. I picked up a can of soda and noticed that it was cold. Over the previous five weeks, the soda was always warm, and we had one tray of stale pastries. Because it was Media Day at the WSOP, Harrah's pulled out all the stops including feeding all of the fresh blood a batch of decent food.

The farce continued during the Main Event press conference and Hall of Fame inductions, which Harrah's abbreviated to help promote a press junket for an upcoming Hollywood film. The brief Hall of Fame ceremony honored two superstars of poker, Billy Baxter and T.J. Cloutier. T.J. had won over 100 tournaments and was a two-time WSOP Main Event runner-up. Billy Baxter, the seven-time bracelet winner (all in lowball) spoke in his slow Georgia drawl during his brief acceptance speech. The pros regularly dubbed the lowball event "The Billy Baxter Benefit" because they knew they were essentially donating their entry fees to him.

The promotion of a new poker movie entitled *Lucky You* during the second half of the press conference made me want to puke. The director, Curtis Hanson (*L.A. Confidential, The Wonder Boys, 8 Mile*), explained that he tried to capture a part of Las Vegas that was often absent from all of the other films that were shot on location. Nicky read over 2,000 scripts in her duties as a studio executive and, according to her, word on the street indicated that *Lucky You* was on the verge of bombing and the producers desperately needed some buzz.

"Hollywood gave poker films a $100 million chance to succeed with *Lucky You*," Nicky explained. "On paper, it looked like everyone's dream poker film. An Academy Award-winning director in Hanson and an Academy Award-winning screenwriter in Eric Roth. Major stars in Eric Bana, Drew Barrymore, and another Oscar winner in Robert Duvall. A $60 million budget, a worldwide marketing campaign, and distribution courtesy of Warner Bros. *Lucky You* had everything you can possibly have going for you when it comes to getting a movie made. But all the money in the world, or at least in Burbank, couldn't solve the film's biggest problem – it just wasn't good. If a movie is good, people more often than not tend to go see it. It doesn't matter if it's about poker, the apocalypse, or hot-air ballooning. If *Lucky You* was good, even a little bit good, I really believe it could have found some sort of audience."

116

The angelic Drew Barrymore introduced the trailer and a special sneak preview. I watched one scene and within thirty seconds I knew the film was doomed.

* * * * *

PokerStars provided me with a free hotel room at Treasure Island for the duration of the Main Event as a part of my compensation package. The Rio was less than a five-minute drive away and the conveniently located TI drastically reduced the commute for Nicky and me, guaranteeing that I'd get an extra hour of rest every night. I would need all I could get.

During the Main Event, days began at 8 a.m. with an automated wake-up call. I frantically edited the last bits of my dispatches and emailed the articles to different editors. By that point, I was writing for over a dozen outlets including a couple of shill sites under a pseudonym. I would depart the hotel at 9:30 and take my seat in the media room between the spots reserved for Otis and Wil. We had limited seating and sometimes Ali and Mad would have to share a spot on the food banquet tables. With two hours to go before the noon start time, I cranked out two quick articles and updated Tao of Poker. I also inspected the list of the players in the event to point out specific PokerStars qualifiers to our photographer, Rob Gracie.

Before the start of Day 1A, rumors circulated around the hallways that an online poker room had taught a monkey how to play Texas hold'em and that they planned on entering the monkey into the Main Event as a publicity stunt.

"Are they really going to let the monkey play?" I asked media director Nolan Dalla.

Dalla responded with a stern, "A fucking monkey is not, nor will ever be playing in the World Series of Poker."

Why not let the monkey play? After all, the Main Event was populated with thousands of amateurs who had no idea what they were doing anyway. The 2006 Main Event attracted a record number of 8,773 players with Day 1 divided into four flights to accommodate the entire field. Harrah's surpassed expectations with an $82.5 million prize pool. A whopping $12 million would go to first place. The online poker rooms funneled thousands of satellite qualifiers to the WSOP. PokerStars came in at the top of the list, sending more players than any other site. With so many online qualifiers, the PokerStars Blog had its hands full. Otis devised a system and split up the Amazon Room into quadrants. We were all responsible for keeping tabs on our individual sections.

My writing assignment for Day 1A was to follow members of Team PokerStars and the sponsored celebrities. Norm MacDonald and Wil Wheaton represented just a handful of the Hollywood types who were playing such as James Garner, Tobey Maguire, Mekhi Phifer, and porn star Ron Jeremy. Rick Solomon, the guy seen long-dicking Paris Hilton in her infamous sex video, also made an appearance in the Main Event field.

Without a warning, the Nevada Gaming Commission (NGC) came down hard on the online poker rooms twenty minutes before the Main Event was scheduled to start. It would not permit any players or online qualifiers to wear anything that contained a dot-com address on it. The NGC prohibited online gambling sites from branding anything with dot-com logos throughout the entire Amazon ballroom. The result was mass confusion during the first hour. Marketing reps scrambled for black tape to block out ".com" or they found new shirts and hats that complied with the newly enforced NGC guidelines. Most players simply turned their shirts inside out and laughed at the absurdity of the issue.

A couple of the pros were involved in prop bets that were settled during the Main Event. Joe Sebok and Gavin Smith agreed on a point system for all of the WSOP preliminary events. Whoever had the lowest score had to show up at the Main Event wearing a different costume each day. Gavin had a better summer which meant that Sebok had to wear a bear costume and a diaper while he played in the Main Event. On the other three starting Day 1s, Sebok walked around the tournament area dressed up like the comic book superheroes of Gavin's choice: Robin from Batman and Robin, Spider-Man, and Wonder Woman.

Ryan Kallberg, a writer and film critic from Los Angeles, was one of my friends playing on Day 1B. After churning out a substantial profit at the online tables, he had decided to take some time off from writing to focus on playing tournaments for a living. He had the necessary skills to be a successful player – meticulous money management, a passion for the game, and a cool temperament – all of which served him well. Earlier in the year, he won an event at the L.A. Poker Classic at Commerce where Nicky had 5 percent of his action. I staked very few players mainly because I didn't trust them to pay me off if they won, but Ryan was a stand-up guy with talent. He was a worthy investment and I bought 1 percent of his Main Event action for $100. At the start of Day 1B, Ryan found himself in front of the cameras for the majority of the afternoon having drawn the same table as Brad Garrett (from *Everybody Loves Raymond*) and Dax Shepherd (then most famous for his stint on the MTV show *Punk'd*).

118

Adam Stormwind, a friend from New York City, was among the thousands of qualifiers from PokerStars. We had both worked together at the Metropolitan Museum of Art a decade earlier and frequently played in a regular home game that rotated from my apartment in Brooklyn to another friend's apartment in Manhattan. Back then, we played low-limit stakes, mostly seven-card stud variations and multiple wild card games. Stormwind had recently moved to Las Vegas after quitting his job at the museum. He was attempting to fulfill his dream of being a professional poker player while supplementing his income as a poker dealer on the side. He deposited a couple of hundred dollars onto PokerStars and parlayed that into a seat into the WSOP Main Event. Like thousands of other qualifiers, Stormwind and Ryan both had a shot at winning $12 million.

On Day 1C, I followed Louie Anderson for my assignment with PokerStars. The actor-comedian and host of *Family Feud* was stopped constantly for photos and autographs and he accommodated every last request. Early on in the tournament, Louie found himself in hot water, falling victim to the controversial "F-bomb rule."

"I didn't think I did anything wrong," Louie explained. "I muttered 'fuck' under my breath and didn't think it was loud enough that anyone heard."

But the vigilant dealer had indeed heard Louie's F-bomb and dutifully informed the floor staff.

"You got to be fucking kidding me," Louie said when the floorman told him that he had to sit out for ten minutes. His response typified my entire Main Event up to that point.

Before dinner break, I was alerted to a young player in a PokerStars shirt who had amassed a big stack and jumped out as one of the chip leaders. His baby face and small stature stood out against everyone else at his table. He looked like a little kid playing at his father's home game. I tapped him on the shoulder and asked him his name.

"I'm the sorry. My English no good," he said in a very thick Italian accent.

"Your name," I asked.

"Ah, I'm Dario!" he said.

I handed him my note pad. He scribbled down "Dario Minieri" and said that he lived in "Roma." I thanked him and returned to the media room with the information. Otis soon figured out that the 21-year-old from Rome, Italy was a Supernova (the highest distinction of frequent players on PokerStars) and had accumulated enough frequent player points to purchase a Porsche. Dario was one of the many Magic: The Gathering players who had successfully made the transition to online poker. In a short time, Mineri became one of the highest-volume players on PokerStars, yet he looked like he hadn't reached puberty.

On Day 1D, Otis and I hit the wall at 2:30 p.m. We needed something to lift our dour spirits. I bought a flask of vodka at the gift shop and we filled up cups with ice, vodka, and orange juice. The homemade screwdrivers took the edge off. At 4:15 p.m, Nicky tapped me on the shoulder and reminded me that it was almost time for a smoke break.

"Wow, so stoners actually get high at 4:20, it's not just a myth?" asked Wil.

"But of course," Nicky said, before she leaned over and lowered her voice. "Even though it's always 4:20 in my world."

Wil was bummed out that he did not advance to Day 2 of the Main Event, but on the plus side, it meant that we saw more of him. After a full year as a tournament reporter, the novelty of being around the biggest names in poker had worn off. However, I had a few moments every day when I completely geeked out because I was seated next to Wil and Otis. Both are sensational writers and their presence challenged me to write better. Even though we were working on the same team, we pushed each other constantly. That healthy competitive spirit resulted in better coverage.

Although the professionalism of our crew kept Otis off of work tilt, he still struggled with being away from home for an extended time. As a group of us were walking into the Tilted Kilt for dinner, I spotted a tall striking woman in a sleek black cocktail dress and high heels walking towards our motley crew.

"Hi Pauly!" she said as we were about five feet from each other.

It was Erica Schoenberg, the former volleyball player turned poker pro.

"If one more hot chick says hello to you in the hallway, I'm gonna put my cigarette out in your eye," Otis said.

On Day 3, Ryan started with a short stack and tripled up early on. He and Jesus Ferguson sat at the same table, but instead of being intimidated by the former world champion, Ryan busted Jesus in front of ESPN's cameras. Fewer than 500 players advanced to Day 4, and both Ryan and Stormwind survived the money bubble and made the cut. Unfortunately, their amazing runs ended on Day 4. Stormwind grinded his way to a 455th place finish out of 8,773 players and collected $26,389, a hefty sum considering his minimal investment of $30. Ryan finished in 410th place and won $30,512. As one of Ryan's backers, I collected 1 percent of his winnings – $305.12.

* * * * *

The WSOP had exploded into a money-making machine for the bulk of the poker industry. The prize pool was generated by the players, minus a small fee of $5.2 million that Harrah's took out to cover "operational costs." The WSOP attracted corporate sponsors and partners – Milwaukee's Best, Party Poker, and Corum Watches – and yet, none of that money went back into the prize pool. No matter what, the house will always win. The sponsors splashed their banners all over the Amazon Ballroom while the online poker sites continued to blur the lines between prostitution and advertising. Ultimate Bet was flagged for hiring a 16-year-old model to work in its hospitality suite. Even degenerates like Foiled Coup had to question the ethics on that one.

Sex and gambling are a lethal combination. The whoring, financial and otherwise, went on everywhere. Vultures circled the Rio. Immoral agents, slick managers, shady online poker sites, scumbag lawyers, and gold-digging pieces of ass all tried to chummy-up to the money winners during the breaks. Broke family members, old coworkers, former high school chemistry lab partners, and every other scam artist on the West Coast were all crawling out from under their rocks and trying to grab a piece of the final table players. These were the worst angle shooters; lazy fucktards trying to cash in on the newfound celebrity and financial success of friends and family. I felt bad for the remaining players who were on the verge of being ruthlessly exploited and betrayed by people they thought they could trust. The dregs of society hung out on the rail ready to beg, borrow, lie, or cheat their way into a piece of the $12 million first-place payday. One guy in a cheap off-the-rack suit hung out on the rail with his shoddy used car salesman smile. He was a "poker agent" who had been promising players that he'd make them a huge star. Next to him stood a smoking-hot blonde who kept a keen eye on the tournament's progression. One look in her dead eyes and you knew she'd sell out every single ounce of her depraved soul to get her hands on a big wad of cash, sucking and fucking with all her might until she got there. She was pure desperation.

As if dealing with these fuckers wasn't enough, there was a potential scandal brewing that involved $2.41 million in chips being mysteriously added to players' stacks prior to the final table. A couple of players received extra chips, including Erik Friberg and Richard Lee. Michael Craig pointed out the error to me, while Amy Calistri and the Poker Shrink jumped on the story and launched an investigation. Most of the time, poker writers are little more than fluffers hired to make the entire industry look cool. However, Amy and the Poker Shrink were determined to solve the extra chips mystery. After crunching the numbers, it was obvious to them that the discrepancy in chip counts was not due to an error by the floor staff during the color-up process (the original explanation from Harrah's was that the "mishap" occurred when the 5,000 denomination chips were removed from play). Word on the street was that one (or more) staff members were paid off to add extra chips to the stacks of certain players. To this day, no one knows the exact truth about the extra chips shenanigans.

The majority of the poker public had no idea about the extra chips because everyone focused on the final nine players. Allen Cunningham was the only big-time pro remaining in the hunt for $12 million. Flipchip had written an article before the WSOP began picking Cunningham to win the 2006 Main Event. For over a decade he had watched the always quiet and humble player rise through the ranks of poker. He felt that Cunningham was an expert at surviving events with massive-sized tournament fields and that 2006 was his year to win it all – and it was looking like he might be right.

Cunningham was part of a wave of new players who surfaced on the Las Vegas scene in the mid-1990s. At the time, Cunningham's crew of young twenty-something players included Phil Ivey, John Juanda, Layne Flack, and Daniel Negreanu. All were roughly the same age and became a support system for one another, and amazingly all five would eventually become multiple-bracelet winners, a testament to their collective talents. At the time of his final table appearance, Cunningham had won four bracelets and made fifteen final tables at the WSOP. Over the years Cunningham became known around the circuit as one of the nicest guys in poker, but was often overlooked by the media because he was so quiet. In a city full of manic thieves and sinners, the always-serene Cunningham was a true gentleman who finally had a shot at poker immortality.

Jamie Gold from Malibu, California had previously worked in Hollywood as a talent agent and as a reality-show TV producer. He frequently played in the big cash games at the L.A.-based casinos and knew Johnny Chan from those circles. In the days leading up to the final table, Chan had been spotted on the rail coaching and advising Gold. By the end of Day 4, Gold had taken over the lead. He had played remarkably well with his erratic style and his trash-talking, which got

122

under the skin of his opponents, persuading them to fold when he was bluffing and enticing them to call when he had them beat.

The rest of the final table included Erik Friberg, Richard Lee, Paul Wasicka, Doug Kim, Rhett Butler, Michael Binger, and Dan Nassif. Friberg, a Swede, was the only international player at the table. They were from all walks of life and included a recent Duke grad, a bookie, a former bartender, an insurance agent, and a theoretical physicist with a Stanford Ph.D. The spectrum was pretty well covered.

I arrived four hours before the scheduled start time. A couple of the guys from Aerosmith (not Steve Tyler or Joe Perry, but the other guys) stood around in the media room and performed vocal exercises before they went inside the Amazon Ballroom and sang the National Anthem a capella. Before they left, I asked them if they were going to segue into *Sweet Emotion* and they looked at me like I was high. I was, of course, but that didn't excuse them from snubbing my question.

The final table played out inside the Amazon Ballroom on an expanded version of the featured TV table where the set was modified to accommodate more seating. The Milwaukee's Best Lounge was moved to an area next to it so fans could drink and watch the action from large lounge chairs. I split time between watching the final table live and from a feed in the media room because I didn't have a specific place to sit in media row. My access was technically restricted to the media room, but I knew my way around the TV set and I found different spots to hide out where I could see the action and not get caught by overzealous Harrah's interns or security guards. The vastness of the Amazon Ballroom allowed more spectators, but the wide open area lacked the intense energy of cramped Benny's Bullpen.

At the dinner break, only five players remained. Gold had added to his lead and held more chips than the other four players combined. Cunningham was still alive but had a huge gap to make up if he was going to challenge Chan's protégé in any significant way. Shortly after 2 a.m., Cunningham hit the rail and busted out in fourth place. With the most experienced and skilled player at the final table gone, Gold had to hold off two more players. After Gold knocked out Michael Binger in third place, he found himself with a 7-1 chip advantage over Paul Wasicka, an online pro from Colorado. The heads-up battle lasted a couple of hands and Gold took down the Main Event title winning $12 million, the largest-ever payout in a poker tournament.

It didn't take long to filter out that although Gold was awarded $12 million, he had made a verbal agreement to split his winnings with Crispin Leyser, a TV producer and poker instructor from the U.K. Gold and Bodog arranged a deal by which they would buy Gold into the Main Event, provided he found them a few poker-playing celebrities that Bodog would also buy in to the Main Event for promotional purposes. Gold enlisted Leyser for help in securing celebrities in exchange for 50 percent of his total winnings. (Interesting side note – Leyser had to sue Gold for his share of the money, and the two settled out of court for an undisclosed amount.)

I finished up the last of my articles and columns by 5 a.m., and Nicky and I joined Michalski and his girlfriend for one last drink at the Hooker Bar. We had checked out of our hotel room before the final table began and were set to return to Grubby's apartment in Henderson for the first time since the Main Event had begun two weeks earlier.

As I drove along the 215, I glanced in the rearview mirror and saw the outline of the Las Vegas Strip. The Luxor's light was no longer visible as the sun slowly crept over the mountains. I smiled. How could I not? The 2006 WSOP had been seven weeks of pure lunacy, and it was finally over.

Chapter 20

August 2006.

The daily events at the WSOP are like attending an AA meeting that never stops. Everyone has a worried and demoralized look about them and most need spiritual guidance after living a bankrupt existence for one day too long. The media room reminded me of an Irish wake. Everyone was raging drunk, talking loudly, and telling wild stories about a dead guy while another group huddled together in the corner and sobbed uncontrollably.

I've traveled the world with a lot of interesting, funny and entertaining people in my life but the folks I bonded with during seven weeks of the WSOP were in their own class. They kept me sane and entertained on the tough, sad, and dark days. Because we worked in close quarters, an instant camaraderie developed, and on the good days the job seemed like we were at summer camp. Wil likened the experience to shooting a movie on location. Michalski thought we were more like plane crash survivors. Flipchip called us grunts entering the jungle for the first time. All I know is that I'd gut salmon in a frigid Alaskan fishery seven days a week for sixteen hours a day (without piss breaks) if one of them asked.

Bright lights, puerile city. I was numb to everything around me and didn't even blink when I passed the buzzing craps tables, the cocktail waitresses sedated on Valium, and the disgruntled slave-wage dealers. Las Vegas, home to the absurd and peculiar, where you can order a Mai Tai at 5 a.m. from a bartender named Sully or pay a working girl to take a shit on your chest for $300. Sometimes you can find both at the same bar.

People forget that underneath the flashing lights of fabricated Las Vegas, the underbelly of society operates in the shadows; the trigger-happy cops shot first and asked questions later, the gangbangers roamed freely in North Las Vegas and gunned down enemies, the skinny crack whores blatantly strolled along Trop, and hundreds of immigrant day workers hung out in the parking lot at Home Depot. They will paint your garage or cut someone's fingertips off – for the right price. Discussing the subject of muscle-for-hire, Michalski said, "I know a Vietnamese guy in Dallas who will take care of your problems for $1,500. They're cheaper than the Russians, but they do a messy job."

I filed that bit away for later, it might come in handy someday.

* * * * *

Grubby had become a legend during his two-year stint in Las Vegas, and he had acquired a great number of readers who lived vicariously through his blog, The Poker Grub, a collection of well-written posts capturing the winner's high and magnifying the testicle-shrinking losses. We all knew that excessive gambling was sucking Grubby dry both mentally and financially. He was on the verge of unplugging the fridge to reduce electricity costs when he finally caught a break.

A couple of bigwigs at a gaming design company frequently read Grubby's blog. One of the executives was in Las Vegas for business and invited Grubby to join him for dinner and drinks. By the end of the night, the gaming company offered to fly him to Chicago for a formal interview.

Grubby impressed everyone at the home office and landed his dream job — designing slot machines. Despite the low starting pay and having to relocate to Chicago, Grubby had an opportunity to make an impact and revolutionize the gaming industry. He had always wanted to develop a game that became as popular as Wheel of Fortune and Mr. Cashman. Although he was enthusiastic about his new job offer, he had found a home at the radio station and was bummed about leaving behind his personal life in Las Vegas.

Grubby packed light. He planned on selling his furniture and putting the rest of his stuff into storage. However, in the weeks leading up to his move-out date, Grubby kept procrastinating. He was also in the middle of a voracious final gambling binge, and trying to use up all of his comps before he skipped town. During Grubby's last weekend in Vegas, I joined him on a bender that spilled over several Las Vegas casinos and strip clubs — betting on baseball, live poker, Pai Gow, lap dances, video poker, craps, prop betting, slot machines, more lap dances, and even Keno.

I passed out around sunrise and thought I was dreaming when I heard voices. I woke up and opened my bedroom door to see a young married couple walking through the apartment. Grubby was showing them various items that he put up for sale on Craigslist. They recently moved to Las Vegas and were in search of a bed. They paid Grubby cash for his.

"Aww shit," Grubby said. "Where am I going to sleep tonight without a bed?"

"You better hope you don't sell the couch today," I said.

Grubby couldn't get rid of his stuff on Craigslist and tossed the things he couldn't take with him into the trash. It did not take very long

126

until the scavengers appeared. An old lady scurried off with the dumbbells. One of the maintenance guys drove by on a golf cart and snagged the exercise bike. A young couple pulled up in a white SUV and took the bookshelf, and a woman with her daughter jumped for joy when they found Grubby's dishes, pots, pans, and silverware sitting in two banker's boxes. She had moved to Las Vegas from Juarez with her husband, brother and her three kids. Grubby asked them if they wanted his blue couch – for free. All they had to do was take it off his hands. The family had very little furniture and could not stop thanking Grubby for his generosity. Within minutes they acquired the remains of his home furnishings. Every last item.

I wondered how the family was going to react when they found my orange plastic bong and over a hundred bars of hotel soap that Grubby had stolen.

Chapter 21

October 2006.

The Joker put on his Disco Santa Claus outfit (essentially a regular Santa suit with the sleeves and pants covered in tons of glitter and other sparkly things), and we popped a couple of party favors before heading for The Joint at the Hard Rock. The Joker handed out candy canes to gamblers inside the casino and to the rolling kids waiting in line.

The first night of the second annual Vegoose music festival was in full swing with Sound Tribe Sector 9 playing a late show. The entire crowd was lit up like the Christmas tree in Rockefeller Plaza by the time the band took the stage at 1:30 a.m. A girl in a unicorn costume passed out behind us during the first set. She danced vigorously for the first few songs, gyrating to the grooves until she completely lost her marbles. She sat down and fell over to her side. Unicorn down.

Nicky and I bailed at set break to return the room and take advantage of the intoxicants in our system for a couple of hours of carnal pleasure. Fucking on a head full of molly is an entirely different visceral experience. The drug heightens your senses; the littlest touch can send orgasmic shockwaves throughout your entire nervous system.

Just as the eye-piercing sunlight began screaming its way through a tiny crack in the curtains, the Joker, still dressed as Disco Santa, rolled into our room babbling about Alice in Wonderland, Ziggy Stardust, and Rainbow Brite. Apparently he'd met some new people.

While most folks went to church, thousands of music freaks were preparing to converge on Sam Boyd Stadium for the last remnants of Vegoose. The Day 2 lineup was much stronger with a Phil Lesh (The Grateful Dead) and Trey Anastasio (Phish) collaboration that also featured John Medeski (Medeski, Martin, and Wood) on keyboards. The festival was set to climax with Widespread Panic ripping it up for a three-hour set on the main stage. To call the evening highly anticipated would be an understatement.

After a quick shower and a costume change, the Joker returned to Vegoose in his UPS delivery driver outfit. I dusted off my doctor's scrubs and Nicky slid into her best whorish medical professional gear. I hadn't taken two steps onto Shakedown Street, before our costumes began attracting a bevy of solicitations. I couldn't walk for more than five seconds without hearing the faint whispers, "Rolls. Pharmies. Special K. Heady nuggets. Opium. Doses. Molly. Yay."

Shakedown was hopping with entrepreneurial activity sort of like a farmer's market for druggies and hippies. Bottles of Pale Ale, nuggets from Humboldt, grilled cheese sandwiches, mushrooms, Vegoose t-shirts, extra tickets to the late night shows, pipes, and heady crystals were all being hawked. As we navigated the crowded area, I nearly stepped on a tour dog as a spun-out hippie chick with dreadlocks lost the leash trying to keep a hold on her basket of ganja cookies.

I stopped one scruffy kid wearing a tie-dyed shirt. He had a Southern accent and was one of the many Spreadheads in town for Widespread Panic's Vegoose set and their Halloween show the following night.

"Pharmies. Pharmies," he whispered.

"What's up?" I asked.

"Zannie bars," he answered in a twang.

"Break for five?" I said.

"Five for 20," he answered as he put his hand into the pocket of his hoodie and slid me something. I slowly unfurled my hand and saw my five pills. I palmed him a twenty and we both disappeared into the crowd.

For those unsure about what just happened, I'll translate:

"I'm selling pharmaceutical drugs. Are any of you law-abiding American citizens interested in purchasing pharmaceutical drugs?"

"What are you selling?" I asked.

"Xanax. 2mg Xanax pills," he answered.

"If I purchase bulk quantities, can I work out some sort of discount?" I asked.

"Yes. I can sell you five pills for $20."

I was relieved to finally pick up some Xanax. After partying for a few days straight, a fistful of Xanax is a godsend for an insomniac like me. A crusty chick sold me a couple of hits of ecstasy, and I scored molly off of a sketched-out kid with dirty fingernails and a sideways Sound Tribe hat. On our way inside, I was stopped a dozen times by desperate addicts in search of their favorite intoxicants.

"Hey Doc, you got any nuggets?"

"Hey Doc, any pharmies?"

"You selling rolls, Doc?"

"Doc, I have back pain, can you hook me up with medical weed?"

During the Rhythm Devils set, the Joker handed out a package to a bunny with unnatural knockers who attended the festival with a dude dressed as Jack from the Jack in the Box fast food chain. As I tried to scribble notes about the deliveries and simultaneously write down the set list for the Rhythm Devils, I was stopped by more wretched pill poppers in search of party favors. Without skipping a beat, I turned my small notebook to a new page and wrote down a faux prescription.

A screaming frat boy rushed over, "Doc, I need you to hook me up. Vicodin. How about Klonopin or Oxycontin. Doc, you gotta get me some Oxy!"

I wrote down, "100mg Valium," and ripped off the piece of paper from my pad. The frat boy looked down and screamed, "What the fuck? Valium? Fucking Valium? Fuck you Doc! I want something stronger."

"Dude, that's a 100 mg pill! That's enough to knock out a horse."

"Fuck you, Doc!" Then he got serious and pointed at me. "Fuck. You!"

As he stormed off I added, "Don't forget to fill out your insurance forms!"

Shortly before sunset, we met up with Michael Friedman, Johnny Walker, and some of the Joker's Colorado friends at the Ferris Wheel. One of the Colorado girls wore wings with a short red wig.

"Nice butterfly costume," I said.

"I'm not a butterfly," she insisted. "I'm a fairy. The anti-drug fairy. I'm going have to report you because you look like you've been doing drugs."

She was onto me. Our elite unit of party people had swelled into a small army as we migrated over to the Phil Lesh and Trey Anastasio set. Before the music started, I scribbled down something in my notebook in extremely sloppy handwriting – *6:48 Take mushrooms.*

I quickly hit my peak and it was all downhill from there. I'd be chasing that high the rest of my time in Las Vegas. One of the Joker's friends had snuck in a bottle of Jim Beam. I took a couple of swigs and passed it off demanding, "As a medical professional, I advise you to take a swig of the nectar of the Gods!" So much for my newfound healthy outlook on life.

130

Johnny Walker pointed to the dark blue sky sprinkled with glowing white dots. The stationary dots were stars from a distant galaxy and the moving dots were a dozen or so planes jockeying for position at McCarran.

"Look at all those planes loaded with all those tourists," Johnny said.

I tried to count, but was too wasted, and lost track somewhere around 12. Johnny pointed again at the cavalcade of planes waiting to land.

"Bags of money," Johnny said. "Those planes are bringing in bags and bags of money."

Part III

"A casual stroll through the lunatic asylum
shows that faith does not prove anything."
- **Friedrich Nietzsche**

Chapter 22

March 2007.

Derek and I were on the same JetBlue flight from New York City to Las Vegas. We booked the flights separately and were randomly seated in 19D and 20D. Derek shared a row with a white-haired gentleman in orthopedic shoes wearing a "WWII Veteran" hat. My row started out empty, until two extremely loud women with knock-off Fendi purses boarded at the last second. All the passengers stared at a skinny black woman in oversized Chanel shades scurrying down the aisle with a buxom blonde in a pink Juicy Couture track suit trailing close behind. The blonde's botched boob job looked liked she had stuffed two dead pugs under her shirt. Her weathered face suggested that she had been living a hard life of booze, drugs, and whatever else accompanied life on the pole. They were seated right next to me in 20E and 20F.

"I think your brother got a better seat assignment," the old guy sitting next to Derek said. "He got the broads while you got stuck with the old fart."

The old guy was wrong. By the time the plane passed over Ohio, the novelty of sitting next to the strippers had long since worn off. They retired to the bathroom every fifteen minutes (on a five and a half hour flight) to snort lines of blow and the skanks never even offered me a fuckin' bump. The nimble black chick could squeeze by, but the blonde was not as limber. The one time she attempted to climb over me, I was nearly suffocated in a sea of silicone. They drank heavily and the cocaine had them yapping incessantly. The blonde guzzled Skyy vodka and Sprite while the black chick ordered double Bloody Marys.

"Are you going to drink with us?" they squealed every time they ordered another round.

"Nope," I said. "I'm high right now."

"On what?"

"On Jesus."

I've come to discover that when you mention the Lord's name to annoying strippers, they tend to leave you alone. I've also come to discover that I enjoy using "Jesus" as a euphemism for generic Vicodin.

"By the way, where you girls working this weekend?" I asked somewhere over Colorado.

The blonde muttered, "I'm retired."

They constantly rang the flight attendant light, which drew the ire of the visibly agitated crew who did not like being bossed around by shitfaced strippers.

I couldn't wait to get off the plane and hoped that I hadn't contracted Hepatitis C or some other venereal disease during the flight. When we finally arrived in Las Vegas, the blonde shouted, "Time to double down!"

"Looks like you already did," I blurted.

My March Madness crew included Derek, Nicky and Señor. Nicky had driven all the way from L.A., while Señor flew out from Rhode Island. We all stayed at the Red Rock Casino in Summerlin to avoid the insanity of The Strip overrun by drunken frat boys on spring break and other sloppy cannibals from the various flyover states.

Nicky headed into the poker room to play Omaha with WWII vets and we arrived at the sports book three hours before game time to secure good seats for the Sweet 16 games. My buddy Miami Don lived around the corner and he stopped by to gamble and drink with us. He was a regular at Red Rock's sports book and knew the adorable waitress who covered our section. We gave her a hefty tip in advance and she provided lightning-fast cocktail service for the rest of her shift. Even though we were bogged down for the long haul, Derek and Miami Don kicked off the day with double shots of Patron. I eased into the day and ordered a Greyhound because my inner demons have an unquenchable thirst for everything that's bad about Las Vegas.

The word *moderation* often disappears from my brain and vocabulary. It's easier to give in than to do the right thing and quell those Dionysian urges. In the city of excess, there's only one thing to do – surrender to the flow. I travel to Las Vegas to raise hell and win money not act like an angel and a good Catholic. As the pussification of America continues before our eyes, Las Vegas remains one of the few places on the planet you can still get your rocks knocked and let loose on a good old fashioned bender without the self-righteous nitwits raining down their sanctimonious barbs.

Sports betting is the speedball of gambling. The bettor's high is better than cocaine and heroin combined. I howl at the big screens and veins bulge out of my neck. I threaten to have the family of referees kidnapped and killed when they blow a call. I rip out chunks of my hair when players miss free throws. It felt like my old days on Wall Street that were filled with endless screaming, mayhem, and an ungodly desire to make more and more money.

136

"Number 668. Ummm... $3,300 to win $3,000," I said at the betting window, speculating on a bunch of twenty-year old kids throwing an inflated ball through a cylinder. If I won, I'd collect $6,300. If I lost? I kissed $3,300 good-bye.

On the first day, I wagered more money than my old man used to make in a month humping a shitty desk job for an insurance company in Midtown Manhattan. I only won two of my four games in a gut-wrenching session, but won my monster bet on UCLA. Seriously, nothing in this life is sweeter than cashing a monster ticket at the sports book and counting along inside my head with the cashier as she counts out my winnings in front of me. I have to wipe the drool from my mouth and hide my erection as the cashier slides the stack of money toward me.

After riding an intense high all afternoon betting on college basketball, I wanted the buzz to continue. Instead of joining Nicky in the poker room, I bet on four NHL games and two NBA games. I was a greedy action junkie. Live poker is so fucking slow sometimes and it seems I always get stuck next to a drunk idiot with foul body odor who won't stop fucking bragging about how great of a poker player he is, or worse case scenario, he unleashes a barrage of bad beat stories making me want to slit my wrists right there at the table.

Miami Don called our cocktail waitress "The Mush" because her picks were so bad that everyone instantly wanted to bet the opposite. Fade the mush.

"Who do you got?" Miami Don asked.

"Memphis with the points and the money line. I also like Florida and North Carolina," answered the Mush.

Derek winced because he had bet big on North Carolina. When she walked away I whispered, "We're doomed."

I sprinted to the betting window. That's when you know you are in trouble – when you find yourself fading picks from a clueless cocktail waitress.

The second day of college basketball began perfectly but ended in a nightmare when I experienced a $6,000 downswing in the treacherous UNLV game. Las Vegas is one of the largest cities in America without at least one professional sports team, and by default, the Runnin' Rebels of UNLV are the biggest game in town. The sports book at Red Rock was packed with a rambunctious sea of UNLV fans and alumni proudly dressed in red clothing. Luckily, I bet on the same side as the crowd and hammered UNLV heavily. The Rebels looked good in the first half until Tajuan Porter from Oregon decided to play the game of his life. Every three pointer he nailed was a tiny little dagger piercing my heart. When the game ended, Porter had dropped 33 points on UNLV including eight three pointers.

"Talk about a bad beat," Miami Don lamented after he lost a couple of bills on the game. He quickly ordered a round of cocktails for the table to soothe the pain.

Someone once told me, "It's better to be pissed off than pissed on." But that mantra could not change the mean streak that illuminated my eyes as I grew increasingly livid. Best way to solve an anger management issue? Drink right through it.

The UNLV loss wiped out all of my profit from the first day. I stewed in a pot of gambler's rage. I tore up a couple of my losing tickets and watched the small pieces of paper flutter to the carpet. If I had been alone at home when I suffered those losses, I would have punched a hole in the wall or tossed an entire litter of kittens into the microwave. Consumed with ire, all I wanted to do was head-butt the lone Oregon Ducks fan in the sports book.

Chapter 23

April 2007.

The Fontana Room at the Bellagio Casino is not a bad place to call your office. Even though I was wedged up against the back wall underneath one of the gigantic plasma screens and my laptop barely fit on the tiny table more suited for hobbits than a tournament reporter, I couldn't complain. Behind me, out the window overlooking Las Vegas Boulevard and The Strip, I could see the majestic Bellagio fountains with the faux Eiffel Tower in the background. Right in front of me sat the greatest show in poker – Phil Hellmuth.

"Best no-limit hold'em player in the world," he often claimed.

At the time, the Poker Brat was a ten-time bracelet winner and the youngest WSOP world champion at that time. Love or hate him, you can't take your eyes off the guy who is often the tallest player in the room. Aside from Mike Matusow, there's also no one louder in poker.

Since I began covering tournaments I've witnessed Hellmuth kick over chairs, call hundreds of his opponents donkeys, proclaim that he can dodge bullets, and walk off the TV stage at the WSOP Main Event over to media row just to ask what BJ and I were writing about him.

In the previous two years covering the WPT Championship, I've never had a better seat. To my left sat Hellmuth, berating everyone within a twenty-five-foot radius, and to my right sat Jamie Gold, the controversial 2006 WSOP Champion, playing nearly every hand and talking just as fast. Both players were constantly jawing at their tablemates and when they grew bored of that, they talked shit to each other.

Hellmuth arrived ninety minutes late in true Hellmuthian fashion, and sat down at his table just as players went on their first break. He walked outside to the veranda to chat with Gold who sat at a table eating a jumbo shrimp salad. John Bonetti, dressed like an old-time NBA referee wearing black sweat pants and a black and white shirt, pulled Hellmuth aside and quickly told him about Gold's bluff.

Gold had been sitting at a difficult starting table that the Poker Shrink dubbed "The Champions Table." It included Hoyt Corkins (2003 WPT Foxwoods Champion), Maureen Feduniak, Adam Weinraub (2007 WPT Invitational Champion), Tuan Le (2005 WPT World Champion), Jamie Gold (2006 WSOP Champion), Francois Safieddine, Tony Cousineau, Abe Mosseri, and Scott Clements (2006 WSOP bracelet winner). England's John Duthie, the EPT creator and the first player to ever win £1 million in a televised poker tournament in the United

Kingdom, was moved to the table late in the afternoon along with 2004 WPT Champion Martin de Knijff.

Tuan Le knew he had drawn a nightmare assignment as he sat to Gold's immediate right. Le's hellacious day began with a monster bluff from Gold during the first level. The blinds were at 50-100 and the players began with 50,000 in chips for a tremendously deep-stacked tournament. There was no need to play ultra fast with such a slow blind structure. Both players, however, have a penchant for playing any two cards, especially Le, who is known as a cagey and unpredictable player. Le had checked on a board of 2s-2c-Jh-7d-4c with five or six thousand in the pot. Gold looked down at his stack and announced all-in. Le sat and stared at the board for several minutes as a panicked look blanketed his face. A wall of media reps quickly surrounded the table. Camera crews fought for position as Gold paced back and forth behind the table.

"Will I be the first player out?" Gold asked the media.

When he was told that no one had busted out yet, he turned to Le and said, "I've got a huge hand. I don't know if it's taking you this long maybe you have a huge hand, too. If you do have me beat, it'll be an amazing call."

Le said he had pocket kings, but I never believe anything a poker player tells me. Le reluctantly folded and tossed his cards into the muck. Gold flipped over 6c-3s and flashed a crooked politician's smile as he raked in the pot while a stunned Le sat there like a man who had just crapped his pants.

"He was about a minute away from sending me home. It wasn't looking good," Gold said.

After hearing about the bluff, Hellmuth instantly challenged Gold to a prop bet. If Gold advanced to Day 2, Hellmuth would give him $5K at 3-1 odds. If Gold busted out, he would have to give Hellmuth $15,000. Hellmuth tossed him a Bellagio $5,000 chip to hold on to.

"I expect to get that back plus fifteen more," he barked.

The two traded barbs, insults, and back-handed compliments before Hellmuth announced, "You're the only one in the room who had the balls to bluff Tuan Le. Every hand that I'm in with Tuan Le, I make sure I have the nuts. But you pulled off a bluff. Every time you bluff Tuan Le, I'm going to give you $500. Cash."

Gold accepted the bounty and within a few minutes he called Hellmuth over. He successfully bluffed Le, and Hellmuth peeled off five $100 bills from his roll.

Twenty minutes later Gold shouted, "Phil, you owe me another $500."

Hellmuth handed Gold more cash and Le sat there like a sullen muppet. Besides jawing back and forth with Gold, Hellmuth gave his tablemates plenty of guff while critiquing their play.

"You throw away A-K and this donkey shows you 5-6 off suit. They think it's a good play. They don't know how bad that is," he scolded one player.

After Hellmuth flopped a set with J-J and turned a boat, he took a nice chunk of one of his opponent's stacks and admitted, "I was setting you up all day for that hand and you walked right into it. That's why I broke all those records at the World Series. I know my customers."

While Hellmuth and Gold put on a show in the Fontana Room, a lot of curious eyes were focused on the nymph-like Anna Wroblewski. The 21-year-old had come out of nowhere to win a preliminary event at the Bellagio one week earlier. Born in Vietnam, Wroblewski was adopted by a family in Chicago. She moved to Las Vegas at the age of 19 and played around town illegally before she went broke and returned home. She took another shot at Las Vegas when she turned 21, but lost her bankroll a second time. Determined to stay in Las Vegas, she found a job in the service industry grinding out a $10/hour salary. She borrowed $400 from her boss to play in a cash game, winning enough to pay him back. Then she bought into a satellite at the Bellagio, which she won, and secured an entry into a $3,000 no-limit tournament. She proceeded to finish in first place in that tournament and collected $337,000. That's chump change for some poker pros, but it could take her up to a decade to earn that much waiting tables.

Wroblewski bounced all over the room and out to the veranda a couple of times. Two degenerates at the adjacent table had a $50,000 prop bet going on Wroblewski's weight. The over/under was set at 90 pounds. She double fisted beers and talked incessantly as the rest of her table sat in silence.

"Why isn't anyone else talking?" she asked.

"Because we were waiting for you to stop," said Irish pro Padraig Parkinson.

She played with a ton of confidence and took the early chip lead. She sent Jeff Madsen packing after she flopped a set of deuces against the two-time WSOP bracelet winner. She added still more chips after dragging a pot with just Ace high.

"Don't you hate it that I keep doing the right thing? They all said that I was a calling station," Wroblewski joked as she sniffed out a bluff from one of her opponents.

At one point, Wroblewski knocked back a shot of Jagermeister chased by a glass of Red Bull. Most of the day, she sat at her table on two stacked chairs and swigged a bottle of beer. Despite her heavy alcohol consumption, she finished Day 1 as the chip leader.

* * * * *

Over seven tables filled with media reps were crammed into the far side of the circular Fontana Room. There was barely any room to squeeze through the labyrinth. With photographers, cocktail waitresses, floor staff, and players walking back and forth, it was impossible to get close to the action. Flipchip popped in and out and grabbed several photos, while I sat at the PokerNews table with the Poker Shrink, BJ Nemeth, Amy Calistri and Nicky.

Snoopy and Jen Mason from Blonde Poker were covering their first-ever U.S.-based WPT event and sat at the European press table along with Benjo, a French poker journalist who I had met in Monte Carlo. As I walked out of the Fontana Room a quick flash from a camera blinded me. A woman twice my size wearing a fanny pack and a WPT visor snapped three photos in a row as I stumbled around struggling to regain my vision. She was trying to get a picture of Doyle Brunson who was lumbering out behind me. I nearly grabbed Texas Dolly's crutch and speared the overzealous tourist in the ribs.

The players filtering out into the casino area were mobbed by hundreds of fans, friends, and family members. The frantic scene is all too common at major poker tournaments. Our celebrity culture worships anyone they see on the boob tube, including poker players. In the 21st century, the autograph has been replaced by the photograph as people fumbled with their camera phones instead of fumbling for pens and paper.

The air quickly filled with cigarette smoke. It had been over ninety minutes since the last break. Pros chain-smoked and told bad beat stories to their friends while they fought off the fans. More camera phones appeared out of nowhere as fans grabbed a piece of any poker pro they could find. One young woman got groped by Devilfish as they posed for a photo near the slot machines. Another guy and his nine-year-old son took a photo with Scotty Nguyen who held a beer in one hand and put his other arm around the kid.

"Excuse me," asked one forty-something guy with a beer gut the size of a boulder as I made my way through the crowd. "Is Gary Greenburg playing?"

"Gary who?"

"Gary Greenburg. That guy who gives all his money to those African kids."

"You must mean Barry Greenstein," I corrected him.

"Yeah, Gary Greenstein," he said.

"No. He played yesterday, but his son is over there," I said as I pointed to the Fontana Bar where Joe Sebok talked with Gavin Smith.

I rushed over to the sports book and put in a couple of bets on the NBA playoffs. I also bet the Yankees heavily since they had not been swept in Boston in almost a decade. All of my bets seemed like a lock, but true to form I went 1-3 with my picks and I was quickly stuck a grand.

Earlier in the day, Benjo pulled a $50 bill out of his wallet and asked me to put a bet down for him. Because Tony Parker, the point guard from the Spurs was also French, we bet on the Spurs. The Spurs won but did not cover the spread. We lost the bet.

"What have you done to the poor chap?" Jen Mason said in her very proper English accent. "He's been in America for two days and he's picking up your bad habits!"

"Strips clubs are next," I answered.

Benjo took the Spurs beat well and got his money back and then some while sweating French pro David Benyamine. Two drunk fans on the rail offered him $100 to poke Benyamine in the stomach. Benjo walked over to Benyamine and explained the situation in French. Benyamine nodded his approval and Benjo poked him in his gelatinous middle region. Benjo returned to the rail and collected a $100 bill.

"Easy money. Who are we betting on tomorrow?" Benjo asked.

* * * * *

"Fuck!" Hellmuth screamed as the pot was pushed to Canadian pro Shawn Buchanan.

"Fuck!" he screamed again and slammed his fist on the table.

I couldn't tell whether the outbursts were genuine or fabricated. Regardless, for twenty minutes, Hellmuth spoke so loudly that you could have heard his whining across the street at the Paris casino. The media vultures flocked over to feast on the Phil Hellmuth show.

"This motherfuckin' kid just bluffed off 200K to the best player in the world! Nice play, genius! There's no way you are going to last the day," Hellmuth said as he pointed at Buchanan. "Playing against the best players in the world and bluffing off your stack with K-7? Nice play genius. You're supposed to be busted."

"Who's stacking the chips, Phil?" needled Amnon Filippi, a New York City pro who sat at the adjacent table.

"Sit down you baby," another pro shouted.

"Fag!" another pro screamed.

Hellmuth ignored the catcalls from the other tables and stood up.

"Sucking out on me? I can see right through your soul," he said. I tried my best not to laugh. "I'm at the top of my game and you suck out on me."

"Learn to take a beat," said Buchanan who was visibly rattled after waking up the sleeping giant.

"I'm playing for $4 million and history, pal. What are you playing for? The way you're playing you won't last until the end of the day. Everyone knows not to bluff me. They tried yesterday. Time after time and I picked them all off with Ace high. Bottom pair. Second pair. Didn't matter. I always knew when they were bluffing. Make sure you write that up on the internet," Hellmuth said as he pointed directly at me.

Chapter 24

May 2007.

I rented a furnished apartment close to the Rio at the Del Bocca Vista, a gated community that kept out gypsies, meth heads, and other vagabonds. Inhabited by many online poker pros, the sprawling complex featured dozens of identical two-story buildings filled with hundreds of condos. Most of them were empty; either up for sale or available for rent.

"Fuck!" I screamed.

Nicky and I had been in our new apartment for less than ten minutes when I accidentally knocked a mirror off the wall and sent it crashing to the floor. Even if you aren't superstitious, broken mirrors in Las Vegas are a bad omen.

The number 13. A black cat. A $50 bill. Someone touching your head. What do all of these things have in common? Bad mojo. Bad luck. Within an hour of the mirror incident, the internet in the apartment went out, I lost $300 playing poker, and I scratched Nicky's new car trying to pull out of the parking space.

"Fuck!" I screamed again as I inspected the damage.

"I'm gonna drive," Nicky said. I eventually calmed down on the way to play poker at Red Rock Casino. I put my name on the wait list. The kid at the desk called my name and said, "You're at table 13."

The illusion of control allows gamblers to feel more comfortable about their fate. By eliminating anything associated with bad luck, superstitious gamblers think they've gained a slight cosmic edge over the casino and other players. Their x-factor is supposedly their good luck symbols or other items that attract positive energy. People engage in ritual after ritual believing that they directly influence the outcome of their gambling ventures. That's why old ladies at bingo parlors bring along their good luck trinkets.

Once you believe in one superstition, you instantly become a slave to the unknown. I have one quirk that involves $50 bills and refuse to carry them in my wallet after Grubby told me that $50 bills were bad luck for gamblers. I never really found out exactly why, but as the saying goes, "Better be safe than sorry."

I try and avoid unlucky people because listening to their bad beats in life is probably the least entertaining thing in the universe. Jean-Paul Sartre explained in his play *No Exit* that hell was enduring other people.

My personal hell? Locked in a small room listening to poker pros bitch and moan about their bad beats for the rest of eternity.

Sartre's character Garcin said it best: "I made my choice deliberately. A man is what he wills himself to be."

If I incurred any bad luck during the 2007 WSOP, the broken mirror would not be the root cause; any bad luck would be brought on by my own choices. That year, I went after a big paycheck and took a position with Poker News. Bluff Magazine had secured the exclusive media rights from Harrah's, which meant Card Player and Poker Wire were out. Bluff brought in Poker News as a media partner to handle live updates and chip counts. Media access at the WSOP was restricted once again, however Bluff and Poker News had free reign of the entire tournament, which meant I had unfettered access to everything.

Poker News became an integral part of documenting the world's most prestigious poker tournament. John Caldwell deeply respected the remarkable history of the WSOP, and he assembled a team of reporters that featured some of the top names in the business. Jonno Pittock, a former tournament director at the Crown Casino in Melbourne, Australia, spearheaded the reporting team which included myself, BJ Nemeth, Nicky, the Poker Shrink, "Tropical" Steve Horton (a comic book writer from Indiana), and my friend "Mean" Gene Bromberg (a writer from Pittsburgh). Flipchip and Amy Calistri were responsible for photos along with Felipe, a photographer from Portugal whom I worked with during the EPT Grand Final in Monte Carlo. Justin Shronk, a multi-media guru from Philadelphia, headed up the video team which included Tiffany Michelle, an actress from L.A., as the on-camera talent.

Before the WSOP began we sat through a series of long meetings to iron out a game plan. Our collective goal was to provide top-notch coverage that was better than anyone had ever seen before. The WSOP had been expanded to 55 events, and each individual tournament lasted three days. Nicky, Tropical Steve, and Mean Gene focused on Day 1s. No one covered a final table better than BJ and the majority of final tables were his assignments. Caldwell assigned me the most difficult task – Day 2s. It became my responsibility to provide comprehensive coverage of Day 2 of each event from the middle to late stages before reaching the final table. Inside of two years, I'd gone from being a solo mercenary to working in a corporate structure and trying to maintain my sanity in a newfound middle-management position.

* * * * *

I walked across the sizzling asphalt of the parking lot behind the Rio Convention Center and felt like a repeat offender resigned to his fate on the first day of yet another 47-day prison term. Flashbacks buzzed my baking brain as I sweated my way through hundreds of parked cars with random poker-themed vanity plates like "ONADRAW" or "FLOPNUTZ."

"Sweet Jesus, what the fuck is this line for?" I muttered to Nicky.

Players stood three across in a registration line originating inside the Amazon Ballroom and stretching all the way past the entrance by the Rotunda. I found the media office and stood in that line for over an hour while exchanging pleasantries with familiar faces that I had not seen since the previous year. "So who you working for this year?" was the most popular question. Jobs in the poker industry are constantly shuffled every few months and people rotate in and out of positions with different media outlets and online poker rooms.

When I finally reached the head of the line, I was handed the wrong badge and media credentials. I sighed, and took the botched badge as an indication of a crappy year ahead of me.

In the first big gaffe of the WSOP, the Poker Kitchen moved indoors to one of the ballrooms and set off the smoke alarms when cooks fried up the kangarooburgers. A group of Scandi pros had gathered at one of the tables in front of the kitchen and left behind a large bucket of French fries. I offered Tiffany Michelle $50 to eat the entire bucket in less than twenty minutes. She agreed and chowed down. The fact that the soggy leftovers originally belonged to Thor Hansen and Per Ummer did not deter her. Almost 17 minutes later, and an hour before the first cards of the WSOP had been dealt, I lost my first prop bet.

"This is going to be a long summer," I said and handed Tiffany her money.

Because I was working for the official coverage team, I did not sit inside the media room as I had the previous year. I returned to the floor and took a seat in between Flipchip and Mean Gene at a skinny table covered with black cloth at the end of the Amazon Ballroom. The tournament room appeared much darker than in previous years. Massive banners hanging from the ceilings blocked much of the overhead lighting. Harrah's sold every piece of available space in the ballroom to advertisers, but accomplished one good thing by adorning the Amazon Ballroom with colossal portraits of previous Main Event champions. When people asked me where I sat, I told them, "Look under Berry Johnston."

I had become a glorified data-entry clerk. A team of college students working as field reporters collected hands and chip counts, and I in turn, published them on the website. Everyone was overwhelmed at first, especially some of the kids who had never seen some of their favorite pros in real life. Some were star struck while others were intimidated. One flustered reporter never returned after the first dinner break. Luckily, I had a few solid reporters who worked with me for the bulk of the summer: Dave (a Filipino kid with loads of tattoos from the mean streets of Flint, Michigan), Drew (the goalie from the UNLV hockey team), and Zeke (a journalism student with atrocious handwriting from San Diego). They were a diverse crew who saved my ass on numerous occasions.

The Rio also used an outdoor space where they set up toilets and a massive tent. You could always find dozens of chain smokers huddled under the sunshade across from the makeshift toilets located inside two trailers. The white tent previously housed the Poker Kitchen, but in 2007 was changed to "The Poker Tent" with fifty poker tables to be used during the $1,500 donkaments, second-chance tournaments, satellites, and for all of the events with a 5 p.m. start time.

Nicky drew the difficult assignment of covering the first tournament inside the Poker Tent. The room was supposedly air conditioned, but the doors were constantly open so the tent failed to retain any cold air. After experiencing a couple of minutes of hot and humid air inside, I quickly renamed it "The Poker Sauna."

"Close the door!" bitched one iPod kid with wraparound sunglasses.

"Can we please do something about the heat?" another player complained.

A sweating Nicky flashed an exasperated look as she struggled to find a steady internet connection inside the hellish room.

"Aren't we lucky? Seven more weeks of this."

"Shoot me now."

Chapter 25

June 2007.

"Does anyone know where I can get a gun?" I asked out loud.

"I wish I could help you," Michalski answered.

I cursed myself for not calling Joo-Chan's gun guy when I had the chance two summers earlier. Despite my extensive search for weapons in the media room, I was unable to secure any firearms, although I did score a couple of painkillers in exchange for some of Nicky's medicinal marijuana. I was worried that a potential all-out gang war between Tony G and Barry Shulman, the publisher of Card Player, would spill over onto the floor of the Rio. Card Player had lifted chip counts from the Poker News website and Tony G went ballistic. He wrote a chilling (and comical) post on his blog outing Card Player for its dirty deeds.

"I am from the street and when you steal from me, you are playing with fire," Tony G wrote. "This is no different than taking money out of my pocket when it was all I had, which wasn't that long ago."

Because I worked for The G, I figured I was a potential target. I didn't want to get clipped in the parking lot during a drive-by shooting between the Shulmans' personal security detail and The G's Lithuanian thugs, or possibly shanked in the bathroom by a Card Player intern while taking a piss.

Card Player and other outlets were caught red-handed after I entered fake names onto the Poker News chip count page and they copied every one. For example, Card Player listed my brother in the chip counts at the same moment he was on a flight from Maine to New York City. I used Derek as bait and Card Player's interns fell for it. Of course, he got a big kick out of seeing his name on Card Player's chip count page in between pros Justin Bonomo and Burt Boutin. It didn't end with my brother because I used the names of musicians from some of my favorite bands such as Phish and Galactic. I also used a couple of dead guys.

"Why is Sailor Roberts in the chip counts?" Nicky asked. "You know he's dead, right?"

Of course I knew that. But the interns at Card Player who stole the chip count didn't. We got a hearty chuckle out of Sailor Roberts. By the end of the day, Tony G got a call from Barry Shulman who offered a sincere apology and a promise to adhere to the stringent guidelines set by Harrah's going forward. I had been a part of the sting on Card Player, and they knew it. I could see it in their crossways glances here and there. I may not have been able to find a gun, but that didn't stop me from carrying around golf tees. They seem so innocuous, but can be turned into a deadly weapon in a pinch.

* * * * *

"There are a lot of holes in the desert," was an expression I've heard many times in Las Vegas. Those holes keep a lot of people in line.

The first major story of the 2007 WSOP surrounded the disappearance of Vietnamese pro Vinny Vinh. In the $1,000 No-Limit Hold'em with Rebuys event, Vinny Vinh completed Day 1 as one of the big stacks. I never saw him but those who did said that he looked awful. The next day, he failed to show up. His stack was blinded off and he managed to finish in 20th place. The chatter on blogs and internet forums was cluttered with possible explanations.

"He looks terrible. Scary actually," Daniel Negreanu wrote on his blog. "He's lost a ton of weight and it looks like he is suffering all the symptoms of possibly crystal meth or something along those lines. He looks half dead."

"He was emaciated and appeared like he had aged years in the course of a month," said Shane Schleger, a pro originally from New York City. "I'm assuming it's the result of some kind of hard-drug problem, but I have no real insight."

"He looked like he was on a different planet," added Shannon Shorr, a pro from Alabama.

As lurid tales made their way around the Rio, players and media speculated on Vinh's disappearance. One whisper even said he was staying at a sister property of the Redneck Riviera. Anything could have happened in those roach motels: robbed by tweakers, rolled by a crack whore, or overdosed on a bad batch of cheese, face down and ass up in the john, just like fat Elvis.

Drugs are the quick escape from reality, and crystal meth keeps a 24-hour city like Las Vegas pumping. Although poker players aren't juicing up with performance-enhancing drugs, many are jacked up on some sort of pharmaceutical cocktail. Sure you have a few token potheads who like to drag a little weed from time to time in the parking lot, but they're harmless. They'd rather be at home with the bong in one hand and a mouse in the other multitabling ten $500 SNGs. The cokeheads are easy to spot, constantly fidgeting at the tables and running into bathroom stalls

150

every fifteen minutes. The nicotine junkies constantly watch the clock and count the seconds before the next break so they can power-drag three Camels. Then there are the Jesus freaks, high on Christ at the tables. Very few drugs bind to neural receptors quite like religion.

Junkies of all types and from all walks of life filled the Amazon Ballroom, hooked on poker and intoxicated by their own vanity, power, money, sex, drugs, religion, or popularity. It didn't matter what the "thing" was, people were hooked in general. In a city full of temptations, some spiral into the abyss and never return. The few who survive are never the same. Vinny Vinh was just one of a thousand players walking that fine line. It looked as though Las Vegas was claiming yet another casualty.

On some days, just before sunrise, I would swear I could see the ghost of Stuey Ungar wandering the hallways of the convention center at the Rio. Some mornings, I'd spot him cleaning out the trash. Other nights, he'd be bartending in front of the Poker Kitchen. Sometimes, my peripheral vision caught a glimpse of him dealing a satellite or standing guard near one of the cages. Most of the time he hung out on the rail sweating the action in the biggest cash game in the room.

Stuey Ungar was the greatest no-limit hold'em player of all time. That's not just a half-baked statement coming from a hack poker writer. The men who knew him and played with him are the ones responsible for bestowing the accolade. The legend of Stuey Ungar has been solidified courtesy of colorful stories about a kid from New York City with a voracious appetite for action who took Las Vegas by storm in 1980. The invincible gin rummy prodigy could not find a decent gin game because no one would play him. Stuey turned to poker instead, crushing the games and quickly rising to the top. There are plenty of heroic gambling tales to tell, including the ones about his three World Championships, but the number of sad and pathetic ones is even greater. Those somber stories are usually told with disappointment as the storyteller paints a desperate picture of Stuey in the years leading up to his death.

Was it only Stuey's self-destructive behavior that killed him or was Las Vegas an accomplice?

Instead of snorting a few lines in a bathroom stall late at night to stay awake, Stuey used on a regular basis and transformed into a raging cokehead in a 24-hour city that profits on every human weakness. It's no wonder that several of his friends bet on whether or not Stuey would make it to his fortieth birthday.

At the 1990 WSOP Main Event, Stuey had amassed a monster chip lead and went back to his hotel room to party. His backer, Billy

Baxter, frantically showed up the next day when Stuey was absent from Benny's Bullpen. Baxter soon discovered that Stuey had suffered an overdose and could not play in the rest of the tournament. Stuey had a big enough lead that his idle stack advanced to the final table before he was blinded off in ninth place.

Flash forward. For the second time in two weeks, Vinny Vinh's stack sat at his table without him behind it. He failed to show up for another Day 2, this time in the $2,500 Short-handed No-Limit Hold'em Event. The floor supervisor opened up Vinh's sealed bag of chips, quickly stacked them up, and left the table. My gut told me Vinh was strung out somewhere, probably close by, but millions of miles away from home.

I had seen it happen dozens of times before in my own journey through life. Some folks slipped, and when they did, it was head first into the deep end. The lucky ones stumbled out of their alcho-narco stupor barely alive. The weak ones? You show up at their funeral a few weeks later with a knot in your stomach the size of a bowling ball as you look their loved ones in the eye and say, "I'm sorry for your loss."

The dealers began the process of blinding Vinny Vinh's stack off. Because it was a short-handed event, his stack decreased at a faster rate.

"He's the tightest player left in the tournament," Mimi Tran joked.

Every ninety seconds or so, another person would come up to the media desk and ask, "Where's Vinny Vinh?" Players, media reps, and spectators bombarded me with the same question and it put me on tilt.

"How the fuck should I know?" I snapped a dozen times.

I was pissed off because my biggest fear about Vinh had become a harsh reality. Vinh was not pulling off a psyche-out by arriving a few minutes late. He wasn't going to be coming in at all. I accepted that fact ten minutes into the tournament. He was a goner. Everyone else thought that good would triumph over evil and there would be a warm and tender Hollywood moment when Vinh would swear off drugs for the rest of his life and race into the room with his NA sponsor while his long-lost family cheered from the rail. Call me a cynic, but that sappy shit only happens on a Lifetime Movie of the Week.

David "The Dragon" Pham walked up to me around 6 p.m. The amicable Vietnamese pro always wore sunglasses and slid them down as he looked me in the eye and said, "Vinny didn't show up today?"

The gloomy glint in The Dragon's eye told me that he already knew the answer, yet he asked anyway.

"Nope. He got blinded off in 22nd place."

"What the fuck?" he said before he muttered something in Vietnamese and walked away.

Photographers took pictures of Vinh's empty chair. He was long gone, somewhere deep into the thirteenth hour of a serious bender. Crystal meth? Crack? Cocaine? Pills? Booze? All of the above? Table #72 in the Amazon Ballroom was the last place you were going to find him. You'd have better luck looking in the bathroom of the Oasis Motel where in November of 1998, they found Stuey's corpse with $800 in his pocket. The official explanation was that he died of a heart attack, but Stuey's friends would tell you that he died years before.

Vinh's empty chair finished in 22nd place out of the 42 players who survived Day 1. He did not play a single hand on Day 2 and won $12,468.

* * * * *

"Eskimo just pissed himself at the table. He can't feel his left side," Otis said before disappearing into the crowd.

I had never seen Otis that upset before. Paul "Eskimo" Clark, a pro originally from New Orleans, served as a medic in Vietnam before he showed up on the tournament circuit in the late 1980s. He won three WSOP bracelets and collected over $2.6 million in tournament earnings over his career.

The life of Eskimo Clark had taken a downturn. Because of his poor money management, he had become known around Las Vegas as a "broke dick." Eskimo had skills enough to win him seven figures over his career, but he was nowhere close to being the player that he once was. No one willingly wanted a piece of his action. He was looking more like a bum standing out in front of your local 7-Eleven panhandling for change instead of a three-time bracelet winner.

Eskimo was a visible warning to every young poker player – be vigilant about how you handle your bankroll, because if you're not careful, you'll end up just like Eskimo. He spent his mornings hanging out in the hospitality suites to scam a free meal and spent the rest of the time wandering the hallways of the Rio hoping an old friend on a winning streak would toss him a $100 chip out of sympathy.

Eskimo was riddled with health issues. He collapsed on Day 2 of the Razz tournament, and Clark County paramedics rushed to revive him.

Eskimo wanted to play through the pain and refused a trip to the hospital. He played on and advanced to the final table. Before the final table began, Commissioner Jeffrey Pollack encouraged Eskimo to seek medical attention instead of playing. Eskimo declined again. I was told through the grapevine that at that point Harrah's made him sign a liability waiver to continue.

America loves underdogs. Movies like *Rocky*, *The Bad News Bears*, and *Hoosiers* send tingles up and down our spines. Many of us hoped that Eskimo would win another bracelet the week after collapsing in the Poker Sauna. The reality was a sad one. He was deep in debt. A group of gamblers stood on the rail waiting to collect their cuts. One look at their faces and it was easy to speculate about the countless unseen others who were owed. Eskimo looked moments away from the Angel of Death sucking out his last few breaths as he busted out in fourth place. The vultures circling his dying carcass did what vultures do. They swooped in and picked apart whatever meat was left over.

I don't know how much money Eskimo owed the others. When you're running bad in Las Vegas and piss yourself at the tables, you should probably take that as a hint to skip town as soon as possible. But a guy like Eskimo was jammed up in a tough spot. What sorts of jobs are available for 60-year-old degenerate gamblers? Was he going to flip burgers at McDonald's? Eskimo had to play cards to climb out of debt – even if it killed him. Whether through bravado or pure stupidity, he was never going to leave those poker tables. Another desperate soul forced into desperate decisions – the Vegas *sine qua non*.

Chapter 26

July 2007.

I had three days off during the entire WSOP and decided to play poker on my first day off all summer. Caldwell and Tony G agreed to back me into one of the $1,500 no-limit tournaments, otherwise known as a donkament because the low buy-in attracts mobs of atrocious amateurs. I was dead money like most of the 2,500 players in that tournament, but Tony G wanted to give me a bonus for busting my ass during the first half of the series. I should have stayed at home, slept in, and caught up on freelance assignments, but I couldn't shake that jones to play cards. At least I didn't have to fork over any of my own money. Many friends and pros who played in the donkaments had suggested that I loosen up and accumulate chips early on if I wanted to survive. In the previous two years, I never made it past the dinner break in any of the WSOP events that I played. To motivate myself, I made last-longer bets with Felipe and Michalski, who played in similar events.

The last player to be seated at my starting table was Bertrand "ElkY" Grospellier, the first Supernova on PokerStars. ElkY, a former professional video-game player from France, migrated to South Korea where he crushed the gamer scene. He quickly mastered online poker and often played 20 tables at once. One pro told me that ElkY was stuck $250,000 playing online poker since the WSOP began. Even if the rumor was true, it still didn't change the fact that ElkY was the most dangerous player at the table.

I sat two seats to ElkY's right. From the first hand, ElkY played fast and aggressive because the rest of my table was comprised of passive weekend warriors. One guy placed an intriguing photo near his stack.

"That's a dead deer and that's my grandson," he proudly said. Yes, only in Texas do they point out the dead animal before their blood kin.

I bullied ElkY in a few pots to let him know that he needed to pick on the other players. I didn't have to worry about ElkY when he busted out early trying to make a move. But shortly after ElkY's elimination, C.K. Hua, a Vietnamese-born pro from California, sat down to my immediate left. C.K. had his small black man-purse slung over his shoulder. It dawned on me that I had never seen him without it. Every time I walked through the cash game area, C.K. would be playing Chinese Poker for $100/point with his man-purse faithfully strapped to his side. He loved gambling and was known for his loose-aggressive play. He quickly went to work showing no mercy to the amateurs at my table. I tried chatting him up and asked him to show me what he had inside the bag. He smiled and refused.

I got in trouble trying to re-steal with Kc-Jc and ran into a player with J-J. I stood up and prepped myself to leave because I was all-in and way behind. I caught a break, however, when the board ran out 8-6-5-7-4 and we tied for the pot with a straight.

"You're still alive," said C.K. "You can sit down now."

"Sweet Jesus!" I screamed.

At the dinner break, I had just around 10K in chips and had won both of my last-longer bets. Because our apartment at the Del Bocca Vista was located a couple of blocks away, Nicky and I went home to relax. My t-shirt and dress shirt were both soaked with nervous sweat. I tried taking them off, but Nicky protested.

"That's bad luck," she said.

"My attire has nothing to do with what cards I get," I insisted.

"You sure about that?"

Like an uxorious husband I caved and continued to wear the sweaty shirts. We spent the rest of the break ripping bong hits on our porch and I formulated a simple plan – double up against C.K., who was among the chip leaders with almost 50K.

When play resumed, only 570 out of the 2,778 original players remained. I would have to fade half of the field to make the money in my first major event. And it was going to be a rigorous task because Eric Hershler, the reigning WPT L.A. Poker Classic champion, had been moved to my table. We didn't even get settled in after the dinner break, before C.K. was pushing me around. I tried stealing his big blind with 5-3 off-suit and he moved all-in.

"50-50," he said, goading me to call.

I folded and he flashed 7c-7s. He had figured me for over cards. Good to know.

"Fifty percent," he said.

"Next time, I'll call," I promised.

Ten minutes passed and I found 7c-7h. I raised 2.1K from the cutoff. C.K. reraised to 7.1K in total. Everyone folded to me. I stared at C.K.'s hands. He wore a bracelet. I don't know from what event, but he happily displayed his jewelry. I tried to put him on a range of cards, but

C.K. could be holding any two. Then I thought about what was in his black bag. *Cash for Chinese Poker. Cell phone. Vinny Vinh's stash? Nah. What the fuck was in that man-purse?* I shook off those distracting thoughts and decided that I wasn't going to let anyone, especially C.K. Hua, push me around. I counted out my chips and looked up. A swarm of media surrounded the table. If I busted, the entire world would know about it within ninety seconds of the hand being posted on the internet.

"I'm all-in," I said.

"I call," C.K. quickly responded.

"Do you have a pair?" I asked.

He shook his head and showed Ad-Jc. I tabled my pocket sevens and he winced.

"Fifty percent," I said.

"Fifty percent," he said.

We both stood up as the dealer fanned out the flop. It missed C.K. On the turn, he picked up a gutshot straight draw and I had more bullets to dodge. The river was a blank and I doubled up. I accomplished exactly what I set out to do and was finally above the average stack.

C.K. counted out my chips and shoved a couple of his stacks my way. I couldn't speak. My hands were shaking like an alkie before his morning fix. All I could think was "What the fuck is in C.K.'s bag?"

* * * * *

Caldwell gave me the afternoon off to play on Day 2, but we both assumed that I would bust out before dinner break and head back to work. As I unbagged my chips, I thought about a couple of lucky hands that I won on Day 1 when I was a tremendous underdog, including one against French magazine publisher, Georges Djen.

I started out in Seat 6 with the small blind. Julie Deng (who made the final table in the Ladies Event) sat to my left in the big blind, with Erica Schoenberg, Men "The Master" Nguyen, and Robert Cheung (semi-pro from Vancouver, Canada) all to my right. "Action" Bob Hwang sat across from me. I had met him in Atlantic City when I covered an event for the Borgata Casino two years earlier. Action Bob was one of the nicest guys in poker, and it was a relief to know two people at my table.

Erica made her living as a professional blackjack player (along with beach volleyball pro and model) before shifting her focus to poker. Erica and I knew each other through my brother, Derek. A couple of years earlier, they worked together on a website called Card Squad. Her fiancé, French pro David Benyamine, was sweating the action along with Patrik Antonius. Normally, I was the one standing on the rail and the role reversal was surreal.

During the first orbit, I found Ah-As. I knew if I shoved all-in, everyone would fold. With Cheung and Men in the blinds, they were guaranteed to call a small raise even if they knew I had Aces. With the blinds at 1K/2K and 300 antes, I bet 5.5K. Everyone folded to Men and he called. Cheung also called from the big blind. The flop was Ad-9h-4d. Men checked and Cheung fired out 12K. I peeked at my cards and moved all-in for about 25K.

Men stared at the flop and muttered something before tossing his cards toward the muck. Cheung quickly held out his left hand about eight inches above the felt over the flop. The suspended hand was his way of signaling the dealer for "time" while he made his decision. His abrupt Jedi move freaked me out. I attempted to breathe normally and avoided eye contact. Cheung looked down at his cards, played with his chips for about ten seconds, then folded. As the dealer pushed me the pot, Men said, "Show me your A-4."

"Nah," I said.

"Come on, why don't you show me what you had?"

"Read about it on my blog tomorrow," I answered.

I moved up to almost 50K while Erica went on a rush and busted two players. After only a couple of orbits I saw that my stack had quickly slipped to under 30K again. I desperately began looking for a spot to make a move. Erica raised to 9K. I figured that I might be able to push her off that hand if I moved all-in with my Ad-9d. I shoved my tiny chip stack toward the center of the table. She took a couple of seconds and called. She tabled 9c-9s. I was behind and needed help.

Here's how BJ Nemeth described the action on Poker News: *"The flop comes Qd-5c-4d, and McGuire picks up a diamond flush draw. The turn card is the 3c, and McGuire also picks up a gutshot straight draw, and he has 15 outs going to the river. But the last card is the 8c, and Schoenberg wins the pot with her pocket nines. Paul 'Dr. Pauly' McGuire is eliminated in 119th place, earning $4,740. He also receives a bonus prize -- a hug from his friend Erica Schoenberg."*

During our hug, Erica whispered into my ear, "You were the only player at the table I didn't want to knock out."

158

"Then why did you call?" I whispered back.

All that work for a hug and $4,740. Well, a little less cash than that. Since he staked me, I had to give Tony G half of my winnings.

Chapter 27

July 2007.

The effects of the Unlawful Internet Gambling Enforcement Act (also known as the UIGEA, a piece of legislation tacked onto the Port Security Act that outlawed transfers between American banks and online poker sites) rippled through the WSOP when the total number of Main Event entrants failed to surpass the 2006 number. The online poker rooms sent fewer satellite qualifiers than in previous years. And, even though PokerStars gave away more seats to the Main Event than it had the year before, only a quarter of those winners were predicted to actually show up and play. Prior to the UIGEA, the online poker rooms bought their players directly into the Main Event. All the qualifiers had to do was show up and play.

After the UIGEA, the registration responsibilities fell upon the qualifiers, who had the $10,000 buy-in plus spending money transferred to their online poker accounts. Thousands of qualifiers opted to keep the money instead of playing in the Main Event because of the complicated and tiresome registration process. Many players thought it was a hassle to withdraw $10,000 from the online poker account, wait for the check or transfer to clear with their banks, then make another transaction – either wiring $10,000 to the Rio's cage or withdrawing the entire amount in cash and then flying to Las Vegas with the money so they could register in person at the Rio. Not everyone had the patience to complete the process.

Players also kept their Main Event buy-ins for other reasons. Many satellite winners ended up pissing away their prize money before they had a chance to withdraw it. Some took a more cautious approach and restricted their play to smaller buy-in events. Others were cock-blocked by their wives and forced to use their winnings on household matters. Whatever the reason, things had changed at the WSOP because of the UIGEA – and not for the better.

The opening day of the 2007 Main Event was more subdued than in previous years and the mood resembled a preliminary event. For the majority of the WSOP, our reporting team at Poker News had been over-extended, but we were fully staffed for the Main Event with all hands on deck. I was teamed with Nicky and four junior reporters. After doing the rounds of our section, we honed in on a couple of C-list celebrities that included Janet Jones, a.k.a. Mrs. Wayne Gretzky. I was shocked that she was playing since she had recently been implicated in a major gambling ring during a federal investigation called "Operation Slapshot."

Nicky circled Jones' table a few times to gather information for a fashion report.

"Oh my God, I'm obsessed with her enormous quilted silver lamé purse. And she definitely had some botox and other work done," Nicky said pointing to her breasts.

Jones was reliant upon medical enhancements to maintain her stunning looks after squeezing out a couple of The Great One's offspring. Even Devilfsh, the British pro with a notorious penchant for young women somewhere between "barely legal" and "old enough to drink," was impressed. During Jones' table change, Devilfish stopped in the middle of a big hand to gape as she passed by.

"Who's the fuckin' blonde?" Devilfish asked and pointed at Jones. The Littlefish in his pants evidently liked what it saw.

"Wayne Gretzky's wife."

"Who the fuck is Wayne Gretzky?" he shot back.

* * * * *

"It's poker on Valium," I told Michalski during a smoke break, voicing my thoughts about the tedium and tepidness of Day 1.

"You can never write enough about the weather," he replied.

Inspired by the timely Hemingway quote, I vowed to rant about the 120-degree sweltering weather on Poker News. On my way back in from the parking lot, I passed the dealers' smoking porch, which Benjo described as, "Depressing and full of people bitching about bad beats. It's sad enough to hear players tell bad beats. It's even more awful to hear dealers tell them."

Dealers were an odd sort. Some of them were players who took a shot at going pro and missed, so they ended up humping a crappy dealing job while waiting for a chance to get back in the game. Jealous dealers were often critical of the play of the top pros. At the same time, however, dealers witnessed pros at their lowest points imaginable including many of the stars and legends. Dealers knew that all of the media hype was bullshit, which made them even more glum.

Two of them were looking up at a plane flying over The Strip with a sign that read, "Congrats to the newest member of Team PokerStars Daniel Negreanu."

"What a donkey!" one of the dealers bemoaned. "What's a bigger waste of money for PokerStars? Hiring that plane or signing Negreanu?"

I continued using the service corridors that Wil Wheaton and I discovered in 2006 in our efforts to avoid the congested hallways. The back corridor was filled with a couple of huge refrigerators, bins of ice, condiments on shelves, shiny coffee pots, stacks of Diet Pepsi, and dozen of boxes of energy drinks. Boxes of apples and oranges and crates filled with bananas and potato chips sat on caged steel shelves. A separate steel shelving unit held hundreds of pieces of linen and table cloths for the different banquet rooms. If I took a banana would anyone notice? Apparently the Rio's staff stole ladders more than anything else in the service corridors; they were the only things locked down.

I passed the sparsely populated dealers' room and nearly tripped on three large jugs of water sitting on the ground. Empty coffee cups and a copy of Poker Player Newspaper were scattered nearby. The corridor also included a TV set, broken lights, and even a plate of half-eaten buffalo chicken wings perched on the edge of a chair. I turned the corner and passed the Bluff Production room, squeezed by a few large wooden crates to reach the cluttered area belonging to ESPN and 441 Productions, and continued walking until I passed the graveyard for wobbly chairs and poker tables with limp legs and large spill stains. Twenty chairs were stacked one on top of the other and a dozen of these pillars hugged the wall. Many times I would sneak in between the chairs and an equipment crate to write in peace for ten minutes, far away from the insanity.

When I opened the doors to the Amazon Ballroom, I took a deep breath and jumped into the tumult. Sometimes, I could block out the eardrum-piercing sounds and everything would go quiet as I lost myself in writing, but most of the time, writing was impossible. The chaotic madness of the WSOP was enveloping. The sound of clattering chips is distinct, like the roar of the trading floor at the N.Y. Stock Exchange or the deafening sound of the subway screeching to a halt in Times Square. If someone played me versions of ambient sounds from different poker rooms, I could easily pick out the Amazon Ballroom from the rest. Besides the chips, there are thousands of other layered sounds to drive people crazy. Dealers shout out to announce a newly emptied seat. A player screams, "Yes!" as he sucks out on the river to avoid elimination. The ESPN cameras rush over to a table as Humberto Brenes whips out a miniature shark and screams at the top of his lungs "The Chark is hungreeeeeeeee!"

When you combine it all, it sounds like little more than an orgy of fornicating geese.

162

* * * * *

Phil Hellmuth tried to make his late entrance into the Main Event a bigger and bigger spectacle every year. He was supposed to be sitting at a table in my section, but per usual, he was fashionably late and missed former New York Senator Al D'Amato kicking off Day 1D with the traditional, "Shuffle up and deal!"

Originally, Hellmuth concocted a plan whereby he would drive a race car down the hallway of the Rio and exit wearing a black NASCAR jumpsuit adorned with patches from his different sponsors. When he couldn't get permission from Harrah's to drive a car indoors, he settled on driving up to the back entrance greeted by an escort of eleven models representing each of his eleven World Series bracelets. Hellmuth had finally broken his three-way tie with Johnny Chan and Doyle Brunson for most bracelets at ten, after he had won a $1,500 donkament for number eleven.

The day before his flight in the Main Event, Hellmuth practiced driving the Ultimate Bet race car in an empty section of the Rio's Convention Center parking lot. The race car included an oversized decal of Hellmuth's face plastered on the hood. Hellmuth didn't get too much to time to admire his own image before he lost control and crashed te race car into a light pole. Conspiracy theorists on the 2+2 forums and jaded reporters slumped at the end of the Hooker Bar suggested that the incident was rigged and a carefully planned publicity stunt, but everyone from Hellmuth's management team at Poker Royalty insisted the accident was quite real. Hellmuth loves to brag about dodging bullets, but he couldn't dodge a light pole.

With the race car demolished, Hellmuth took a limo to the Rio as part of his grand entrance. At 2:20 p.m., Hellmuth finally arrived at the Main Event over two hours late. I stood outside on the steps in the 115-degree heat sweating my balls off as I waited for his pompous arrival. Hellmuth exited the limo, linked up with the eleven models, and paused for a few photos as the ESPN cameras recorded his every move. Fans swarmed around him and he signed autographs. The frenzied media, ESPN's crew, fans, agents, managers, Harrah's suits, and PR people slowly made their way down the corridor. Hellmuth entered the Amazon Ballroom with his entourage of models trailing behind him. He took his seat, shaking hands with the gentleman next to him.

"This is fucking ridiculous," said Nolan Dalla, who had also grown weary of Hellmuth's antics.

Hellmuth gingerly sat down. He looked stiff and wasn't his usual tempestuous self.

"He's hurting with whiplash," Hellmuth's agent Brian Balsbaugh mentioned. "But you know what he told me? 'I've won tournaments when I was hurt before. I've won bracelets in more pain.'"

Sore or not, rigged or not, Hellmuth failed to make it to the dinner break. Players actually cheered when Nolan Dalla announced his elimination to the crowd.

* * * * *

I was keeping my eyes on an erratic Vinny Vinh. Most of us in the media waited for him to explode. One by one, relentless reporters stopped by his table giggling, pointing, and jeering like he was the baby with lobster claw hands at a carnival freak show. We're a country comprised of suckers for dramatic stories involving characters of ill repute. We revel in the misfortunes of others with the same habitual morbid fascination that compels us to slow down and look for dead bodies when we pass a car wreck on the freeway because we think it's neat.

Vinh was originally scheduled to play on Day 1B and never showed. Supposedly, he was in the hospital and his backers (under the guise of friends and relatives) pleaded with Tournament Director Jack Effel for a refund. Effel returned the money as rumors swirled around the hallways and the media room suggesting that Vinh was in rehab. In a post that I wrote on Tao of Poker, I even alluded to the fact that "hospital" was a code for rehab. We thought it was the end of the Vinny Vinh story. We were wrong.

Vinh magically appeared on Day 1D. He quietly sat down and slowly built up a stack. Chops from Raw Vegas TV was able to snag an interview with Vinh. When Chops asked why Vinh had skipped so many Day 2's, he mumbled something about a dispute with his backer. Photographers fluttered by the tables to snap pictures of the exhausted Vinh. He rested his head on the table in between the sporadic moments when his inner poker savant took control. In those moments, he picked up pots and demonstrated flashes of the brilliant player who had earned over $2.3 million during his career.

At 8:30 p.m., Poker News reported that Vinh's stack was 34K. He didn't return from dinner and everyone thought the worst. Just six hours earlier, the media were rubbernecking in front of Vinh's table and now they were returning one by one to take photos of the empty chair. My suspicion was that he had taken a nap at dinner and slept through the break, or it was worse and he was passed out in a cheap motel after snorting too much _____ (insert drug here).

Speculation and gambling on whether or not Vinny Vinh was going to show up on Day 2 ran wild. Yet once again, the Amazon Ballroom was set abuzz when word got around that Vinh had been spotted in the building. Lance Bradley, a Canadian journalist from The Poker Biz, snagged Vinh for an incoherent interview before he took his seat.

"I can't win," Vinh told Bradley. "If I win this year, I die. So I'm not gonna win. These Vietnamese guys, they find me if I win. So I'm not going to win this year. Next year though, I win. This year I'm too crazy."

On the morning of Day 2, I received an email written by a pro refusing to give me his name. I couldn't tell if the source was legit, pure bullshit, or if I was being set up. The pro said to expect Vinh back during the Main Event because he was stuck with a couple of people including many well-known pros and bracelet winners.

"The people he owed money to would make sure he was there because that was the only way they ever figured to get any money from him," the anonymous pro wrote. "They have taken everything he owns, beaten him, locked him up, drugged him, chased him between Vegas and wherever he is from. They have also tried to make sure he has no money so he can't get anywhere... I think that he was locked up with no access to anything but drugs, including very little food."

The tipster also suggested that Vinh skipped out on Day 2 in the preliminary events because he knew that Harrah's put aside his prize money and he could collect his winnings at a later date.

"It's a trick that plenty of old-school gamblers employ to avoid making good with backers who are hounding them," Flipchip explained when I showed him the anonymous email.

Vinh's arrival on Day 2 surprised everyone. While his opponents unbagged their chips, he calmly ate an ice cream bar and looked over the table. With a paltry 3,200 chip stack, he moved all-in on the second hand of the day. After busting out, Vinh ducked underneath the ropes and vanished into the crowd.

Chapter 28

July 2007.

"Are you on 'ludes? You look like you're on 'ludes," Steve Rosenbloom said as he carefully studied my eyes like a cop administering a roadside sobriety test.

"Quaaludes? Are you serious? Does anyone actually do 'ludes anymore?"

My Chinese astrological chart indicated a successful yet sickly 2007. As the year progressed, the prediction took on more and more validity. Despite the UIGEA, Tao of Poker was flourishing and Poker News had compensated me well as a lead tournament reporter. However, it seemed like I was perpetually either just kicking a cold or trying to get over a new one. I had also pulled a muscle in my right arm that I aggravated in Monte Carlo, followed by a strawberry-colored rash that appeared on my shin shortly after Nicky and I first arrived in Las Vegas in late May. I was having some other odd symptoms like teeth-grinding pains in both of my ankles and my right knee. I limped around like a washed-up prize fighter and couldn't help but wonder whether the expanding rash and the joint pains were related.

Sans medical insurance, I decided to look everything up on the internet. A couple of medical websites suggested that I might have the gout, a disease brought on by excessive heavy alcohol consumption, a poor diet, fatigue, and stress. After a good five minutes of self-recrimination, I immediately curtailed my drinking at the Tilted Kilt and altered my diet – no more bacon and red meat. Otis immediately noticed the drastic deviation from my usual feeding habits.

"I think I might have the gout," I said as I rolled up my pants leg and showed him the rash.

"You got that rash, too?" he said.

"What do you mean… too?"

"Without fail, a rash shows up in the same place on my leg the day after I arrive in Las Vegas. Every single time. I have no idea why it's there, but it goes away with Gold Bond ointment."

After taking his advice, the Non-Gout Otis Rash disappeared in less than three days. Because I didn't have the gout, I resumed my WSOP diet of bacon and booze. I solved one health issue but I couldn't shake my chronic cold.

I had acquired an extensive collection of medications during my international assignments; nasal decongestants, severe cold and cough caplets, nighttime flu, sinus headache relief, and free samples of different allergy meds such as Allegra and Claritin. During overseas gigs, I made it a point to purchase the medications containing pseudoephedrine, a chemical that many pharmaceutical companies in the U.S. were forced to remove from their over-the-counter products. Tweakers hoard pseudoephedrine and use it as a base to cook up batches of meth. In addition to being popular with meth cooks, Sudafed was also a drug of choice among professional hockey players until it was banned. Training rooms all over the NHL used to have gigantic bowls filled with little red pills to give the players a boost on the ice. If you're sleepy, you pop two Sudafed pills and forty minutes later you'll feel a little buzz and within two hours you'll be wide awake and stay that way for many hours.

During the 2007 WSOP, I logged a minimum of 90 hours per week for Poker News. One week when we were short-staffed, I clocked 130 hours at the Rio and that number did not include the hours that I put in for Tao of Poker. During that stretch, I was sleeping an hour a day and surviving on my supply of international Sudafed to lift my exhausted demeanor. It beat drinking the sludge-like coffee in the media room or spending ridiculous amounts of cash at Starbucks. I couldn't find anyone with Adderall, and snorting crushed up No-Doz pills was out of the question. I tried it once in college with less than desirable results – a bloody nose and a case of the shits.

The diluted speed-like effects didn't seem to be detracting from my writing ability so I continued taking them. "What the hell," I thought, "Some of my favorite writers penned their best works all jacked up on speed." Supposedly, Jack Kerouac cranked out *On the Road* in three weeks while crocked to the tits on Benzies.

Nasty side effects were the downside to over-the-counter meds. Irritability and edginess seemed to be my middle name. The mere sight of tourists in Hawaiian shirts and spectators with cameras dangling around their necks annoyed me. It felt like my skull was being crushed by a vice every time a pro bitched about a bad beat. Plus the booze hit me harder when I mixed in the meds, which is exactly what was happening when Rosenbloom wandered up and accused me of hoarding the coveted and archaic quaaludes.

"I got these Dutch cold pills that make you feel pretty groovy, but that's about it," I said.

Every couple of hours, I consumed copious amounts of ganja to handle the bombardment of inane questions from spectators who were forever wandering up to the media desk as though I were the human version of Google. Every few minutes I wanted to scream, "Do I have a sign on my head that says, 'Ask me stupid fucking questions?'"

Felipe, one of the Poker News photographers, was from Portugal and able to get away with muttering "No speaka English!" in a thick accent and people would leave him alone. However, I didn't have that luxury. I was usually left barking curt one-word answers. Some days, I became the Poker News complaint line and pros lined up to get their chance to bitch and moan about how someone at Poker News fucked up their bust-out hand.

Working on the floor of the Amazon Ballroom every day gave me a better sense of what was really going on in a tournament, but I missed my friends in the media room. The only time I was able to see them was when I popped by to chat before my shift began or when they ventured out to the floor. That's why I cherished the late night hijinks with Otis.

During the EPT Grand Final in Monte Carlo, Otis and I initiated a tradition where we drank a beer at the start of the last level of play for the night. We would retreat to the bar overlooking the Mediterranean Sea and waited for up to ten minutes before the callow French waiters served us. At the WSOP, we continued the tradition and raided the stand-up bar in the hallway. The Bulgarian bartender served us Coronas with limes in plastic Milwaukee's Best cups. We stepped outside to hang out on the dealers' porch and savored every sip of our late-night beer during our few minutes away from the mayhem inside.

I noticed an ashtray-trashcan combination that sat at the bottom of a flight of steps. I suggested a prop bet and watched as Otis' ears perked up. The top of the trashcan was approximately the size of a laptop. The hole for the trash was located in the center flanked by two ashtrays that had become graveyards for hundreds of cigarette butts. We wagered on achieving one of three things: $20 to hit any part of the garbage can with the lime, $100 if the lime landed on either part of the ashtray, and $250 if we successfully threw the lime into the actual can.

We stood on a landing about twenty-five feet above the trash can. After the first few rounds, we understood the difficulties of throwing a lime wedge into a small hole. You had to compensate for the crosswind and adjust to the lime's downward trajectory. Those little intricacies transformed a lark of a bet into a challenging contest. Alexander Pope said it best, "What mighty contests arise from trivial things."

Lime Tossing evoked a flood of adolescent memories. Even though we were two thirty-something adults, we ran up and down the

168

stairs with youthful exuberance as we chased after beat-up limes. By the end of the night, my fingers were sticky with lime juice, and little flecks of pulp coated my laptop. The lingering odor of limes surrounded me for the rest of the night. From then on, we continued our tradition of a beer during the last level, but added a compulsory round of Lime Tossing as an additional sport.

I developed different strategies to try and gain an edge. I squeezed the limes and drained the juice to make them lighter and more controllable. Until that fateful point in the series, I was stuck for over $200 because of various failed "throwing things" prop bets. Thanks to the birth of Lime Tossing, however, I was slowly able to recover those losses because of my newfound ability to hurl citrus fruits with uncanny accuracy.

After being locked up inside the loony bin for twelve straight hours trying to make douche bags look like rock stars with flowery fodder, Lime Tossing was the day's only opportunity for us to gamble and relax. The life of a poker reporter is sort of like working on the set of a porn movie – after being around naked women for an extended period of time, you can't help but excuse yourself to rub one out. At some point, reporters have to unleash all that built-up energy and gamble on anything, especially after seeing so many bad players win oodles of money. It's a serious downside to working in the poker industry and a big reason why some reporters were always broke. They blew their paltry paychecks in the pits or at the poker tables because they were unable to control that calamitous urge to gamble. Otis and I needed to find a medium where we could compete, because deep down we were both action junkies. Lime Tossing filled that void.

"It was so meaningless," Otis said, "that it actually became important to us. Sometimes it was the most important thing we did all day. Some days, it was just two guys throwing fruit. Either way, Lime Tossing was bigger than the WSOP, bigger than Vegas, and bigger than the two of us."

Chapter 29

July 2007.

When I visited Australia at the beginning of the year, the entire poker room (aptly called the Las Vegas Room) at the Crown Casino in Melbourne was packed wall-to-wall with Aussies, Kiwis and players from other Asia-Pacific countries, as well. That's when I knew that although poker had suffered a huge setback in America courtesy of the UIGEA, the poker industry overseas was in the midst of its own glorious boom.

When I flew to Monte Carlo in March to cover the EPT Grand Final, I was more than impressed with the setup. The media room was massive, at least five times the size of the media room at the Rio, housing a substantially smaller concentration of European media reps. Poker had already been popular in the U.K., Ireland, and France for a few decades. Yet, like an outbreak blossoming into a full-blown pandemic, online poker was rapidly sweeping Scandinavia (Sweden, Norway, and Denmark in case you didn't know), Germany, Italy, Russia, and other Eastern European countries. Many Swedes often boasted that per capita, they were the best poker players in the world. The Finns, Danes, and Norwegians naturally said otherwise. As you read this right now, there's a bunch of sixteen-year-olds in Norway with bankrolls approaching seven figures. What will happen when they turn 21 and visit Las Vegas for the first time?

When it comes to betting on Main Event players, I can't help but lean towards the Scandis. Over the previous years, at least one Swedish player had gone deep at the Main Event. In 2007, the Swedes failed to advance to the final table, but Philip Hilm from Denmark carried the Scandi torch. At the time, bookies were listing the young pro as the favorite to win because he held nearly all the chips at the start of the final table. Scandis have a reputation for playing erratically and being difficult to read at the tables. The fearless Hilm loved playing big pots.

The final table represented many different nations and continents. The flags of Canada, Russia, and South Africa were in constant motion as fans displayed their nationalistic pride. During big hands it often felt like you had been dropped into the middle of the World Cup with all of the thunderous chanting and rowdy drinking. The highly visible South African contingency wore green shirts that read "Everybody Loves Raymond" in support of their local hero Raymond Rahme. They draped flags over their shoulders and wore them as capes while frequently screaming "Ship it to Africa!" whenever Rahme won a pot.

Alex Kravchenko, a 2007 bracelet winner from Moscow, had a substantially smaller cheering section. They were waving the Russian flag and also singing in Russian, but I had no idea what any of it meant. Tuan Lam's friends and family each held miniature Canadian flags and would break into a chorus of "O, Canada" whenever he won a pot.

The first 60 hands of the final table flew by faster than anyone in media row could have imagined. A wave of giddiness swept over us, because after seven weeks of insanity, we all wanted to go home. Badly. Everyone, including me, secretly wished for a fast final table, but I tried to mentally prepare for the long haul because the 2005 and 2006 Main Events had lasted somewhere around 13 or 14 hours. The space in front of the media room became a refuge for luggage. Many members of the European press had checked out of their rooms and were planning to catch cabs to the airport as soon as the final table ended.

With four players remaining, it appeared as though the final table might be completed by midnight. Jerry Yang had captured over 55 percent of the chips in play while Kravchenko hung on with a short stack. He held the distinction of being #1 on the All-Time Russian Money List, and he showed everyone why he was one of the toughest and baddest motherfuckers on the block. You couldn't miss Kravchenko wandering around the Amazon Ballroom clad in his black Adidas jumpsuit. You almost expected to see an old Soviet regime CCCP stamped on the back. He carried a cold and blank expression on his face and glanced at you with the eyes of a sniper. We developed wild theories borne out of exhausted delirium that Kravchenko was a hit man for the Russian mafia who had come out to Las Vegas to whack Vinny Vinh or collect a monster debt from Eskimo Clark.

How Kravchenko survived for so long was beyond me, but he slowed down the action for many hours fighting off his would-be executioners. Eventually, Yang took out the Russian in a classic race with pocket eights versus Big Slick. Considering Kravchenko was consistently short-stacked during the final three days of the Main Event, his fourth-place finish was truly amazing.

Two hands after Kravchenko's elimination, Yang quickly took out Rahme in third place when he snapped off Rahme's pocket kings with A-5. The heads-up match was set between Yang and Canada's Tuan Lam, a former poker dealer turned pro. In sharp contrast to the fight put up by Kravchenko, Lam played passively at the final table, just trying to stay out of Yang's way. After 36 hands, Yang emerged as the winner and collected $8.25 million.

Originally from Laos, 40-year-old Jerry Yang lived in California with his wife and six kids. He worked as psychologist and social worker and was a relative newcomer who concentrated on low stakes. He had never played in the WSOP before and won his Main Event seat through a $225 satellite at the Penchanga Casino in California. Yang had the most karma points coming into the final table because before any cards were dealt he made a public commitment to donate 10 percent of his winnings to the Make-a-Wish Foundation, Feed the Children, and the Ronald McDonald House. He also indicated that he was going to use some of his windfall to help other people in his community.

Yang's family members sweated him enthusiastically. One of them sat on the floor and constantly prayed. Yang was a very religious person himself and could often be seen praying as he awaited the outcome of big hands. During his post-victory interview with ESPN, Yang constantly spoke about how he could not have achieved what he did without the help of God.

"I had a feeling inside," Yang said, fighting back tears. "I kept praying. If God could help me, I knew I could win. I had a funny feeling inside that I could do it. I thank the Lord. The glory goes to him. Thanks to the heavenly Father, I am here today and victorious. With this money, I can do a lot of good for people out there who need the help."

"Are you having the best day of your life?" asked ESPN's Norman Chad.

"My family tried to escape Laos and we failed. They (the communist regime) hunted us down. Then we escaped to Thailand. When I found out that we were going to America, it was the happiest day of my life. It was the first day I found freedom."

"Do you think this is the most poker that the Lord has ever watched over?" Chad joked.

"The Lord was watching over me," said Yang. "When I had 4-4 and I was all-in I prayed, 'Lord, give me a set.' Then the flop had a 4 and I survived that hand. I have seen the miracles of God at the World Series of Poker."

When he was asked about his future, Yang said: "When I made the final table, I called my boss and told him I needed a few extra days off. I plan to go back to work – to give my two weeks notice. My wife works the night shift. I told her that she doesn't have to work anymore. We have six small children and we want to make sure they get the best life and education."

Sometimes rays of hope appear within the dark side of humanity that dominates poker. Guys like Barry Greenstein (Children, Inc.) and Phil Gordon (Bad Beat on Cancer) worked hard to help charitable causes. PokerStars teamed up with the cast of *Ocean's Thirteen* and helped raise money and awareness for the humanitarian crisis in Darfur. Plenty of players like Kenny Tran, Scotty Nguyen, John Phan, and Liz Lieu helped their families and communities in Vietnam. They literally feed villages with their winnings while most of their American counterparts blow their cash on strippers and degenerate gambling. Yang was going to use it to help ease the burden of those who needed it most. Could it be that the poker gods are paying attention, after all?

In a time in America when politicians pandering to the religious right were influential in brandishing online poker as a society-corrupting evil, a devout Christian like Jerry Yang demonstrated that poker could be a conduit for good. Sure, poker is a form of gambling, but so is trying to beat the stock market. Heck, praying to an imaginary being is the ultimate gamble. What's the difference between shoving all-in with Big Slick vs. middle pair and believing in God? I don't see any. Both are coin flip situations. God either exists or doesn't. That's a race situation that churchgoers gamble on every single Sunday.

I've long given up the quest to determine whether our original creator was Allah, Buddha, Jesus' dad, or some alien scientist who cross-bred themselves with apes. Maybe an all-powerful force exists or maybe it doesn't. The existentialist in me believes that we live in a gloomy, random, and godless universe. Spending so much time in Las Vegas only strengthens these notions.

The most important conversation I had during the entire summer occurred when I was on the verge of going off the deep end of life tilt during one of the breaks for the $50,000 H.O.R.S.E. event. It was around 3 a.m. and the lights of The Strip glistened in the background as Benjo and I stood on the dealers' porch. I initiated the conversation and asked him something about Jean-Paul Sartre banging Simone de Beauvoir. Benjo replied with a weird story.

"Simone de Beauvoir made Sartre take a holiday in Southern France because he was too burnt out after experiencing hallucinations, specifically one about a lobster following him around. He had been abusing too much mescaline and felt the residual effects of that drug. For years, a lobster followed him around everywhere and it nearly drove him insane. He finally confronted his own reality and made the decision that he was not going to see the lobster anymore — and the lobster vanished and ceased to exist."

I had a moment of clarity and felt as though I had finally figured out what Sartre was trying to teach. Well, not "exactly," but felt I was definitely on the right track. Sartre said that we have to make a choice in life and not just about what we do, but what we believe and what values we hold. Those choices are not going to be made for us, nor should they be dictated by those around us. One day, Sartre decided to stop seeing the lobsters and they were gone.

If Jerry Yang thought that he won $8.25 million because of God's help, then so be it. Was it God or luck that brought him a six on the river to come from behind and beat Tuan Lam? I was not going to debate it. I didn't need to. After all, any role that the hand of God played in the final outcome ended up great publicity for all of poker. The way I see it, according to the words and actions of the newly crowned WSOP champion, The Lord *must* love poker. God had helped the good guys siphon money from the morally reprehensible bad guys in order to redistribute it among the poor and needy. How could it not be so?

While seeking a shortcut through life, I found poker as a viable way to obtain quick cash. You gain a deeper sense of satisfaction when you win money through gambling than when you earned it by humping a job for someone else. I was willing to put money on the line, and the payoff was exhilarating and intoxicating. The risks are greater and so are the payoffs, thus, the attraction of living the bohemian lifestyle or becoming a professional poker player. Gambling gives you a smug sense of self-accomplishment that makes you walk tall because you feel like you have the testicular fortitude to gamble on yourself instead of putting on a stiff suit and tie and taking guff from an inept boss.

The illusion and myth, however, were much different from the reality. I lived in two cities simultaneously. There was the Las Vegas everyone saw on TV and in the movies; the romanticized version where dreams could come true and people partied their asses off. Then there was Lost Vegas; the miserable, desperate side of the world that few people lived to tell you about. If you open your eyes wide, you'll find losers everywhere. Everywhere. In line at the buffet. Your Pai Gow dealer. The drooling old lady in the keno parlor. The frat boy wearing sunglasses at a micro-limit poker table. The hookers selling their snatches all over town. Everyone is juiced up on their vice of choice; sports betting, slot machines, blackjack, roulette, craps, and even poker. Every aspect of the Las Vegas empire is, was, and will forever be built on losers' money. Construction crews work around the clock and build more megalithic casinos funded by little pieces of your dignity. The bright lights on The Strip? Paid from your Grandma's losses at the slots. The gaudy facades? Paid by your uncle's dice throws.

The demons mercilessly poke pin-sized holes in your soul and all of your warmth, creativity, and morality oozes out to become part of a stream of hopelessness that flows all the way back to Lost Vegas. Just when I was ready to give up on humanity, Jerry Yang taught me a lesson in faith, in the middle of a casino, of all places.

Chapter 30

September 2007.

Key West, Florida.

A fucking rooster woke me up.

I managed to avoid puking, chugged bottled water and quickly popped two Motrin followed up by a generic Vicodin. I sat down at the table near the window overlooking Duval Street, and looked through my digital camera. Like a scene out of *Memento*, I slowly pieced my life back together using random images, mostly taken at the Irish bar. The strip clubs we'd ventured to had a strict "no photography" policy. Sadly, there were no shots of that debauchery.

I grabbed the wad of cash out of my pocket. It looked healthy until I unfurled it and began counting. Wait, where did all the hundreds go? All the twenties had been replaced by singles. What the fuck? I did some quick math and figured out that between the Irish bar and a trip to two strip clubs, I had blown almost $500.

Key West has the vibe of a Caribbean island without the color. The streets are flooded with sunburned white people clutching souvenir bags filled with cheap rum and chintzy t-shirts with old Papa Hemingway's face plastered on the back. The AlCantHang Compound was off the beaten path, down a secret alley off a side street, far away from tourist central. Those poor fuckers at the real estate agency who rented the house had no idea what they were getting into because twenty-five lunatics were about to descend upon Key West to celebrate AlCantHang's fortieth birthday in a party to end all parties.

When AlCantHang plops down at an Irish bar, everyone present knows that they are about to be knee deep in a serious mind-altering drinking binge. There is no pretense. All actions undertaken are your sole responsibility, and yours alone. The best you can hope for is that your liver manages to escape with minimal damage and that the hangover the next day is not so devastating that you end up awake at sunrise cuddling the toilet bowl with the worst case of the dry heaves since the early days of the Clinton administration.

We joined the hordes of horny men and other desperate souls climbing the slippery wooden staircase to reach the Classy Joint, a local strip club on Duval Street. It was large with a stage in the middle of the room flanked by two poles on either side. Twenty or so chairs surrounded the stage and a long bar nestled against the back wall. The hallway off to the side led to the Champagne Lounge, a room for private dances,

176

furnished with red velvet couches where adult entertainers performed under sultry red, purple, and pink neon.

Big Mike, AlCantHang's wingman who is the size of an NFL lineman, scouted out a spot and we set up camp near the stage and started handing out bills. He tipped a minimum of $5 and up to $20. "We were conditioning the natives," he explained.

Because it was our first night in Key West, we wanted it known that we were going to be in town for a week. Recklessly splashing around money established the fact that we were not tightwad day-trippers looking to see tits and ass for next to nothing. Within minutes, the attention of all the talent in the Classy Joint was under our full control. The rest of the customers became secondary to the AlCantHang Experience. Big Mike took care of our waitress with a sizable pre-tip and she responded with an endless barrage of beers and shots of SoCo. The attractive Cuban woman wore a tight red top. Seeing the skanky pieces of naked meat on stage made her the most sophisticated woman in the club.

"How come you don't dance?" Big Mike asked.

"I'm a mommy. Mommies don't dance. Would you like to see your mommy dance?" she said.

"Are you kidding me? That fuckin' bitch? I'd love to see her actually get off her lazy ass to make a dime," Big Mike said.

Most of the strippers were average looking and could potentially find work at a second-tiered joint in Las Vegas. The luckier ones might be able to get on the afternoon shift at one of the bigger clubs, but for the most part, the dancers who joined our party were the cream of the Key West crop.

Most strip clubs in Las Vegas implement a strict hands-off-the-dancer policy. The majority of the girls at Spearmint Rhino aren't going to shower you with special attention unless you shower them with $100 bills. The Las Vegas girls are all business and if you want to engage in any sort of unsportsmanlike conduct, you'd better be prepared to fork over big bucks for an adventure in the VIP room.

At Key West establishments you pay $20 for a naughty lap dance, which includes relentless crotch grabbing and having your face pummeled by fake breasts. We lost random members of our group from time to time as they disappeared with a stripper into a black hole, eventually reappearing with messy hair and wry smirks on their faces.

I befriended one girl from the Czech Republic who stood about five-foot ten with dark hair and natural breasts. She reminded me of actress Phoebe Cates and had a tattoo of a scorpion on her ankle. What looked like four cigarette burns peppered the inside of her thighs. By the second lap dance, we were discussing a Czech author, Milan Kundera, as she stood upside down on her hands and rubbed her shaved crotch on my chest. It became very obvious that she had never actually read Kundera's books, she just knew the titles. I didn't really care because I was hammered and rambling.

"Your country was invaded by the Soviets," I said. "They set up a puppet government that eventually crumbled after the Berlin Wall came tumbling down. Your former nation-state behind the Iron Curtain was broken up into two republics and instead of remaining in your new land of freedom, you fled to Key West where you strip for a bunch of old farts who are in town for a few hours while their cruise ship is docked. Or you're grinding away for horny servicemen on leave, taking every cent of their slave wages that our government pays them."

"I like the warm weather," she cooed. "And I'm trying to earn enough money to bring my mother here."

Of course, it was the old routine she was trying to sell. The American bimbos use law school or business school as their faux cover. The foreign ones bring up their struggling mothers and highlight the hardships in their native lands. My guess was that this one migrated to Key West to hook a big whale, perhaps a lonely and retired businessman with a yacht and multiple million-dollar homes.

"Everyone loves their mothers," I said. "Don't you love money?"

"Of course," she said as she continued to dance to a random hip-hop song with fellatio lyrics.

"But do you love money more than your mother?"

She paused and said, "I love them equally both."

"But your mother is still washing dirty underwear for tourists in Prague, right? If you really loved her, she'd be in paradise with you, washing dirty underwear for tourists in Key West."

She was a hustler, and a decent one at that. She didn't blink or try more words to get me off the topic. She grabbed my junk and twisted my nipples until I begged her to stop.

Part IV

"But he who cannot reveal himself cannot love,
and he who cannot love is the most unhappy man of all."
- Søren Kierkegaard

Chapter 31

May 2008.

You always remember the last time you were in Las Vegas. I'll pause for a moment while you close your eyes and let your mind wander.

...

So what was it like to feel the pile of chips in that monster pot you won? Did you taste the savory sushi? Could you smell the cheap stripper perfume? Hear the relentless cacophony of slot machines? Feel the thickness of desperation that filled the artificial air?

You look out the window of your car with the intensity of a leering deviant. The Luxor light captures your attention, a poignant beacon of promise where the unreliable patron saints of gambling gather: St. Coulda, St. Woulda, St. Shoulda. They jeer at your unanswered hopeful prayers. Blurry images of The Strip remind you of psychedelic Crayolas as you speed down the mountain at 92 mph towards the muted glow.

Your fate silently awaits your arrival under ominous incandescent lights. You went to Las Vegas instead of visiting the largest ball of twine because Vegas offers something no other place on Earth can deliver: the chance that *this time*, it will be your turn to get lucky. That's why you chase the long shots and try to live out your wildest dreams. The rush of a lifetime. You want to cash out racks and racks of chips and commandeer a thick-necked security guard to escort you to the cage.

You didn't go to Las Vegas to make love. What was your ultimate goal? To have an orgasm so intense that it wakes up everyone in your hotel. That's how you ended up with the frigid fist-master that you hired after calling the number on the card that the midget illegal immigrant porn slapper shoved in your hand as you walked past Casino Royale.

As the city raced to implode its past and expand, abandonment and foreclosures swept through residential areas like a deadly virus. New strip malls, and the shallow symbols of commerce they represent, infested the landscape, yet many of them remained empty. The skies are invaded by shining high-rises that no one can afford because nearly everyone is cash poor and has shoddy credit. The surplus real estate is gobbled up by sheiks and businessmen from Dubai who sleep on piles and piles of cash – profit on America's morbid addiction to oil and opulence. Our nation pissed away its wealth on gaudy SUVs and watermelon tits, and my pampered generation of party crashers became nothing more than a nauseating morass of used car salesmen and fame-whores trying to get one last high before the soiree ends. Better make mine a triple shot of tequila. Shit, just give me the whole bottle and I'll take it home with me.

Rush in and rush out. Hit and run. Vegas quickies are recommended, because sustained visits can cause permanent brain damage as one year of Las Vegas time tends to turn East Coast intellectuals into blathering space monkeys.

Las Vegas reminds me of Ayn Rand's crumbling society in *Atlas Shrugged*. System overload. Every few weeks, another construction worker dies on the clock and another dazed spirit haunts the next wave of looters and moochers. Those voices inside your head are not subliminal messages pumped out through the casinos. No, those are real voices from the beyond. The Las Vegas Valley is ripe with anguished ghosts who mercilessly tease and torment you. I'm ambushed by the gambling demons in the worst places, like at the precise moment that I decide to leave the Pai Gow table, my good senses suffer a massive seizure, paralyzed by greed that violently pumps through my bloodstream as the sensible part of me vanishes.

I frolic. I conquer. I stumble. I crash hard. The missteps rip me apart like shrapnel. The nonstop gambling action soothes me like a lick of ice cream on a hot summer day.

After my previous trip to Las Vegas with my brother and Señor for March Madness, I fled Sin City faster than a refugee evacuating Milosevic's Serbia. Over the previous two years, Las Vegas viciously beat me down every time I showed up. I wasn't exactly looking forward to another ass-pounding.

Nicky and I loaded up her car and drove four-plus hours before arriving in Summerlin, one of the first planned communities in the Las Vegas suburbs. In a part of town where it seems as though everyone lives in subdivisions hidden behind grey concrete walls, our palatial compound was nicknamed Sheckytown. Thanks to newlyweds John Caldwell and Jen Leo, we finally had a swanky place to crash during the WSOP. Our summer accommodations included a backyard pool, hot tub, and a new Wii entertainment system. I really don't require much to get work done, just a lamp, a desk, and a chair. My roomies were generous enough to set me up to write in an isolated area. After my stint at the Redneck Riviera, I felt like Siddhartha lounging in a suite at the Four Seasons.

I declined a generous offer from Caldwell and Tony G to work for Poker News' official coverage team for a second year in a row. I didn't want the insane workload and tremendous amount of responsibility. My days as a live blogging monkey were over. After accepting big paychecks in 2006 and 2007, I once again had the freedom to return to my roots and focus solely on Tao of Poker, over which I had 100 percent creative control. If anyone was going to profit off of my blood work, I wanted to make sure that it was me, and only me.

At the onset of the 2008 WSOP, the online poker industry was close to hitting rock bottom with cheating scandals at Ultimate Bet and Absolute Poker (where some owners had access to superuser accounts that allowed them to see their opponent's cards). I knew that such ugliness was just the tip of the iceberg, yet I continued to play online poker at PokerStars and Full Tilt. They were in the business to make legitimate money, but that didn't mean my opponents were 100 percent honest. We live in a Machiavellian world, and Las Vegas is the perfect example of immoral means justifying indulgent ends. Yes, cheating in poker had always existed for longer than any of us have been alive. Cheating is the fattest elephant in the room and a harsh byproduct of the highly competitive and lucrative nature of the game. When millions of dollars are on the line, you never know whom you can trust. Sure, the majority of online card rooms curtail cheating and their security teams frequently bust players who break the rules. However, you rarely hear about the slick ones getting away with it. The powers that be really don't like media types hyping stories about cheating scandals and would prefer that everyone just ignore and forget about them.

I had an intense disdain for the metamorphosis of the poker industry, yet I was ready to burrow deeper than ever before. Creative types have to go where the money is if they want to survive. My friends who are real journalists at newspapers and magazines are paid paltry sums compared to the ridiculous money I was paid to crank out fluff piece after fluff piece. I knew that the bubble had burst and the federal government was breathing down our necks, so I needed to grab as much money as I could before it vanished. That's why I stuck around. Besides, I had no other place to go. Outside of Las Vegas and the gambling industry, I was virtually unemployable.

I wouldn't consider myself a purist per se, and I'm not completely anti-corporate. I actually loved it when Dylan went electric. Harrah's did many positive things to advance the WSOP brand and continue in its tradition, but along the way there were the not-so-positive things that made you cringe. Poker has a rich history full of colorful characters that were, and are, some of the greatest card players of all time. Harrah's made a grand gesture in trying to pay homage to former WSOP champions by hanging banners containing their portraits all over the Amazon ballroom – but you could barely see them. The champions banners were obstructed by dozens of advertisements for a third-rate energy drink, a peanut company, multiple online poker rooms, poker magazines, a beer company hawking tasteless swill, a playing cards manufacturer, and a designer watch company. In Japan, artists create murals to honor their Sumo champions. These murals are hung in public places like train stations where people can stop and pay homage to those whom they admire and wish to emulate. What was the point of the poker portraits if no one could see them?

The corridor in the Rio's convention center was prime real estate. Pizza Hut and Krispy Kreme rented space, and inflatable beer cans cluttered the halls. Sapphire, the largest strip club in Las Vegas, rented a booth that was populated by lazy leftovers from the afternoon shift with C-section scars and smudged tramp stamps. After emerging from the Inflatable Beer Forest, I caught a glimpse of the new harem of Milwaukee's Best girls adorned in their updated 2008 outfits. Evidently, the suits at Beast headquarters ditched the skanky look and dressed their models in less revealing and less tantalizing outfits. Shit, they might as well have been Mormon wives from rogue polygamist compounds in Utah. Walking by the new Beast girls was like watching a porno with all the penetration shots edited out.

Some obvious improvements at the WSOP included color-coded table numbers, which helped alleviate confusion on days with multiple events. The Poker Tent was ditched to the delight of the players and was replaced by the Poker Kitchen. Three big-screen TVs were installed in the media room. I wanted to be closer to the action and opted for the elevated press box, which allowed a clear view onto the floor of the Amazon Ballroom. The top level was headed up by Nolan Dalla, and I usually sat in between Michalski and Tiffany Michelle. The front row was filled with the Poker News' coverage team and European media including Benjo and the rest of the French reporters.

On my first day back, I reconnected with old friends and bumped into people I had not seen in weeks, months, and even years. That was the fun part, catching up and talking to people from all over the spectrum – media, players, floor staff, dealers, suits, interns, readers, and even a few odd locals. Sadly, Amy Calistri skipped the entire event for the first time in over a decade, and Otis was working a reduced schedule and wasn't slated to arrive until midway through the WSOP.

The most difficult change to overcome was the extinction of the Tilted Kilt. Management finally closed its doors and our favorite gin joint was replaced by a McFadden's franchise. I sat down at the bar and nursed a pint while I took note of the changes. The lack of scantily clad waitresses was depressing and the wanna-be Elton Johns at the dueling pianos instantly annoyed me. It was obvious that once Otis arrived, we needed to find a new place to unwind during dinner breaks.

184

Chapter 32

June 2008.

"Archie Karas showed up with just $9 in his wallet," said Tom Sexton, pointing over to Karas' table.

Tom and I were often teamed up together at the 2007 WSOP when we worked for Poker News. During breaks in the action, he'd tell me mind-blowing stories about the poker scene in the 1970s and 1980s, particularly the seedy side of Las Vegas that has been glossed over. Most of the stories involved his brother, poker pro and WPT announcer Mike Sexton, and the illustrious Stuey Ungar.

The corporations running Vegas do an amazing job at cosmetically enhancing the place, but if you want the straight dope on Sin City, you have to rely on the oral history from grizzled veterans like Tom Sexton, Flipchip, and others who survived the war of attrition on the casino floors and in the back alleys. Thirty years ago, if your conduct was deemed uncouth, you got the beat down of your life in a dismal alley behind Glitter Gulch. The troublemakers caught on quickly. The ones who didn't would find their fate at the bottom of a ditch somewhere in the desert. For most contemporary poker players, their biggest worry is getting flamed on the 2+2 forums. They would soil their shorts if they had to step outside and settle things in the parking lot instead of acting like whiny pricks for the cameras.

Archie "The Greek" Karas is legendary for turning $50 into a $50 million bankroll before losing it all. When the 2008 WSOP began, Karas was flat broke as he began his comeback. Someone staked him in the $10,000 World Championship of Seven-card Stud and he secured funding for a couple of other events, including Razz. At one time, Karas was regarded as the world's best Razz player, and I'm sure in the eyes of many, he still is. I vaguely recalled Karas' final table appearance in the Razz event at the 2005 WSOP, but I hadn't seen him since. Out of 158 starting players in the stud event, he was among the 80 who advanced to Day 2. Karas ended Day 1 with almost 55,000 in chips, which was good enough for a spot in the top 20 overall.

Archie Karas grew up in Greece and ran away from home at 17. He worked various jobs on different ships as he sailed around the world. While on a stop in America, Karas jumped ship and never went back. With a limited English vocabulary, he eventually showed up in Los Angeles and quickly learned English and Spanish. He squeaked by on a modest income by hustling in pool halls and bowling alleys but soon realized he could make more money at the poker tables.

In his 20s, Karas was a rounder in high-stakes games at different Los Angeles card rooms. His bankroll always fluctuated. He would run it up to over a million in a couple of months and then go busto in a single weekend.

"Archie was widely known to win and lose a million dollars as much as fifty times over. When (he was) broke, he would find a new backer to start over," Sexton said.

"One day I might be driving a Mercedes, and the next day I might be sleeping in it!" Karas said.

In December 1992, Karas had hit rock bottom when he lost the last of his $2 million bankroll. He had $50 to his name and did what any action junkie would do – he gassed up the car, drove through bat country, and headed straight to Las Vegas. When Karas arrived at the Horseshoe, he spotted a friend and boldly asked him for a $10,000 stake so he could sit in a $200/$400 Razz game. Karas' reputation easily secured him funding.

"Archie came out of the gate blazing and tripled his money in three hours. He quickly went over and paid his $10,000 personal loan off plus a 50 percent profit for the happy investor," Sexton said.

Within three hours of his arrival in Las Vegas, Karas raised a bankroll. It would only be the beginning of his rollercoaster ride.

"Archie had more gamble in him than any person I ever met," said Jack Binion, former owner of the Horseshoe Casino.

Karas would shoot pool against anyone for up to $40,000 a game. On one occasion, he took down a gambler for $1 million after four lengthy sessions of nine-ball. Karas was hot, yet his opponent kept reloading. Finally, on the fifth attempt, Karas took a tremendous hit and lost all his profits plus an additional $740,000. In 1992, $740,000 was a sizable amount. Karas' backer unsuccessfully tried to convince Karas to skip out on the debt by staging a fake robbery; however, Karas was an honorable gambler and a stand-up guy. He went to his box at the Horseshoe, withdrew $740,000 in cash and paid his debt.

Karas' backer immediately dropped him and Karas returned to hustling pool. It wasn't too long before he ran his bankroll up to $1.2 million. One evening at a pool hall, he beat a high-stakes poker pro for $500,000. After a prodigious ass-whipping where Karas had the edge, the pro suggested a heads-up poker match. Karas agreed.

"I took that money I won shooting pool and went on to win $3,000,000 more playing poker in only a few days. We started at $4,000/$8,000 limit seven-card stud and quickly moved up to $8,000/$16,000 limit hold'em, which was unheard of in those days," Karas said.

During a three-month period in 1993, Archie Karas battled the best poker players in the world and turned $7 million into $17 million. His extraordinary feat has been called "The Run" and is considered the greatest single winning streak in poker and one of the most noteworthy accomplishments in the history of Las Vegas gambling.

"When I started, I easily had a $7,000,000 bankroll and my confidence was on top of the world," Karas said. "I remember getting ten racks of $5,000 chips, which is $5,000,000, and putting them in the middle of the poker room on a poker table at the Horseshoe. I was ready to take on all comers in poker, and this stirred up a lot of interest. Poker's most colorful character, Puggy Pearson, began to circle the table chanting, 'Step right up here, boys, and help yourself to some of this easy money... $5,000,000 just waiting for you... step right up!' Puggy was comical... like a carnival barker, continuing, 'Archie will take on all comers... step right up to his office!'"

Stuey Ungar accepted Karas' challenge and they played a heads-up Razz match. Lyle Berman staked Stuey $500,000 for that game, which didn't last very long. Karas demolished him.

A couple of days later, Chip Reese took a shot at Karas in a session of Razz. That match lasted eight hours and Reese lost $500,000. After a dinner break, Karas returned to the poker room where Stuey and Berman were waiting for a second crack at him. Karas destroyed Stuey again and took an additional $700,000 of Berman's money, bringing his total winnings *for that day* to $1.2 million.

The next evening, Reese took a second shot, only to lose to Karas. Again. The Greek was unstoppable.

"The most money I ever lost in a single night of poker was $2,022,000, playing $8,000/$16,000 limit against Archie Karas," Reese said about that ugly session.

During "The Run" both Johnny Chan and Doyle Brunson took cracks at Karas, but both came up short.

Karas reflected, "Many of my opponents want to add games or play half Razz and half seven-card stud. I want to play one game only, so Razz being my best game, the opponents usually played seven-card stud 90 percent of the time. Once Johnny Chan wanted to add a few games, and I quickly said, 'John, I'm not looking to add any games. I'm looking to take one away. If you want to play another game, let's play six-card Razz.' He went for it and lost a quick $300,000! If you're a great Razz player, playing six-card Razz is even more of an edge. You have to be quick-minded and smart in this shark-infested world in order to survive. Like a boxer, you have to protect yourself at all times."

One night, Karas experienced a bloody awful run in which he found himself stuck $11 million. He was still tilting the next day when he showed up at the Mirage to play Reese and blew through his buy-in. He had to borrow $2 million from Reese just to stay in the game.

"I've never loaned $1,000,000 to anyone in a poker game, let alone $2,000,000," Reese said.

Karas was an obvious exception. Reese knew he was good for it so he loaned Karas the money. Karas promptly lost it all to Reese and after a trip to his box at the Horseshoe, Karas paid his debt. The two would never play heads-up again.

"I had to start playing dice and baccarat more," Karas explained. "I played and beat the best poker players heads-up, including Chip Reese, who I must have played 25 matches against. Word spread quickly how tough I was to beat, and I couldn't find anyone to play with after a while. I had to start shooting dice, and ended up running my $17 million bankroll up to over $40 million as a result."

Craps is the devil's game and Karas never saw a craps table he didn't like. Tom Sexton explained, "My brother saw Karas lose $1 million in about five minutes at the dice table in 1993."

"The most I won in one session was $12 million, but that night I was already stuck $4 million first," Karas said. "I netted $8 million for the evening. I went up and down for over two years, winning $5 million scores on the dice tables on many occasions."

Karas was on top of the world until dice and baccarat finally decimated his bankroll. It was only a matter of time before he was left with nothing.

"There was a three-week period of time where I lost $30,000,000, which I could never fade," a regretful Karas said.

When Karas was down to his last million, he headed to the Bicycle Casino in Los Angeles and played against Johnny Chan. Lyle Berman backed Chan, but both Berman and Chan played heads-up against Karas, alternating every two hours. Karas decimated the tag-team duo and doubled up. However, his inner action junkie could not prevent him from heading straight to the craps tables where he pissed away the entire $2 million along with what little dignity he had left.

Karas faded away into obscurity after that humiliating moment. His name is whispered from time to time and many of his feats are often dismissed as urban legends. He will be the first to tell you that he should have stuck to poker, but the games dried up for him, and his incorrigible thirst for action led him to the table games where he was an overwhelming underdog. The house always ended up with Karas' money.

"If I had known there was a poker boom right around the corner," Karas said, "I would have parked $10 million to the side, even if I had to wait ten years to play. Poker has always been my bread and butter. I'll point out that between 1992 and 1995, who could have guessed there was going to be such a boom in poker by 2003? Back then, I couldn't wait three hours to get in action. Dice is the fastest action in the world, where I could win or lose a million with one roll."

The legendary Nick "The Greek" Dandolos died broke and was last seen playing $5 poker in a California card room. Archie "The Greek" Karas didn't want to go out in a similar way. Tom Sexton wrote a series of articles about Karas for Poker News, befriending him during the interview process. During their long talks, Karas reflected upon his Shakespearian rise and fall, and he rediscovered the itch to play poker once again.

For his comeback at the 2008 WSOP, Karas showed up in Las Vegas with $9 in his pocket and riding a wave of nostalgia. He carefully navigated his way through Day 1 of the stud event and returned among the chip leaders for Day 2. As the field thinned out, Karas' stack failed to increase and he suddenly found himself among the short stacks. Karas' comeback fizzled when he busted out in 23rd place, only a few spots from the money.

One week later, Karas entered the $1,500 Razz tournament. It was his best game and he definitely stepped up his play, advancing to the final table. Unfortunately for Karas, it ended up being Barry Greenstein's day to win. Karas finished in seventh place and won $19,477, certainly small potatoes compared to his $50 million bankroll of days past. At least, a five-figure score was a step in the right direction.

Karas played a couple of other events at the WSOP but could never get anything going. He flew under the radar for all of Day 1 of the Main Event and advanced to Day 2 with a modest stack. However, he could not pick up any momentum and was among the throngs of players who were eliminated on Day 2. Karas silently made his exit out a side door of the Amazon Ballroom. That's the last I ever saw of him.

* * * * *

The afternoon began for Phil Ivey with Day 2 of the $5,000 Deuce-to-Seven Rebuy Event. He was in for $60,000 worth of rebuys and add-ons, but he made a disappointing and early exit. Ivey bought into another tournament at 5 p.m. and had his back worked on by a masseuse during the first hour of play. When the basketball game started, Ivey could not sit still. With the Lakers down 2-0 in the NBA finals, Ivey was intensely watching Game 3. He supposedly greased the floor guy to turn off the tournament clock and put the Lakers-Celtics game on the TV instead. Ivey held a keen interest in the game after he made a $2 million prop bet with an unnamed "very rich" Russian businessman. When the intriguing word got out about Ivey's wager on the Lakers, the media vultures sweated Phil Ivey, who in turn sweated the basketball game.

Ivey stood up, paced back and forth around his table, and constantly checked his BlackBerry. I've never seen Ivey exhibit such an abundance of emotion and anxiety. Ivey hated not being in control of his own destiny. Watching him squirm, I got the sense that he was the type of guy that would throw on a Lakers jersey and try to win the game himself.

The Lakers prevailed that night and Ivey breathed a temporary sigh of relief. The $5,000 buy-in poker tournament was an afterthought compared to the $2 million wager. Ivey's bet was brazen; especially in the wake of the Herculean scandal involving Tim Donaghy and other ex-referees who were accused of fixing NBA games. But that's why Ivey is regarded by many as one of the most awe-inspiring professional gamblers in the world. Even in the face of overwhelming odds, he has the testicular fortitude to wager ridiculous sums of money. Others surely see it as approaching the apex of degeneracy.

Ivey also wagered millions in bracelet prop bets with Ted Forrest and some of the regulars in The Big Game at the Bellagio. The moment after Daniel Negreanu clinched a victory in the $2,000 buy-in limit hold'em tournament and won his fourth bracelet, he reached for his mobile device and texted Ivey. The two had $200,000 riding on which one of them would win a bracelet first. Negreanu won $204,000 for first place in the tournament, only $4,000 more than he had won in the prop bet with Ivey.

When the Celtics eventually defeated the Lakers to win the NBA championship, Ivey kissed $2 million goodbye in a moment that can only be referred to as "stomach-churning." Earlier that week, he had lost $1.1 million shooting dice with Barry Greenstein. Alongside the $200,000 he coughed up to Negreanu, Ivey lost around $3.3 million inside of seven days. It seems very bad, but then again, this is Phil Ivey, a stupendous poker player and a fearless gambler who could easily win a couple of million in a single weekend.

Humanity is often held together by a tiny thread. Professionals like Ivey were on top of their game in 2008, whether it involved tournaments, cash games, prop bets, golf bets, bracelet bets, craps or sports betting. But what keeps them from evolving into the next cautionary tale? Charmed luck can only be pushed so far before it pushes back. Just ask Archie Karas – if you can find him.

Chapter 33

June 2008.

Day 22 of the WSOP began like the previous 21. I drove to the Rio and parked in the back, hiked across the sizzling asphalt, and passed the usual group of chain-smoking dealers. I set up my laptop in the press box and realized that I had forgotten my power cord.

"Fuuuuck!"

I didn't want to disturb Nicky, who was fast asleep on her day off, so I rushed out of the Rio and drove back to Scheckytown to fetch my power cord. I was on autopilot and retraced the same route that I had been driving for over three weeks. I approached the intersection of Desert Inn and Rainbow with the air conditioning on full-blast when the car in front of me slammed on the brakes in order to avoid a collision with a fire truck rumbling through the red light. I pumped the brakes on my car as it careened into a Ford Focus. My glasses shot off my face and onto the floor as I braced myself for an airbag deployment that never came. Luckily, the guy behind me had enough room to stop without rear-ending me and condemning me to a hospital visit. I was in one piece.

A young woman in her early 20s with purple hair and black polish on her nails had the shakes so bad she could barely light her cigarette. She insisted that she and her passenger were fine, but we were all thinking the same thing: "I am the luckiest fucker in Las Vegas today."

The twisted hood of my rental car looked like an almost perfect triangle. The mangled bumper was scattered around a ten-foot radius. The entire front end was totaled with multicolored liquids leaking all over the road. I stared at the swirling greens and reds as I called both Caldwell and Nicky and told them I was okay.

A young motorcycle cop, looking fresh off a tour in Iraq, arrived at the scene and asked me to move the car because we were blocking traffic. The engine started but the car didn't move. He radioed for a tow truck then wrote me a ticket for driving too close. A hysterical Nicky showed up ten minutes later with tears streaming down her face.

I kept thinking about how events would be different if I hadn't forgotten my power cord and had never left the Rio. Over the ensuing weeks, I had existentialist seizures and questioned the absurdity of my journey as I wasted away inside casinos for endless hours. I felt as though the accident was a second chance and a sign for me to think about moving on to other fruitful writing adventures.

I returned to work even though I probably should have taken the day off. After a couple of hours, the stiffness and soreness overwhelmed me. My friends gathered up whatever medications they could find to get me through the day. One online poker pro hooked me up with Oxycontin, but with specific instructions: "Dude, I know you party a lot, but be very careful. Just a nibble at a time. Anything more will kill you."

A friend of mine recommended a crooked doctor who accepted patients without insurance and was notorious for dispensing pain medications, no questions asked. Mob doctors don't exactly practice in aesthetically pleasing offices in the burbs and this office was on the fringe of the ghetto with bars on the windows. The house next door had an ominous foreclosure sign on the front lawn but a psychic in the house across the street had a sign in the front window that said P-Y-S-C-H-I-C. At least that error made me chuckle.

I opened the squeaky front door to my new doctor's office and stepped back in time 20 years. I stood inside a small living room that acted as a waiting area. The worn-out carpet contained repetitive designs in clashing colors: pistachio, chartreuse, and sepia. A portly Hispanic nurse behind a window knocked on the glass partition and she motioned for me to come over. She slid a bunch of forms underneath a slot and demanded $150 in cash up front before the doctor would even see me.

The nine people seated on folding chairs in the room were fixated on an old TV tuned to an episode of *Law and Order*. An old black guy in the group looked legitimately sick, but the rest of the patients were a transparent and sad group of pill poppers. One tweaker seated across from me had bright red and orange flame tattoos covering his arms. He stepped outside three times in 20 minutes to smoke a cigarette before he was finally called. A skanky stripper with juggernaut breasts spilling out of her top sat down and asked me to help her fill out the forms. She was either too lazy or couldn't read, and I wish I could say I was surprised when it became clear that both were true. I was too uncomfortable to care.

A husky nurse in pink scrubs called my name and led me into a small examination room where she recorded my vitals and left. Over the next 15 minutes, I read a couple of golf magazines and noticed that the doctor subscribed to Poker Player Newspaper. I found my article on page 22. An elderly Chinese doctor walked into the room and we made some small talk about the accident. He said that I should fight the ticket and recommended a good lawyer. I wondered if he got a kickback for the referral?

He inspected my back and suggested X-rays. I told him I didn't have insurance and needed to get back to writing and covering the WSOP. He recommended a triple cocktail that included an anti-inflammatory, muscle relaxer, and painkiller called Lortab (just another fancy name for Hydrocodone, otherwise known as the active ingredient in my favorite painkiller Vicodin). I drove to the drugstore, purchased generic versions for half the price and then returned to work.

A week after the accident, I realized that I was more injured than I had first thought; I was going to need a whole lot more of those powerful pills... oh, yeah!

* * * * *

The instructions on the pill bottle said "Take 1 tablet every 4-6 hours." I usually took that dosage when I was abusing Vicodin recreationally, but since I was suffering from back pain, I doubled and tripled the recommended dosage. I began thinking that perhaps I was experiencing side effects. I saw things that were not there, like visions of a single ant crawling across my Sheckytown desk. I felt things that were not there crawling on my skin. Was I becoming a hallucinating junkie or just extraordinarily aware?

One ant scurried across the desk. Then another. I stopped writing, grabbed my mini flashlight, and launched an investigation. "How are they getting up there?" I wondered as I crawled around on the floor. "Aha! They were climbing up the legs. But where did they come from?"

I felt like the Crocodile Hunter on *Animal Planet* as I stalked a trail along the floorboards all the way to the front door. I silently exulted, "Mother of God. There's a whole nest of these fuckers! I've found their staging ground!"

I squished a dozen of them with my foot and left the dead as a message to any others that might dare to venture into my territory. For the next three days, the ants launched insurrections under the cover of night. I bought ant traps at a local grocery. Ants were supposed to go in, eat the bait, take it back to the nest, and all the other ants would die. I placed two traps by the legs of the desk to catch them on their ascent and one near the front door. The overall number of ant sightings initially declined, but three days later they returned with larger numbers in a vicious counterattack. I stood around in a pharmie daze and carefully observed their movements. Not a single ant stepped inside the traps. Ants crawled over them or simply went around. Their recon unit was obviously well-trained and had issued warnings to the others.

The ants launched their version of the Tet Offensive while I worked a 16-hour day at the Rio. Waves upon waves infiltrated the house and marched through their network of tunnels underneath the front-door floorboards, along the foyer and front room, and along the hallway before taking a sharp right turn into the kitchen.

When I got home, I found ants in places I had never seen them before. I declared to Nicky in my best General Patton voice, "It's time to escalate the war and engage in chemical warfare. That is the only effective way we can deal with this insurgency."

The attacking platoons of ants were trying to cut off our food supply, a simple war strategy dating back thousands of years and just as effective today. Faded on painkillers and unable to drive, I begged Nicky for a lift to the store to buy war supplies, but she didn't want to go after her exhausting shift at the Rio. I told her to inspect the front lines herself. She took one look in the kitchen and said, "Let's go."

After ten minutes of stumbling around the grocery store we located the strongest weapon in their stock – hornet and wasp spray. I told Nicky to go to sleep while I confronted the enemy on the front lines downstairs. Luckily, Caldwell and Jen Leo were away that weekend and I was clear to pull out the stops.

With one push of the button on the black can, I unleashed a heavy stream of industrial-strength death. Thousands upon thousands of ants were annihilated in a matter of seconds. Within three minutes, the battle was over. The air filled with the smell of the deceased enemy and a repulsive chemical odor (reminding me of that foul stench that you encounter while driving through New Jersey on the turnpike). I surveyed the carnage and thought of the charred highway in the first Gulf War where the U.S. military lit up the Iraqi army retreating from Kuwait.

I did not go to sleep. I applied a fresh coat of war paint, resupplied my opiate receptors, and waited over the doorway with my black can of death anticipating a last gasp counterattack from the enemy. And I waited… and waited… and waited… and waited…

Chapter 34

December 2007.

Bad Blood and I were both in Las Vegas to hang out for the annual bloggers' gathering with a private tournament scheduled for Saturday afternoon at the Venetian. As Friday spilled into Saturday morning, I discovered I was still wide awake. I grabbed breakfast and sat down to play poker at the Imperial Palace with some friends who were getting an early start to the day. Around 11 a.m., Bad Blood sent me a cryptic text message.

"There are very few people who can handle *The Procedure*," Bad Blood texted. "You're one of them."

In his South Carolina home town, Bad Blood created a ritual where he skipped out of work an hour early, headed to the bar, went to a strip club, and finished off the evening with poker. Booze. Women. Cards. In that order. *The Procedure* was born.

Bad Blood had handpicked me to join him for a Las Vegas installment of *The Procedure*, and had commenced phase one at the Sherwood Forest Bar inside the Excalibur. I immediately cashed my chips and bolted out of the poker room, fighting my way though a gathering of cowboys in town for the rodeo finals. A light rain sprinkled as my taxi roared down Las Vegas Boulevard.

"The rain brings out the nipples. I love wet t-shirts on tourists," the driver commented, pointing to a group of girls walking The Strip without an umbrella.

"Speaking of nipples," I interrupted. "If a guy like me wanted to head to a strip club and check out the noon shift, which one would you recommend?"

"The Rhino," came the quick reply. "At this hour, that's where you'll find the better girls."

"Or the strung-out ones," I mentioned.

"That too."

I gifted the horny cabbie a fat tip and suggested that he get some relaxation therapy when his shift ended. After all, cabbies know all the best rub and tug places in town. I burst into the Excalibur and passed a line with hundreds of rodeo fans who waited for a cab to take them to the Thomas & Mack Center.

I fought the crowds of obese tourists rolling themselves to the buffet and found Bad Blood deep into his third dirty martini. I took a seat, ordered a Southern Comfort, and we proceeded to catch up on life. I wasn't able to spend nearly the amount of quality time I would have liked with friends since I fell into the poker industry, but it was a sacrifice that inevitably came with the job.

Grubby was the third and essential member of *The Procedure*. He was in charge of getting us to and from the Rhino. Because he was playing in a craps tournament at Bally's, he delayed the starting time for our mission. He eventually swung by the Castle and chauffeured us to the Rhino.

The Rhino, the Bellagio of strip clubs, seemed unusually empty for 1 p.m. on a Saturday. We sat down and three strippers immediately appeared from the shadows. Two jumped up onto the laps of Grubby and Bad Blood as a waitress took our drink order.

"Red Bull and vodka," I said.

"The breakfast of champions," the waitress said.

A blonde in stilettos, who stood a good three inches taller than me, introduced herself as "Joey" before she sat down.

"What do you guys do?" she asked.

"I'm a hot air balloon pilot," Bad Blood said.

"Wow! That's so cool," she cooed. "And what do you do?"

"I'm a writer in Hollywood. We're currently on strike," I said.

"Wow! That's so cool. What have you written?"

"*Daddy Day Care 2*," I said with a straight face as the waitress handed me a drink.

"*Daddy Day Care 2*? That's my kid's favorite movie. Wow! So fucking cool!"

I took less than two sips of my drink before Grubby and Bad Blood disappeared into the back with the two strippers. Grubby left his car keys and his drink. Joey gave Grubby's drink a long look, mumbled something about alcoholism, and asked me if she could have a sip. I said yes but then worried that the stripper might give him Hepatitis B. I realized as she drained the glass that it wouldn't matter. It was easy to see that Joey was the cream of the crop... circa 1992. The booze perked her up a bit and she began telling me horror stories about the previous evening. The cowboys in town for the rodeo liked to look but not pay.

"At least they're mellow," she said.

There were also a massive group of Brits in town for the Ricky Hatton and Floyd Mayweather fight at the MGM, and, according to her, they were a raucous bunch. "I can't tell you how many of them tried to stick their fingers up my cooch and in my ass," she said, as *Paint It Black* by the Rolling Stones blasted on the sound system. "British people are supposed to be polite, but they were fucking animals."

As we retreated to the back room for lap dances, I asked her about the last celebrity she danced for.

"Do you know basketball? Well, Wally Szczerbiak was here. He was such a nice guy. Very shy. He's so tall too. I asked him if he wanted a dance and he said yes. That's when I felt his dick. Oh my god! He had the biggest dick I had felt in years. I kept calling my girlfriends over and screaming, 'Oh my god! You gotta feel Wally's dick!' He was such a nice guy with such a big dick."

Joey danced five songs for the price of three because I negotiated a better deal. You can always haggle with the girls on the afternoon shift, especially when the club is empty. Grubby finally appeared out of the shadows with his stripper who stood at least ten inches taller in her heels. I handed him the car keys, gave a pointed look in the direction of his empty glass, and then pointed over to Joey. Grubby shrugged and his stripper excused herself. That's when he pulled me aside looking conspiratorial.

"She squirted all over my chest," Grubby said.

"What?"

"She was grinding me in her favorite position."

"Which was?"

"She sat on my lap with her back to me. I heard her moaning really loud as she gyrated back and forth. Then she stopped and quickly shifted."

"Why did she stop?"

"To apologize."

"For?"

"Wetting herself."

"Did she get any on you?"

"I didn't feel anything through my pants until she pulled up my shirt and sat on my chest."

"What the fuck? What did it feel like?"

"It was all warm and wet. Then she continued to grind for another song, and then pulled up my shirt and squirted on me."

Wally Szczerbiak might have a big dick, but Grubby brought a Las Vegas stripper to a climax during a lap dance. That's talent. I was more than impressed; I was in awe.

* * * * *

June 2008.

"I'm addicted to pain," she slurred and slowly turned her arm to expose her left wrist. Through the faint light I could see a few marks. She pulled my hand toward her and I felt the roughness of the scars. "It took me almost ten years, but I finally figured out that I'm addicted to pain. I love misery. I can't be happy unless I'm hurting."

"Never swing at the first pitch" was one of the few words of advice my father gave me when I was young. Bad Blood, Mean Gene, and I had only been at the Rhino for 15 minutes and I was determined to heed my father's wisdom. Mean Gene had experienced a brutal WSOP up until that point and desperately needed some R & R. He was scheduled to work Day 2 of the $50,000 H.O.R.S.E. event with Nicky, but I persuaded her to let him skip out on the first hour while Bad Blood and I investigated the afternoon shift at the Rhino. Mean Gene had never done *The Procedure* before, and he made an uncharacteristically impulsive decision to join us at the last moment.

The bar at the Rhino has the best lighting in the joint, and is the one spot you need to be to properly inspect the goods. I bought a round of overpriced drinks while a blonde an inch taller than me attached herself to my hip. I could smell the booze on her breath. Great, how the hell did I attract the drunk stripper? Karma? Bad Luck?

I originally had a choice – a pasty brunette covered in tattoos who looked more like a Suicide Girl than a Rhino dancer. However, I rejected her in favor of the drunken, yet innocent-looking girl-next-door blonde in the pink thong. I should have taken into account the sparsely populated nature of the afternoon shift and swung at the first pitch. I betcha she would've had better drugs, too.

"I've only been taking Prozac for three days," the blonde screamed over an AC/DC song.

That pretty much summed up my visit to the afternoon shift. The stripper was sedated on happy pills, sloppy, and slurring her speech like Albert Finney at happy hour.

Her name was Dylan, too.

"Like the singer?" I asked.

"No, like the *90210* character," she said.

"Seriously?"

"Yes. Oh my God, I'm on the South Beach diet," she blurted out.

She couldn't stay on the same topic for more than 90 seconds and soon the conversation had more plot twists than a M. Night Shyamalan flick. Dylan insisted that she was also OCD, ADD, and definitely suicidal with the mental stability of Courtney Love.

"People think I'm really fucked up," she said.

"Why? Did you kill your husband, fake the suicide note, and then squeeze his band members out of millions of dollars in royalties?"

"Huh?"

"Never mind. So where you from?"

"Oklahoma. Oh my God, the last time I went home, I had not been there in seven or eight years, I saw some old friends from high school and you know what they were doing?"

"Cooking up a fresh batch of meth?"

"Almost. They were huffing propane. Driving around in a car, smoking cigarettes, and huffing propane."

"Did you join them?"

"Hell no."

Some strippers reveal very little and ask lots of questions and let you talk. Others will tell you all of their problems. Dylan unloaded on me. I soaked up her life story and hung on every word. Part of the fun of hanging out with strippers is digging deep and trying to figure out what makes them tick. What tragic event in their life led them down the path toward the pole? I didn't get to play my games with Dylan. She was so drunk she spilled the beans right away, and then some. Inside of five minutes I learned that she was a former gymnast who majored in English at college in Denton, Texas, and got knocked up at 20, forcing her to drop out of school. She can't have any kids after a botched back-alley abortion in Matamoros. Her stepfather murdered her mother over an empty can of Pringles and the psychopath-pedophile knocked up her 13-

year-old half-sister. Dylan was a real life Jerry Springer episode gyrating on my lap and spilling Grey Goose all over my Ecco shoes.

She kept on telling me about how she used to be a gymnast. It was like when a former high school athlete could not stop living in the glory days, telling you the same stories about how they hit the winning shot to win the league championship, or came *thiiiis* close to it. Her mind was frozen on the happiest time of her life – senior year in high school.

"Since I was such an awesome gymnast, I could do all these cool tricks on the pole," she bragged. "But I like to drink, so I don't do them anymore. Oh my God, the last time I tried to get super fancy, I was so fucking wasted that I slipped and fell flat on my face. I chipped a tooth and I got seven stitches in my chin."

She lifted up her chin and let me feel those scars.

"Did you get off on the pain?"

"Yeah. I love the sight of my own blood."

"Do you have a LiveJournal page?"

"What's that? I'm on MySpace. Oh my God, did you see *Saturday Night Live* this week? I love that show."

I looked over at the tall exotic Nordic woman seated on Bad Blood's lap. To my right was a very happy Mean Gene. On his lap sat a dominatrix who could have been an extra from the freaky Merovingian club scene in the last *Matrix* flick. The only things missing were a few firearms. He had the top four buttons of his dress shirt undone and she slipped one hand inside and commenced a scratching motion with a twisted look on her face.

My drunken stripper relentlessly rambled on about total bullshit. I asked to go into the VIP room because I thought it would shut her up. Nope. She kept yammering, even in the middle of a lap dance.

"I used to love Xanax," she said. "When I first took it, I'd get sleepy and pass out. After a while I took so much that all I felt was..."

"You felt normal?"

"Yeah, how did you know? You sound like you have a lot experience with pills. What do you do again?"

"I'm a psychiatrist."

Forty minutes in, she had not asked me my name or what I did for a living. I was bummed. We all had our cover stories prepped and ready to go when we came in. Bad Blood stuck with his usual cover – hot air balloon pilot. I was supposed to be a psychiatrist from Yuma, Arizona, named Nick Papageorgio.

The VIP room was a sickening bad beat. Nothing is more disappointing in life than getting a horrible lap dance, unless it's a horrible lap dance with a schizophrenic depressive who won't shut the fuck up. As we quickly exited the VIP room, Dylan had the balls to ask for a tip.

"Why would I tip? You did a shitty job. You are lucky I didn't ask for my money back. I should have ditched you the moment we met, but I felt sorry for you. When I usually leave a strip club, I go home and jerk off. This time? I'm going home and gonna put on the new Coldplay album and then kill myself."

For the first time since she latched herself onto me, she was dead silent. Free at last, free at last! I stood near the bar and noticed that Mean Gene and Bad Blood were still inside the VIP Room. Day 2 of the H.O.R.S.E. event had begun and Nicky sent me a text saying that I needed to get Mean Gene back to the Rio because their boss was looking for him. I tipped the thick-necked bouncer $20 to help me out. He trudged over to the far corner and told Mean Gene that his time was up.

Mean Gene and his stripper held hands as they left the VIP room. It was an adorable scene, like when two high school kids decided to go steady for the first time.

"Heya Doc, um… um… I'm a little short," he said.

"Sure thing," I said and turned to his stripper. "How much does he owe you? $40? $60?"

"$300," she said.

"$300? What the fuck, Geno, you sex-pot!"

He smirked and shrugged his shoulders as I peeled off three Benjamins and handed it to the latex-clad stripper.

"Oh and don't forget a tip," she said.

I handed her a $20 bill and she gave Mean Gene a kiss on the cheek leaving a trail of cheap stripper perfume as she turned around and disappeared into the darkness. We were nearly blinded by the sun as we made our exit. When my vision cleared, I noticed Mean Gene's messy hair. He had random scratch marks all over his neck and tons of lipstick smudges all over his cheek.

A devious grin illuminated Gene's face as he said, "At least I got her number."

Chapter 35

July 2008.

Nicky and I entered the Amazon Ballroom through a side door to an eerie calm. For the first time since the WSOP began, I did not hear thousands of chips clattering. Nothing. Not a single player in the ballroom. Even the cash-game tables were cleared out around dawn to prep for the $1,500 Donkament. Those tables would be among the first to be broken down and converted back into cash games. Churn 'em and burn 'em. Get the lemmings in, get their entry fees, and when they bust out, keep them around by enticing them with satellites, second chance events, and cash games. More juice. More rake. More donkey feces.

The dealers lined up and reported to the floor manager who dished out their table assignments as another floor person handed over racks of tournament chips. They walked down an assembly line to pick up their necessary items out of small boxes: pens, a dealer button, wristbands for players (to allow them past security), and two decks of cards. With their arms full, the dealers sauntered to their tables and set up their wells. A rep from All In spammed the tables with free samples of their third-rate energy drink, while Charlie the floor supervisor jumped on the microphone and called out to the different sections to see if they needed anything. Within ten minutes, every single table in the ballroom had a dealer silently awaiting the running of the donkeys.

"Okay, we're going to open the doors in a few minutes. It's time to cue the music," Charlie said.

"Anything but that rap shit," one cranky old dealer screeched.

"Play Frank Sinatra!" shouted another.

Two seconds later, I heard the intro to Journey's *Any Way You Want It*. Journey? Are you fucking kidding me? I popped another generic Vicodin as the security guards opened the doors and players rushed in.

"Welcome back to another great day at the World Series of Poker!" exclaimed tournament director Jack Effel over the PA system.

Benjo commented that the best way to spot the dead money was to look for the ones arriving at the table 20 minutes before the start time. Ah, the eager beavers. There were thousands of bright-eyed and bushy-tailed poker enthusiasts flying into Las Vegas from destinations all over North America for their shots at the big time. They might have the necessary skills to crush their local home game in a messy garage at the end of a cul-de-sac, but they were outmatched in Vegas.

Within a few hours, a thousand donators had their stacks decimated as the blood of losers settled in tranquil pools around the room – $1,500 down the toilet. I hoped they remembered to ask for their food comps.

I sat in the press box perched high above the sheep being lead to a merciless slaughter. Casualties made their way down the walk of shame in front of the press box and out into the hallway where they commiserated with their loved ones, spewing bad-beat stories and tales about the fierce damage.

Location is the one of the major keys to any successful business. That's why the Hooker Bar was such a popular hangout. Within a short walk, you could crash a real estate seminar, take a picture with Doyle Brunson, buy an overpriced personal pie from Pizza Hut, pick up a copy of Bluff Magazine, and negotiate a hummer.

The hookers were out in force on Saturday night trying to pick up the sex-crazed punters. One particularly enterprising working girl loitered in front of the Everest Poker suite. She wore a black WSOP t-shirt, tight jeans, high heels, and carried a leopard-print purse. She randomly stopped guys and gave them a hug as they walked by. During the embrace, she whispered her proposition into their ears. I left her in the middle of negotiating a deal with one guy who needed a spanking to work off his bad beats.

* * * * *

Former World Champion Scotty Nguyen drank steadily throughout the entire $50,000 H.O.R.S.E. tournament with an ever-present pack of Winstons at the ready near his big stack. He flashed a game show host's smile for the cameras and threw back his head to let loose another laugh. Scotty's unmistakable cackle reminded me of a dubious villain from a James Bond movie. Tourists on the rail behind Scotty were chugging Milwaukee's Beast and getting drunker by the minute while amateur photographers with cell phone cameras were jockeying for position on the rail, elbowing the drunks in the process. They were on the verge of rioting. And why? Just to watch a bunch of guys play cards.

One side of the Amazon Ballroom was flooded with carcasses from the $1,500 slaughterfest. Call them whatever animal names you want. Donkeys. Emus. Pigeons. Fish. Pigs. Dogs. Rats. They were dead meat within minutes of taking their seats, ending up as quivering masses on the killing floor. The survivors on a play break tracked donkey blood all over the carpet as they trudged through the H.O.R.S.E. area. Harrah's cleaning crews worked around the clock using an extra-strength extract from an exotic Guatemalan fruit to help erase the blemishes.

Poker agents slithered around the H.O.R.S.E. event looking for more fresh blood. Sign up the unknowns. Ride them to the final tables. Get them on TV. Suck the life out of them. Then spit them out and find another wannabe pro to feast on. The true parasites.

Poker is not a sport. It's a card game that takes a tremendous amount of skill and mental toughness to succeed over the long term. Being in good physical shape is a benefit for the individual player, but is by no means necessary for success. Poker is a competition that does not test athletic ability. Besides, no legitimate sport permits you to consume alcoholic beverages while competing or forces you to sometimes randomly play against drunk opponents.

Before hole-card cameras, tournament poker was a horrible spectator sport. The introduction of the cameras added an invigorating element of suspense and drama because viewers know a vital piece of information that players do not – their opponents' cards. If anything, poker tournaments demonstrate the pure essence of reality television programming in an era when most reality shows are manipulated by the producers. ESPN packaged the WSOP as slickly produced "sports entertainment."

To spice up viewership, the floundering World Poker Tour should add wrestling-type features to make poker tournaments more exciting to watch. Permit and encourage physical altercations at the tables. At any given time, a player can hurl a chair at another player or jump across the table and unload with a flying elbow. How cool would it be to see Chau Giang clothesline Phil Hellmuth while he's in the middle of berating a dealer? I would have paid big bucks to see Greg "Fossilman" Raymer body slam Mike Matusow when "The Mouth" talked smack at him during the 2004 WSOP Main Event.

Poker tournaments should also allow animals inside playing area as part of this new rule set. Remember Jake "The Snake" Roberts from the World Wrestling Federation? He'd pull a python out of his supply bag and let the reptile slither around the ring and attach itself to his fallen opponent as everyone in the stands watched in excited horror. The new rules would allow Scotty Nguyen to bring his monkey to the final table. When Scotty blows a special whistle, the monkey begins hurling feces rapid-fire at Scotty's mortal enemies.

As the U.S. economy continues its slide into the shitter, it will only be a matter of time before the Game Show Network shifts its programming philosophy to begin broadcasting cage matches live from Costa Rica where Barry Greenstein and Daniel Negreanu wrestle a crocodile. The bouts will be sponsored by PokerStars and you'll be able to trade frequent player points for a chance to wrestle the endangered species of your choice. Of course, Otis and the Brits will live-blog the action.

* * * * *

Prize pools in the Main Event are monstrous because of the abundance of dead money who are in way over their heads. Most of these guys shouldn't even be buying into a $1,500 no-limit event, but that's part of the magic. Any player at any skill level has a shot at the big time, as long as he or she pays the price of admission. As food and fuel prices hit all-time highs with no end in sight, thousands of gamblers willingly piss away $10,000 on a pipe dream.

Poker pros could not drive fancy cars and live on palatial estates were it not for the dream-chasers handing over their money. Without the influx of the lower life forms into the food chain, everyone in the poker ecosystem would starve and eventually the sharks would be eating each other and becoming endangered species. It's not every day that a new Russian oil tycoon decides to donk off several million to Tony G in a PLO cash game in Moscow. Guys like Andy Beal (billionaire banker from Texas) and Guy Laliberte (CEO and founder of Cirque du Soleil) don't make a habit of risking millions against the best in Las Vegas. The big whales are few and far between, so pros must seek out alternative feeding pools.

The WSOP is Disney World for poker players. Instead of Goofy, Mickey and Donald Duck running around giving out hugs, you have Jesus, Negreanu, and Phil Ivey taking your money. The WSOP is the place where dreams are fulfilled or mortally crushed. Some see the fulfillment of their dreams by simply setting foot in the room. For a player who hasn't been to Las Vegas before, let alone played in the WSOP Main Event, the feeling is electrifying and life-altering. Pure adrenaline. It remains a part of the post-modern American dream where anyone has a chance at fame, glory, and the most coveted award in all of poker.

In the five years since Chris Moneymaker won the Main Event, a phenomenon called The Moneymaker Effect rippled through the cosmos and helped spread the viral phenomenon of poker all over the world. On Day 1A of the Main Event, Moneymaker signed autographs and posed for pics with random fans who waited in line to pay respects to their hero. Since Moneymaker's gallant victory over Sam Farha, over 30,000 players have bought into the Main Event and purchased a ticket to the largest poker lottery in the world. Fossilman, Joe Hachem, Jamie Gold, and Jerry Yang got the bulk of the booty while tens of thousands of players went home empty handed with crushed dreams, hopes obliterated, and the fairy tale over.

Phil Hellmuth was rumored to be arriving in a tank, yet another elaborate entrance for the Poker Brat. Hellmuth's sponsor, Ultimate Bet, had been running a promotion titled "UB Army" in which online qualifiers would join the ranks of UB's pros during the Main Event. Even the almighty Hellmuth was unable to secure a tank. Instead, Hellmuth arrived in a camouflage jeep, and a crush of spectators and media surged forward. Hellmuth stepped out of the convoy dressed as General Patton in full military garb including a battle helmet with 11 gold stars representing each of his 11 bracelets. I almost forgot about the 11 models also decked out in military outfits. They saluted Hellmuth upon his arrival and fell in line behind him during his pompous march from the parking lot to the Amazon Ballroom with a cluster of poker paparazzi and gawkers in tow.

What's next? Helicopter? Hot air balloon? How about Hellmuth riding into the Rio on a donkey? Talk about a priceless moment. Hellmuth can ride the donkey down the hallway while his minions sprinkle flower petals and wave palm fronds along the path to celebrate his stately arrival, like Jesus Christ entering Jerusalem. The poker citizens will greet him with great cries and shouts of "Blessed is He whose ego cannot fit through the door!" Spectators at the Rio will gawk and fight over who gets to keep the donkey shit littering the hallway leading up to the Amazon Ballroom. After tying the donkey to a post near the rail, Hellmuth will regally adjust his Juan Valdez poncho covered in UB logos and slowly take his seat. And after he busts out, the ESPN cameras will follow him as he rides his donkey into the dusty desert sunset.

I can only imagine the snarky headlines... "Ass Rides Ass to WSOP."

Chapter 36

July 2008.

During the opening rounds of the Main Event, a massive shuttle bus carted PokerStars troops, decked out in their branded hats and shirts, from base camp at the Palms Hotel and Casino to the front lines at the Rio. At night, the same bus left the parking lot of the Rio with the dead and injured.

"Seat open, table 28!" shrieked a dealer.

Hordes of wounded warriors hobbled out of the Amazon Room mangled and battered. Some were wheeled out on life support gasping for breath and hanging onto their short stacks. They were the lucky ones. The majority of their brethren didn't make it out alive. Did you know that every PokerStars premium gift bag can be converted into a makeshift body bag? A zip here, a snap there. Bag 'em and tag'em.

The PokerStars Blog team drew the repugnant assignment of cataloguing the carnage. The two Brits on the team, Howard and Bartley, were veteran poker combat correspondents who had covered felt skirmishes all over the globe. All had "the stare" and looked right through you. Alongside Otis, they scrambled across the killing floor every hour to retrieve the online-qualifier carcasses from the pile. You could see the malnourishment of the soul in Otis' eyes. The sorrow. The misery. The agony. He could not shake the post-traumatic stress of constantly being first on the scene after the initial slaughter. If you had to slosh around knee-deep in fish guts and donkey intestines for 15 hours a day, you'd be somber too.

When the online qualifiers won their seats, they thought they'd won a ticket to the big dance. What they really won was a one-way trip to nothingness. Wave upon wave of players fell into the existentialist meat grinder, never to be seen again. By the third flight of Day 1, you stopped minding the smell of rotting corpses and ignored the cuffs of your jeans, wet and stained with blood from the stream bisecting the Amazon Room. The French media called it, "Fleuve de sang des anes," or, *Donkey Blood River*.

You can try to repress the horrific images of the anguish and stash them next to your suicidal thoughts, but they always bubble to the surface and ambush you when you least expect it. I could not escape the faces, like that of a young kid from a small farm in Kansas. He barely shaved and had a girl waiting for him back home, his high school sweetheart. "We're fixin' to get married," he told me. He texted her every break until he exploded into a thousand little pieces. Sucked out on the river. He never saw it coming. One moment, he was cracking jokes about getting to sit at the same table as Jesus and in the next, he was a statistic.

"Seat open, table 43!"

Every night during the Main Event, I was constantly awakened by the screams of those tortured souls as they marched blindly into the WSOP quagmire. You can see the films on TV but you have no idea what butchery is like until you've been hit in the face with an exploding piece of donkey brain matter. I am haunted by the deafening screeches of innocent boys and girls getting their hearts ripped out of their chests while the media vultures stand idly by with smug looks, live-blogging the atrocities.

Donkeys make a distinct yelp in the moment before they die, like a thousand rabbits screaming in one short but horrifying terror cantata. Being caught flat-footed too close to the shrill sound would cue Wagner's *Die Walküre* in my mind as my world faded to black, only to wake moments later in a thick pool of the losers' blood. I drew looks of disgust and pity from my fellow media reps as I tracked the grim remnants up into the press box without wiping my feet.

Remember that first time you drove to Las Vegas from Los Angeles and you saw the lights magically appear as you came over the pass? You were less than half an hour away when the Luxor light shot into the night sky like a beacon of hope. Promise. Faith. Redemption. You're filled with it, ready and willing to leave your old life behind and immerse yourself in a fairy tale utopian landscape. Purple and red flickering lights. Pink cocktails. Wads of greenbacks. Working girls in baby blue dresses with orange purses full of yellow condoms. Buy a ticket and take the ride. Hump a cougar. Hug a porn slapper. Double down on a 14. Make a Jack-high Pai Gow. Play in the World Series of Poker.

Jesus Christ turned water into wine, but the Rio in Las Vegas is the only place where you can magically turn $10,000 into $9 million in less than two weeks time. One lucky soul was on the cusp of achieving immortality. They only had to be the last one standing in the killing fields.

Chapter 37

July 2008.

Otis and I created a new version of Lime Tossing called "In Between the Limes." Throwing a lime wedge into a garbage can while standing on top of a stairwell was much more difficult than we imagined, which meant that money rarely changed hands. Because we both craved any semblance of gambling action, we tweaked Lime Tossing to include realistic scoring possibilities. Using the employee parking lot as a playing field, we split the area into five different zones: two $20, two $80, and one $150. The diagonal lines of a "no parking" area marked the different lime-tossing zones – which were about three feet wide and 10 feet long.

The pregame ritual is always the same. Sometime around midnight, we give each other the secret sign using hand signals from the Navy SEALs. We never leave the press box at the same time because that would draw suspicion. We discreetly abandon our posts and rendezvous at the bar in the hallway. The Bulgarian bartender always serves us Coronas with extra limes. He knows better than to ask why, and we tip him well for his discretion. We then sneak out to the smokers' porch where we vent about work for a few minutes, sip our beers, and wait until the entire playing field is clear before we can begin our lime competition.

I won the coin flip and opted to throw second because I wanted to gauge how the swirling wind affected the limes. The glistening lights of The Strip illuminated our playing field. Otis took one last drag on his cigarette and dropped it on the ground. He fished a lime out of his cup and shook the wedge twice as excess drops of Corona sprayed on the ground. He stepped up, peered into the beckoning night, and took a deep breath. His lime sliced through the wind with the precision of a laser-guided missile. It landed in the $80 zone. Perfectly. No skids. It dropped dead in the middle. Otis pumped his fist and took a satisfying sip of his beer. That fucker had been practicing.

I swigged my Corona and calculated wind adjustments. I squeezed as much juice out of my wedge as I could and unleashed my lime. I threw side-arm because that eased the strain on my back injury and allowed the lime to cut through the tempestuous Nevada wind. The trajectory was not as pretty as Otis'. My wedge bounced once on the line in between the $80 and $150 zone, then skidded a few inches, stopping in the middle of the $150 zone.

"Every time!" screamed Otis followed by a string of expletives.

Otis requested another round for double or nothing. I declined. I got lucky with my toss, so I took the $70 and booked the win. We had to get back to work and could always resume the action the next day. Besides, it's never smart to exacerbate an extreme case of lime-tossing tilt. Too many men have lost their minds and their entire fortunes chasing the citrus dream.

* * * * *

The Poker Shrink and I chatted in the hallways about Adderall, as he kept an eye on one of his clients, Mike Matusow. The drug, usually given to patients with attention deficit disorder, is also popular among students to help them during their studies. A couple of poker pros like Paul Phillips took similar prescription medications to enhance their concentration at the tables. Why wouldn't poker players want to take it? Any edge counts, right? Besides, the WSOP does not drug test players. You can stumble into the poker room all coked up, stoned to the gourd, jacked up, drunk as a skunk, roided up, or faded to the tits… and it doesn't matter.

The Mouth held court at the featured TV table for all of Day 5 and the Shrink always sat nearby. In 2007, the Shrink and Amy Calistri spent a significant amount of time interviewing Matusow for a book, and during their meetings, the Shrink developed an understanding of what made Matusow tick. Matusow suffered from a bipolar disorder after years of his affliction going undetected. Matusow was now fine – as long as he took his meds.

"The Matusow blowups are a thing of the past," the Shrink said. His eyes said he was confident. I remained dubious.

Matusow had recently lost a massive amount of weight in a very short time to win a prop bet with Ted Forrest. The drastic weight loss negatively affected his meds and Matusow struggled to readjust his dosage of Adderall. Too much and he was bouncing off the walls and talking nonstop. Too little, and his mind turned to pudding and he couldn't concentrate.

During the dinner break, the Shrink hung out with Matusow inside the VIP lounge. Matusow paced backed and forth and analyzed his table for the Shrink, specifically ranting that if the players in seat 2 or 3 raised his blind one more time, he was going after them.

"Those assholes think I'm weak, but I'll get them."

Matusow popped another half an Adderall to help him focus for the rest of the evening in front of the cameras at the TV table. Shortly after play resumed, Sean Davis raised Matusow's blind. Davis was one of the players who had been aggressively stealing his blinds, so Matusow did exactly as he promised and moved all-in for his last 540,000. Davis quickly called with A-K. Matusow sheepishly tabled 10-5 and instantly knew he picked the wrong time to make a move. He was on the verge of elimination and let out a stream of curses. The dealer fanned out the flop. The crowd exploded when they saw a 5. Matusow went berserk and flailed around while his vociferous fans howled and stomped their feet. Matusow doubled up.

"I shifted gears at the right time!" Matusow screamed. "It's time to go to work. I feel good!"

The rush. The excitement. The adrenaline. The confidence. Matusow fed on all if it. The more the fans cheered, the higher he got.

"Lemme tell you. I fuckin' suck!" said Matusow as he worked the crowd like a crooked evangelist ranting to his congregation of Sunday morning sinners seeking the Holy Spirit.

Enter Phil Hellmuth. The gates of Hades flew right open. When the smoke cleared the room, Hellmuth sat down with about 1 million in chips.

"Yes! Yes! Yes! Yes!" Matusow screeched repeatedly as he jumped up and down like a little kid at Christmas whose parents had bought him a new bike.

After waiting 44 days for a sure thing, the defining moment of my reporting summer finally appeared. Phil Hellmuth and Mike Matusow at the same table. Right next to each other. With fewer than 90 players remaining in the Main Event, hundreds of inebriated, drooling, blood-thirsty fans waited anxiously for the fireworks to begin.

I grinned and thought to myself, "This story is gonna write itself."

Hellmuth and Matusow. It was like the Roman masses waiting for the Christians to be tossed to the lions. The featured TV table was standing room only with spectators spilling out of the Milwaukee's Best Lounge overlooking the stage. Limbs dangled over metal rails. People on top of people, all waiting for a meltdown, an uprising, anything to titillate their fevered minds. I'm shocked that a brawl didn't detonate in the stands between the loyal legion of Matusow fans and the smattering of Hellmuth loyalists. During a New York Rangers hockey game in the early 1990s at Madison Square Garden, I witnessed a soused and irate group of fans pummel a poor sod wearing a Philadelphia Flyers jersey. The police let the fans tear off his jersey and get in a few cheap shots before they broke it up. New York's Finest then proceeded to eject the clown for inciting a riot. We weren't exactly center ice at the Garden, but we were on the biggest stage in all of poker with seven dwarves at the TV table overshadowed by The Mouth and The Brat.

I had an invitation to watch the madness unfold before me with a front seat in media row. Over the first 15 minutes, Hellmuth remained quiet. He studied his opponents and let Matusow run the show as the table captain.

"I came out to hang out with my buddy Phil Hellmuth. He just got here and he told me how great he is. Now, I gotta sit here and hear it for 90 more minutes!" Matusow yelled out to the crowd. They ate it up.

Hellmuth and Matusow were the two biggest sharks left in the Main Event and they avoided each other. Like boxers in a fixed fight, they danced around throwing half-assed punches. I figured that these two better start giving something, anything, otherwise the voracious fans would mutiny and start hurling empty Beast cans, car batteries, and bar stools at the stage.

While Hellmuth and Matusow avoided each other, Chino Rheem shifted gears and gobbled up chips. The erratic pro from Southern California went from playing like a crazy Asian gambler to a psychotic drunken Scandi. Chino sold a hefty percentage of his action to friends and backers. One of them, Canadian pro Greg "FBT" Mueller, sat next to me as he hovered around media row. He grew happier and happier with each pot that Chino won and went deeper and deeper into the money.

"Chino? He was on tilt. Full blown fuckin' tilt. His chips were going everywhere. But look at him now!" Matusow said.

The featured table players were conditioned to Matusow's bizarro world after playing with him all day. Hellmuth's presence did not intimidate them at all. In fact, they were gunning for the fresh fish. When one player pushed Hellmuth off a pot, Hellmuth's frustration began to simmer.

Matusow tried egging on Hellmuth while working the crowd at the same time. "I object to all of you picking on my friend Phil Hellmuth. Leave him alone!"

I was disappointed with the first hour of the Hellmuth and Matusow show. What a dud. I wanted a refund. It was like getting suckered into seeing that new movie with your two favorite stars that ends up going nowhere. But then it happened. On one of the last hands of the night, an implosion of Hellmuthian proportions burst forth. But it wasn't between Hellmuth and Matusow. Instead, Hellmuth found himself rumbling with Cristian Dragomir, a pro from Romania. Dragomir opened the pot for a raise. He only held 10d-4d but it was a hand he had been successful with earlier that day. Poker players can sometimes be superstitious like that. If a certain junk hand is winning them money, then they will keep playing it until it runs out of luck.

Hellmuth suspected something fishy from Dragomir, so he re-raised him holding A-K. Dragomir flat-called with his 10d-4d. On the flop of 10-9-7, Hellmuth checked and Dragomir bet his pair of tens. Hellmuth stood up and called Dragomir an idiot who was "trying to go broke." With a look of utter disgust, Hellmuth folded his cards face up. An ace and a king hit the felt.

"Show the bluff!" insisted Matusow, trying to stir up trouble. "Show him the 3-8 off suit."

Dragomir accommodated Matusow's request and flipped over 10d-4d. The entire crowd howled. The players at the table, including Chino Rheem, applauded Dragomir for taking a pot from the bully. Hellmuth made the correct fold, but did not react kindly to Dragomir rubbing it in by pumping his fist in the air.

Hellmuth jumped out of his seat and stormed around the final table set screaming, "This is how I lose my money? To this idiot!"

"I'm an idiot with a stack," Dragomir taunted.

"This is the sorry state of poker," Hellmuth continued, "Someone puts 400,000 in the pot with 10-4 and the crowd celebrates like it's a good play. This is the worst player in history and the crowd is cheering. Idiot!"

Dragomir complained to the floor supervisor, who told Hellmuth to settle down. Hellmuth wouldn't stop. Dragomir couldn't take it anymore. He stood up and yelled, "Enough is enough! You are an idiot!"

"You're really out of line," Matusow told Hellmuth, who ignored him.

"This is the Main Event and you are the worst player in history!"

"Hey man, he sucked out on you. I understand, but it's just poker," Chino said trying to calm Hellmuth down.

"To you it's just poker. To me it's my life!" Hellmuth barked.

Hellmuth kept on berating Dragomir, so much so, that tournament director Steve Frezer yellow-carded Hellmuth for his gauche behavior. Frezer issued Hellmuth a one-orbit penalty. Luckily for Hellmuth, it was the last hand of the night and play was over for Day 5.

Part of me thought, "Here goes Hellmuth acting like a dick again!" Then I sat back and nodded in approval. Hellmuth knew it was the last hand of the night and was aware that the featured TV table lacked the zest that ESPN and the leering crowd had hoped for. He knows more than just about anyone else in Las Vegas that poker is not a game anymore – its sports entertainment. No one plays a villain better than Hellmuth.

"Fucking idiots from Northern Europe," Hellmuth screamed. "They don't even know how to spell poker!"

Chapter 38

March 2007.

Tiffany Michelle and I officially bonded during a tough assignment in Monte Carlo. The 2007 European Poker Tour Grand Final started out disastrously when the Poker Shrink (head of tournament reporting for Poker News at the time) threw out his back and had to miss the trip. John Caldwell also stayed behind in Las Vegas to attend last-minute WSOP meetings with Harrah's and Bluff Media. That left me in charge of the Poker News coverage team which included Tiffany, Justin Shronk, and Felipe Pacheco.

Before I left for Europe, Caldwell warned me that Felipe's English was spotty. As a dumb boorish American, I knew zero words of Portuguese, so we sorted out any linguistic issues with an online dictionary and hand gestures. The guy was a machine. He slept even less than I did. He shot photos for 16 hours a day and then spent most of his off-hours playing cash games against Eurodonks.

Justin Shronk was one of the best in the business at splicing together videos and had an uncanny knack for repeating any line of dialogue verbatim from Aaron Sorkin's *The West Wing*. As a product of the Philadelphia suburbs, Shronk was an admitted horrible traveler and had a rough time adapting to the pretentious French Riviera.

I didn't blame Shronk one bit. I prided myself on being a traveler and not a tourist, but out of the dozen countries I've visited while reporting on poker, the aristocratic Monte Carlo experience was by far my least favorite. I only knew a handful of French phrases despite the Jesuits trying to beat it into me for three years during high school. The affluent locals sneered at my jeans, the uber-wealthy jet-setting visitors jeered at my unpolished shoes, and the proletariats humping the service jobs hated me because I was an American. The surly and slow-as-snailshit waiters sent me on tilt when they took up to 15 minutes to serve me a room temperature Heineken that cost €9.

I knew fewer than 10 percent of the field at the EPT Grand Final and was overwhelmed standing in the middle of a ballroom full of unknown Scandi poker players with perfectly messy hair wearing designer sunglasses and garish hoodies. My lack of knowledge of the European players was already an obstacle and the pulled muscle in my arm was only going to add to the burden. I first noticed the sharp pain in Nice when I hauled my bag through Côte d'Azur Airport. I pinpointed the origins of the injury to an incident in Florida a few weeks earlier at the Langerado music festival when I tried to hurl a glowstick onstage at Dave Schools, the bass player from Widespread Panic. I aggravated the injury in France by lugging around my bags and the pain persisted during the entire assignment. The medical situation was compounded by serious ganja withdrawal because I was unable to find a competent source. Plenty of shifty-eyed cab drivers and hustling doormen offered me mounds of cocaine, which would be fine if I wanted to chatter incessantly about my misery, but all I wanted was a couple of hits off a joint to soothe the pain.

I walked to a pharmacy down the street from the casino in search of painkillers. The old lady behind the counter scoffed at my feeble attempts to explain my issue through the use of charades. She must have figured me for a junkie because she refused to sell me painkillers. Instead, she grabbed a tube containing a strange eucalyptus ointment off the top shelf. The ointment smelled like cat piss and bubblegum. It sank deep into my arm muscles, burning like hell.

Because I knew Tiffany was a licensed massage therapist, I told her about my pulled muscle. She worked magic on the heavily damaged area in my arm a couple of times a day. The cat-piss gel, Tiffany's massages, and warm Heinekens got me through the turbulent week.

* * * * *

July 2008.

During a Poker News party at the Bellagio, Tony G and Jeff Lisandro (an Australian pro with a residence in Sicily) agreed to stake Tiffany Michelle in the Main Event. Even though Tony G had backed Tiffany in two other smaller buy-in events, she was still an amateur and he was reluctant to stake her the full $10,000.

"She is a star to me and a great entertainer but not qualified enough as a skilled poker player that I would stake (her) in the Main Event," Tony G said. "No one would want to touch her with that big of an investment on unproven ground. I said to Jeff (Lisandro) that if he put up $4,000, I would put up $6,000, but I would have all the rights to Tiff in terms of endorsement. At the time, it was kind of like buying a lottery ticket. I was pretty excited because I had 35 players in the Main Event and very high hopes that some of them would do very well and win, and what it would all mean to Poker News in terms of traffic and new exposure."

Even for the world's best players, the Main Event is a serious long shot given the sheer number of entrants. When all three parties (Tony G, Lisandro, and Tiffany) agreed to a staking arrangement, none of them expected Tiffany to be the last female standing and have a shot at advancing to the final table. Otherwise, the standard Poker News staking contract that she signed would have been worded much differently with more time spent hammering out any potential ambiguities. For the first few days of the Main Event, Tiffany wore a Poker News patch. On Day 5, things changed.

As a 24-year-old attractive woman, Tiffany stood out in a pack of unshaven and overweight guys who looked like they just woke up from a nap. Naturally, she received more and more attention from the ESPN cameras as she advanced deeper into the Main Event. Her chest became a perfect target for product placement by online poker rooms. On Day 5, both PokerStars and Full Tilt Poker were interested in locking up Tiffany to an endorsement deal for the rest of the Main Event. However, Ultimate Bet won out because of her personal relationships with several people involved with the company. Tiffany dated Dave Stann, a pro on the Ultimate Blackjack Tour founded and run by Russ Hamilton (former WSOP Main Event champion and founder of Ultimate Bet). She was also tight with Annie Duke, a part-owner and spokesperson for Ultimate Bet. Tiffany's agent, Katie Lindsay, a former poker writer from Florida who recently started her own player management agency, arranged the deal with Ultimate Bet.

"By wearing the Poker News logo, Tiffany showed the world that she was part of the Poker News/Tony G syndicate. I got the message, but Katie didn't," said Oliver Tse, another former poker writer turned agent.

In 2008, the running rate to wear an online poker room patch on your shirt or on your hat with 180 or so players to go in the Main Event was priced at anywhere between $10,000 and $15,000. That did not include contingency payments (if she finishes in X place, she gets Y dollars) or bonuses for appearing on the TV table. On Saturday morning before cards went in the air on Day 5, Tiffany added two Ultimate Bet patches; one on a hat and another patch on her hoodie. The Poker News logo on her t-shirt was covered up by her hoodie and Tony G went ballistic. He felt entitled to have a Poker News logo visible at all times. They eventually cleared up that issue and for the rest of the day, Tiffany displayed a triumvirate of patches – Poker News on one boob, UB on the other, and a patch sporting the name of her management agency in the middle.

Only a few months earlier, Nat Arem, a programmer from Atlanta and founder of the Pokerdb.com, discovered a superuser cheating account on Absolute Poker. The superuser was every online poker player's worst nightmare – someone who had the ability to view the cards of everyone at the table – which conferred an overwhelmingly unfair

218

advantage. The superuser pillaged and plundered unsuspecting players for millions of dollars. Because the same parent company owned both Absolute Poker and Ultimate Bet, a group of victims on Ultimate Bet launched their own investigation by inspecting every one of their hand histories. Sure enough, more superusers were discovered.

Players instantly withdrew their money. The 2+2 forums and other websites took vigilant stances against Absolute Poker and Ultimate Bet. The angry self-righteous masses ridiculed anyone's involvement in the scandal including sponsored pros from both of the online rooms such as Mark Seif at Absolute Poker and Phil Hellmuth and Annie Duke at Ultimate Bet. Meanwhile, rival online poker rooms engaged in quiet damage control in an effort to get the entire scandal to blow over. The cheating incidents attracted the attention of national media outlets including *60 Minutes* and The Washington Post. Online poker already had a black eye with the UIGEA and tremendous opposition from the religious right. The last thing the poker industry needed was the mainstream media further sensationalizing the problem.

After some serious and lengthy detective work, Nat Arem fingered the person who appeared to be the main culprit – Ultimate Bet founder Russ Hamilton. Arem announced his findings during the Main Event and the news spread like wildfire. Many poker news sites interrupted their regularly scheduled WSOP coverage to report about Arem's disturbing findings.

"For decades, Hamilton was known in Las Vegas circles as a cheat and overall scum bag," Flipchip said. "Doesn't surprise me that Big Fat Russ was involved."

Suffice it to say, the last gasps of Ultimate Bet's legitimacy flew out the window after Arem implicated Hamilton. Despite the damaging news, Tiffany continued to wear the Ultimate Bet logo and associate herself with the site.

"When Tiff turned up with UB gear on Day 5, it was a total shock," Tony G said. "She told me that she couldn't talk to me, that I would have to talk to her agent, Katie. I don't understand why she would do this to me. Where was Katie when Tiff needed $10,000 to play the Main Event? Where was anyone at all, including UB, when Tiff needed to find a way into the Ladies' Event or the $1,000 rebuy event?"

The UB patch became the source of the disagreement. Tony G felt he was entitled to have a final say in any endorsement deals for Tiffany. At the time, Tiffany didn't see it that way and felt as though she should honor her initial commitment to Ultimate Bet.

"Early on as I kind of started doing well," Tiffany explained, "UB were the first and only site that was interested in throwing something on me and I think a lot of people don't know the inner workings, all of the things that went on. It's easy to have sites jump out of the woodwork when cash symbols start popping up above my head, when I start making it deep. I just have to say early on, way before patches were even issued they said 'You know what, yeah, we want to throw a patch on you and we want to start talking.' So I had to respect and honor that out of everybody else, they were the first ones that were there and they were so supportive all along. When things started getting deep – the business, weird pressure, just everything started coming out of the woodwork, they personally stepped up and were so behind me and handled so much drama for me and they were, I felt, the only ones saying 'You know what, guys? Tiffany is in the middle of the World Series of Poker Main Event – back off! She has really important stuff to do.'"

In the initial days of the Main Event, the chatter about Tiffany Michelle on the 2+2 forums was primarily in the form of "Hot or Not" threads. However, when the Ultimate Bet news broke, she was thoroughly vilified in the feeding frenzy. She was caught up in the endless war of domination among big media entities and online poker rooms; a tiny rag doll that the fat cats fought and bickered over as they scrambled to gain control of the space around her tits and trucker hat.

On Day 6, I spotted Tiffany's other backer, Jeff Lisandro, mucking it up with agents from Poker Royalty, the N.Y. Yankees of poker representation. Founded by former sports agent Brian Balsbaugh, Poker Royalty was the top dog in Las Vegas and represented the biggest stars in poker including Daniel Negreanu and Phil Hellmuth. They had connections throughout the entire industry including a very well-established relationship with PokerStars. All of the small-time agents trolling the hallways at the Rio combined couldn't compete with the dominating influence wielded by Balsbaugh and his company.

After Lisandro finished up with the Poker Royalty guys, he had a long talk with Tiffany's agent. The two walked across the empty ballroom. When Lisandro put his arm around her, I was eerily reminded of the scene in *The Sopranos* where Silvio is ordered to whack Adriana and he drives her out to the woods to finish the dirty deed. I assumed that Lisandro was politely explaining to Katie that she was no longer Tiffany's agent. The wise choice would have been to allow the big boys from Poker Royalty to handle her going forward, with their first order of business signing Tiffany a lucrative deal with PokerStars.

Because Nicky spent almost a decade hip-deep in the Hollywood swamp, I turned to her for the low-down on agents.

220

"I dealt with a lot of agents in my time," Nicky explained. "They are some of the most ruthless, yet sickeningly hardworking people you will ever meet. The client's interest is your interest, and it is the only interest. Everyone else can go fuck themselves. Agents can piss people off and get away with it because they hold the keys to the castle by controlling the talent. Talent is the only real currency in Hollywood. Producers, financiers, studio executives, marketing divisions, publicists? Without the talent what do they have? The genesis of Tiffany's poor handling of her sponsorship deals came with her choice of agent. The deeper Tiffany got in the Main Event, the more Katie Lindsay got in over her head. The more Katie got in over her head, the more people tried to encroach on that agent-client relationship. To put it in Hollywood terms, let's say Tiff had just booked a series regular role on an NBC sitcom but was still represented by a one-man firm in the Valley. The minute that news gets out, bigger and better agents are going to target her. And then her decision becomes – do I be loyal and stay with my friends, the people that supported me since day one? Or do I ditch them in favor of someone who really knows how to advance my career?"

I also overheard a conversation at Scheckytown that I was not supposed to hear on the morning of Day 7. After a couple of hours of sleep, I woke up and headed downstairs to play nine holes of Tiger Woods golf on the Wii. I heard Caldwell talking on the phone and decided to put my eavesdropping skills to work. Tony G had managed to work out an endorsement deal for Tiffany with PokerStars through his connections with the owner. I was blown away when I heard the terms.

"She was going to get millions out of it," Tony G said. "With at least $1 million in buy-ins no matter where she finished in the Main Event. I know that with UB she did not even get a signed contract and UB was her agent's only choice. Before play in her last day, Tiff called me and I was so happy for her to have made it as far as she did. But I told her that no matter what, she couldn't wear the UB clothing. I asked her to please think about what she was doing to us, meaning her relationship with me and Poker News, and she said she would think about it."

Tiffany advanced to Day 7 as one of the final 27 players. With all the negative publicity swirling around about Ultimate Bet, both Full Tilt and PokerStars were heavily interested in endorsing Tiffany. Based on the information that I overheard, all signs pointed toward Tiffany signing a deal with PokerStars. I agreed on wagers with many of my prop bet-happy friends. They even gave me odds on Tiffany wearing a PokerStars patch. It seemed like easy money.

The drama and tension escalated in the minutes leading up to the start of Day 7. No one had seen Tiffany, but Otis confirmed that he was told by his higher-ups to monitor Tiffany for the PokerStars Blog. Tiffany finally arrived with an entourage including her agent and adult film star Samantha Ryan. She sat down at the featured TV table and finally revealed her decision. She continued to wear the Ultimate Bet logos. I admired the loyalty to her friends but it was a questionable business decision. She strapped herself to what many viewed as a sinking ship.

With the November Nine final table delay on the horizon, the WSOP Hype Machine was ready to whore out Tiffany. The last woman standing was a heavy fan favorite, but she generated significant controversy. The quality of her play was questioned by both pros and pundits while her ethics and morals were scrutinized for her decision to endorse Ultimate Bet.

With Phil Hellmuth and Mike Matusow eliminated, Tiffany was by far the most popular player left in the mix. If she became the first woman to win the Main Event, she would be the spark that ignited another poker renaissance in America. The industry salivated at the prospect of hordes of young women players and Tiffany-clones taking up the game en masse.

Tiffany started Day 7 among the Top 5 in chips as she closed in on 10 million. However, she got rattled early on and lost half her stack. She failed to advance to the final table when she ran into Peter Eastgate, a young pro from Denmark. My friend Iggy played in the Main Event at Eastgate's starting table and said that the kid was running over everyone with his hyper-aggression.

Once it got down to the final two tables, Eastgate shifted gears and Tiffany walked right into his trap. Dennis Phillips, an amateur from St. Louis, opened for a 500,000 raise. Eastgate flat-called with A-A. Tiffany found A-J in the big blind and called bringing the pot to over 1.6 million. The flop was A-10-9. Tiffany checked her pair of Aces. Phillips fired out 1 million at the pot. Eastgate smooth-called, which immediately drew Phillips' suspicion. When action returned to Tiffany, she check-raised all-in for her stack worth almost 4 million. Phillips folded J-10 and Eastgate called quickly, turning over his pocket Aces. He had flopped a set and Tiffany was drawing nearly dead. She could not conjure up a miracle and busted out in 17th place.

Tiffany won $334,534 but that was before taxes and before she had to pay Tony G and Jeff Lisandro their cuts. I'm astonished that Tiffany went as deep as she did despite all the distractions and circumstances that surrounded her run at the Main Event. What really should have been a celebration for both Tiffany and Tony G, unfortunately, ended up marred in scandal.

Chapter 39

November 2008.

Over a period of four years, I witnessed the effects of unexpected windfalls – lives destroyed, best friends torn apart, and general poisoning of the soul. Most people understand that too little money can make you do desperate and unthinkable things. Surprisingly few people take the time to think about the same holding true on the other end of that spectrum. In the pursuit of seven and eight figures, once-astute judgment becomes clouded just as quickly. The scene has been repeated in Las Vegas more times than anyone can count.

Poker is a simple game. Played among friends, it can be one of the most entertaining experiences in life. But, the ethical weights and measures change when poker is played for millions and the gross profiteering of corporations overshadow the game itself.

I had a front-row seat to the circus for seven weeks every summer. After 46 grueling, ball-busting days, the 2008 WSOP came to a halt. No bells. No whistles. The ballroom emptied the moment the final nine players were set. The lights in the Amazon Room were turned on the highest settings and the roaches scattered to the farthest corners of the room. No more cries of "All in and a call!" and "Seat open!" I'd heard the last of the shrieks from the animals being led to the slaughter.

Televised poker's ratings were trending lower, and in an effort to juice up ratings for the WSOP, Harrah's and ESPN delayed the Main Event final table. During the off-time, ESPN aired episodes of the opening days of the Main Event leading up to the final table in an attempt to hype the prospects of a "live" final table. In previous years, true poker fans already knew the outcome and some never bothered to watch the final table. With the "semi-live" November Nine final table, there would be less than 48 hours between a winner being declared and the airing of the final table episode.

"All of this leads to a big increase in ratings," BJ Nemeth said. "The current ratings for poker on TV are pathetic by the standards of live sports, and the demographics have been dropping every year since 2004. By turning the WSOP final table into a live 'event,' it will attract a much, much larger audience. Everyone in poker will know the date and time that the WSOP final table airs on TV, and most of us will be watching it with far more excitement than we have in recent years. The contagious nature of excitement will trickle down to the casual fans and even attract some non-poker friends and family who are curious to see what the fuss is about. In the short run, high ratings benefit Harrah's and ESPN the most. But in the long run, high ratings benefit everyone in poker, because it attracts more fans, more sponsors, more money, and best of all for the players, more fish thinking they can do what Jerry Yang did."

"There is absolutely nothing wrong with wanting to increase ratings," Otis said. "It will help us all. I'm all for it. The problem is, in an effort to market poker to a wider audience, Harrah's is making changes to the game that have a chance at affecting the outcome. Simply put, the WSOP is either a sporting event or a reality show. If it's a sporting event, then cover it like one. If it's a reality show, then let's all call it what it is and stop being so high and mighty about it. I prefer the former, but nobody listens to me."

I was vehemently opposed to the final table delay and felt that the Main Event should be played out from start to finish because the delay killed whatever momentum the final nine players had built up. The true beneficiaries of the delay were the big business entities (Harrah's, ESPN, Milwaukee's Best, Bluff, Poker News, PokerStars and Full Tilt). I couldn't chastise them for wanting to make money because that's the sole reason for their existence. However, the suits kept insisting that the final table delay was in the players' best interest because it gave them the opportunity to attract more sponsors. In reality, the delay didn't help the players in any appreciable way. Beyond the major online poker rooms, members of the November Nine were unable to secure the millions of dollars in endorsement deals that were originally projected.

The final table delay had major counterforces fighting against it. The economic slide began in early 2008, led by the real estate market implosion and the first inklings of credit default swaps and other derivatives threatening to bankrupt major international banks and insurance companies. As more Americans began feeling the strain of the financial crunch, the influx of new blood to the game had become practically nonexistent. The escapist element of televised poker seemed a little too absurd as most viewers were more concerned about losing their jobs or keeping their homes.

The sporting world focused its attention on the first-ever Olympics in China, hosted in Beijing. Barack Obama's historic run for the White House was also heating up in late summer. Even some of my hard-core poker friends were caught up in the election fury. They stopped writing about suckouts and shifted their blogging to political punditry.

The ratings on ESPN were positive and the best in years, but the November Nine fell under the radar of the mainstream media. During the 117-day delay, Nicky admitted that instead of counting sheep to fall asleep, she tried to recall the names of everyone from the November Nine. I consistently named eight (Dennis Phillips, Peter Eastgate, Ivan Demidov, Ylon Swchartz, Chino Rheem, Kelly Kim, Craig Marquis, Scott Montgomery... and... um...) but I always seem to miss the elusive ninth (Darus Suharto). I was vaguely familiar with only two players – Ylon Schwartz from playing at the Borgata in Atlantic City, and Chino Reem, a regular on the tournament circuit. The other seven were a mystery to me.

Harrah's pipe dream never panned out. The November Nine did not become media darlings and pose for paparazzi photos while rubbing shoulders with Hollywood A-listers. None of the players made the rounds on the nightly talk shows as everyone had hoped. As much as our ADD-entertainment-thirsty society generally laps up any bullshit you spoon feed them, they did not find the November Nine palatable.

Chapter 40

November 2008.

Otis and I found ourselves lost in the darkness of the Hooker Bar sipping moderately chilled beers. We were sharing travel stories with our British colleague, Sinclair, while classic rock tunes cranked out of the sound system. In the blink of an eye, they appeared. In four sips' time we were outnumbered 3-1 by a spirogyra of working girls.

The prostitution industry was being hit with the full force of the credit crunch and quality tricks were few and far between. Fewer conventioneers means fewer potential clients. It seemed that the three of us were the only marks left in the building as I watched them hover like a flock of famished vultures ready to pick apart any carcass. Their eyes were transparent. Any john, any drunk, anybody in their path would do. We were their imminent prey.

* * * * *

3:35 A.M.

One hour earlier inside the Penn & Teller Theatre down the hall, Peter Eastgate won the 2008 WSOP Main Event. The 22-year-old pro from Odense, Denmark, collected $9,152,416 for first place. Eastgate became the first Scandinavian player to win the Main Event and shattered Phil Hellmuth's long-standing record for youngest world champion.

The post-final table festivities were extremely tame compared to those of previous years because a smaller group of media covered the November Nine. Instead of the usual army of reporters, sites only deployed small elite units of between one and three people to cover the final table. Most of them had scheduled early flights or were on rigid deadlines. They declined the invitation to binge drink until sunrise.

The portly guy in his early 50s with a scruffy white beard reminded me a little of Ernest Hemingway. The working girl who had latched onto him was drunker than Judy Garland in her prime years. The tipsy old whore wore a black satin corset with tight black pants, but the tasteless heels gave her away. She didn't have a New Jersey accent, so the tawdry magnificence of her outfit in Las Vegas instantly told us that she was a pro.

4:20 A.M.

The barkeep served Hemingway round after round of an unidentified fruity drink, some sort rum and pineapple concoction. The old hooker slammed Jagermeister like a frat boy at Mardi Gras and moved to the land Beyond Drunk. The liquor sweeping through her bloodstream was effectively signaled by the marked increase in the volume of her voice, as well as her level of friskiness. She took off her heels, and Hemingway massaged her wrinkled feet. He proceeded to kiss her bare left foot then the right one before inserting three toes into his mouth. He sucked for a few seconds and then licked the bottoms of both her feet. A spume of sexual invigoration seized his better judgment and they began making out. It wasn't erotic like two lipstick lesbians sucking face with one another. It was disgraceful and tasteless even for Vegas' low standards.

As we sat watching in utter disbelief, I found myself quoting from National Lampoon's *European Vacation*. "Dad, I think he's gonna pork her."

Without even breaking stride, Otis quickly returned the next line, "He's not gonna pork her, Russ. "

Hemingway shoved a hand up her shirt as she licked one side of his beard. Papa, he's gonna pork her right up against the Hooker Bar.

* * * * *

5:36 A.M.

The old hooker stood up and almost fell over. We've all been there before. You barely notice it while you're up on the bar stool until you stand up to go take a leak and the excess booze hits you like a ton of bricks. Your legs disappear and you spin around like a Weeble hoping to get lucky and regain your balance before smashing your face into the edge of the bar. The old hooker stumbled back, twirled a few times, and nearly collided with the electronic roulette table.

"She's going to get 86'd," said Otis.

I nodded but not one security guard was in sight. The Rio was practically abandoned. Even our barkeep disappeared for ten minutes at a time. A couple of blue hairs were hidden behind a row of slot machines, but other than that, we were on our own.

Hemingway eventually realized the gravity of his situation and decided it was time to call it a night. The old hooker was reduced to incoherent babbling. She lost all motor function and crashed to the ground. A security supervisor walked by as the snookered Hemingway struggled to pick her up off the carpet.

Otis nodded at the suit and gestured at the old hooker. The suit was off the clock and on his way home. He handed off the responsibility to a security guard who looked half asleep when he reluctantly stopped the two sorry souls. The old hooker leaned up against Hemingway when the guard asked for identification. Her sedentary body lost the battle and she slowly slid down to the floor once again. The security guard scribbled down her name and address on a piece of paper. He avoided all eye contact and didn't even bother asking Hemingway for an ID before letting both of them go.

"This shows the boundless nature of Las Vegas," explained Otis while *Piece of My Heart* by Janis Joplin blasted on the speakers. "All Vegas does is look at it and write it down in case there's a lawsuit or the cops come when she shows up dead. And they let it go on."

As Hemingway dragged the old hooker back to his room we began speculating. Which was more likely? Would she puke all over his bed? Pass out on the shitter? Get sodomized with a remote control? Or have her throat slashed in 14 places? Dead hookers are a dime a dozen in Las Vegas, especially on a Tuesday morning.

Thoughts of an obese necrophiliac dragging a comatose hooker back to his room reminded me about the degradation that shoves Otis over the edge. The omnipresent cycle of endless perversion sends him spiraling into the depths of mega-tilt almost every time.

"This is a depraved and soulless city. And this shit goes on all the time," Otis lamented. "After you spend five weeks here, that becomes real. It becomes your reality. And when you start to accept that is reality, you are living in a world where no one should actually live."

Out of nowhere, Peter Eastgate appeared, walking down the corridor. Only a couple of hours earlier, the Scandi won $9 million and now the biggest swinging dick in Las Vegas was walking around the Rio by himself while an old drunken hooker was being covered in globs of semen and may or may not have choked to death on her own bile.

* * * * *

6:08 A.M.

A middle-aged guy in an orange Texas Longhorns hat sat down at the end of the bar and shoved $20 into the video poker machine. An attractive Halle Berry-esque young woman slid into the stool next to him, pulled out a cigarette, and asked him for a light. I started wondering if those were assigned seats specifically meant for johns and working girls.

Just as we took note of the latest harlot, a gaggle of them showed up at the other end of the bar. Three of them sat near Otis and ordered drinks. Two broke off from the larger pack and made a beeline toward us, flashing seductive glances with every step. They operate in pairs whenever they can; one to do the stroking while the other does the talking.

"You guys looking for a little fun?"

She gave us the standard opening line. I tried to play hardball. "Umm, that's what we were doing before you arrived."

"So where are you from?"

I pointed to Sinclair, a distinguished Englishman from London, and blurted, "He's Irish and I'm from Colorado."

"What's your name?"

"Steve," I said. "I'm Steve from Colorado. I sell propane and propane accessories."

"What's his name?" she said as she pointed at Otis who had his head tucked so far down that it looked like he was sleeping on the bar.

"Cameron," Otis muttered.

"Have you ever been with a black girl, Cam?"

Otis instantly raised his left hand and practically shoved his wedding ring into her face.

"I have," I revealed, trying to rescue Otis.

"Well how about we have some fun?" she cooed.

"How much does fun cost?" I inquired.

"Depends. What do you want to do?"

Both slags were now stroking various parts of Sinclair's paralyzed body.

"How much for a threesome? I want to videotape both you and her tag-teaming my Irish friend."

"We'd both do him, but you can't videotape us," she insisted.

Before I could retort with a counter-offer, she instantly changed her mind.

"OK, you can tape us, but no faces!" she said. "I don't wanna see you getting fuckin' rich by putting that shit up on the internet."

She even demanded that I sign a contract. At that precise moment, Otis noted that we were dealing with a working girl who had keen business acumen. We suspected that she let a previous john tape her and it ended up on YouPorn.com. Otis offered up his services as a choreographer and that's when the negotiations broke down.

"You want a fuckin' cut? You get 10 percent. What's my cut?" she demanded.

"Um, three percent," I said.

"Fuck that!"

Foiled again.

"What's your name?" I asked.

"Tela," she said.

"Tela is the name of a Phish song. Ever hear of that band?"

"The Fish? Never heard of them."

No shocker there. The only other Tela that I'd ever run across was a Siamese cat belonging to my ex-girlfriend. (Later that morning, I'd send her a drunken text that read, "u named your cat after a vegas hooker." Being a third grade teacher at a parochial school in Dallas, she was not exactly thrilled with my drunken wit.)

I steered the conversation toward economics. I wanted to know how the collapse of the subprime mortgage and derivatives markets were affecting the average Las Vegas working girl.

"It sucks," she said. "Business is bad. No one has money. Shit, I might have to actually get a real job."

"Did you vote for Obama?"

"I would have, but I didn't vote."

"Why not?"

"I'm from Oregon."

"I don't know too many black people from Oregon, unless you count the guys playing basketball for the Portland Trailblazers."

"No shit. That's why I'm here. So do you guys wanna have fun or what?"

I sipped a bottle of Amstel Light as four hooker hands continued to stroke Sinclair.

"What the hell is that?" Tela asked.

"Amstel," I said.

"I never heard of Amstel? Is that a cracker beer?"

"It's from Holland."

"Well, finish that weak-ass beer and let's go up to your room and do some real partying."

I rejected her again. Tela stopped messing around and switched to lewder tactics as she unleashed another aggressive sales pitch.

"Don't you want a blow job? All guys want their cocks sucked. Let's go up to your room," she cajoled.

"We can't go up to my room. My girlfriend is sleeping there."

"Girlfriend? Who the hell brings sand to the beach?" Tela asked.

That line always makes me laugh, and the banter ended right there. The hoochies knew when to fold a losing hand and finally gave up. What else could they do? Otis kept flashing his wedding ring. I constantly reminded them about my extremely understanding and wonderful girlfriend who was fast asleep upstairs. Sinclair displayed admirable nerves of steel. He did not blink once, nor did he utter a single word during the ordeal.

"They fancied me," said Sinclair once the storm subsided and the harlots retreated. "I think that under different circumstances, we could have had a noncommercial relationship."

We ordered another round at a time when most sensible people were having a cup of coffee or a glass of freshly squeezed orange juice. The Rio was slowly repopulating. A steady stream of conventioneers with dangling name tags walked by us every couple of minutes on their way to breakfast. Some of them stopped to leer at the bored slags hovering around us.

One of the working girls seated next to Otis received a phone call. She quickly wrote down an address and two of them scurried off. The last of the hussies had bailed and it seemed like a good time for us to document our experiences. I took out my voice recorder and chatted with Sinclair about surviving our encounter with the working girls. Tela and her friend unexpectedly returned and interrupted our discussion. She thought that my mini-recorder was a phone and snatched it out of my hand. She sang along to a Pink song that blasted on the speakers.

"What the fuck? This isn't a phone. Is this a camera? What the fuck is this?" she screamed.

I forcibly grabbed my recorder from her hand.

"You're not videotaping me are you? I'll sue your ass if you're fuckin' videotaping me!" she screamed and stormed away.

* * * * *

7:10 A.M.

"So are you guys finally ready to fuck?"

Tela and her friend returned for a third time to hawk their goodies. They looked fidgety and had a lot less patience. They gave us the nonsexy hard sell. After we declined their advances once again, they darted toward the cashier's window.

"I wanna know where they've been," Sinclair said.

"Doing blow in the bathroom?" was my quick answer.

"They're going to the cage. Why else would they be going there?" Otis said.

"They went on a heater at the blackjack tables and were cashing out their winnings," I theorized.

Otis wasn't convinced. "They were business women who were just paid for their services in chips."

He was right. These girls were savvy veterans. Only MBAs in whoring and hustling would have started talking contracts. With their cash now in hand, they disappeared into a sea of conventioneers.

"This is just a semi-horseshoed bar in a no-name casino in a barely named city in a fucking country that's barely anything in the world," Otis said. "There is a reason why this bar is named the Hooker Bar."

232

Chapter 41

December 2008.

Nine of us stood in front of Craftsteak, a posh eatery owned by celebrity chef Tom Colicchio, located inside the MGM casino. The reservation for twelve was made in AlCantHang's name. He and his closest friend, Big Mike, were wrapping up a binge-drinking session at the sports book. The attractive hostess reminded me of one of the female subjects from a Modigliani painting – angelic with an elongated swan's neck. I slipped her a $20 bill and told her that a few members of our party were running behind.

"Are you Mr. CantHang?" she asked.

"No," I said, "I'm just his assistant. Mr. CantHang is the rock star, and I just cater to his affairs. He'll be arriving shortly with his personal security detail, a gentleman named Big Mike. When you see him, you'll understand why he's called Big Mike."

"I'll make sure that Mr. CantHang is seated immediately," she said. "And if there is anything else that I can do to make your dining experience any more pleasurable, please do not hesitate to ask."

I successfully bluffed Modigliani's model. A couple of minutes later, she returned with AlCantHang shuffling behind and clutching a tumbler filled with Southern Comfort. Big Mike sauntered behind AlCantHang with a menacing gait. We had a full table including my brother Derek, Nicky, and some of my closest friends in order to celebrate the impending nuptials of our dear friends, Gracie and Pablo.

Our ensuing dinner was fantastic with hysterical conversation and scrumptious Kobe beef. About midway through our three-hour meal, AlCantHang excused himself to have a cigarette. He wandered up to the hostess and asked where he could smoke since both Craftsteak and the Studio Walk area just outside of the restaurant were nonsmoking zones. She pointed towards the casino floor and asked him if he needed a security escort. Al respectfully declined the escort, but complimented her and the rest of the staff on their sensitivity to the needs of a celebrity.

The bill arrived and I picked up half the tab because I saw it as our version of The Last Supper. Less than 12 hours later, I was lit up like a Christmas tree and stumbling back to my room when I got a call from American Express. The fraud prevention department flagged the transaction at Craftsteak as suspicious activity. I explained to the customer service rep that indeed, my gold card was in my possession.

"Yeah, that was me. I fuckin' loooooooooove steak."

* * * * *

I shook Nicky for about two minutes before she finally grumbled.
"What?"

"You gotta see something."

It took her another two minutes to crawl out of bed. I stood in front of the window in our room at the MGM and pointed at the mountains surrounding the Las Vegas Valley. The L.A. born-and-bred blonde rubbed her eyes a couple of times. She stood in silence for a few seconds and blurted "Is that snow?"

A shimmering blanket of pristine white powder covered Red Rock Canyon and the rest of the distant mountains. Michael Friedman called to tell me that three inches accumulated in his backyard in Summerlin. The temperatures were a few degrees higher on The Strip and a wintry mix of rain and melting granules splattered against our window. An unexpected winter storm blasted Nevada. Flights at McCarran International Airport were delayed with thousands of passengers stranded. The storm dumped snow in the higher elevations and blocked Cajon Pass on I-15, which we had to cross to return to home base. An alternate route to L.A. would have taken twice as long and neither of us wanted to drive in crappy weather for eight hours without snow tires.

I had only seen heavy rain in Las Vegas a couple of times, and snow? Never. Flipchip lived in Las Vegas for decades and mentioned that it snowed once a year but that it rarely stuck to the ground. A snow storm consisting of a couple of inches (what folks back East would call "flurries") occurred only once every ten years or so. A harmonic semblance of peacefulness and purity fell over Las Vegas after an unexpected display of Mother Nature's power. When the storm ended, we were greeted by clear azure skies and immaculate snowcapped mountains.

The unusual winter blast was stacked neatly atop the harsh economic storm. The most popular tourist destination in America sat virtually empty. Commercial landlords bled money as strip malls struggled to fill vacant storefronts. For several consecutive years, Las Vegas had been declared America's fastest-growing city until all of that heralded growth came to an abrupt halt. Now, Las Vegas teetered on the verge of becoming America's fastest-imploding city. Entire neighborhoods became ghost towns overnight. U-Haul and other self-serve moving companies ran out of trucks as residents fled the state. Las Vegas used to be the largest receiver of their one-way truck rentals. No more.

The local convention business suffered greatly when corporations slashed their budgets and opted for regional locations instead of Las Vegas. Airlines scaled back their Vegas routes. Even the lavish Wynn and Bellagio were offering deep discounts to fill vacancies. Cabbies took a hit as many sat idle in long lines up and down The Strip. Bartenders, waitresses, and dealers in the pits saw a drastic reduction in gratuities. Even the working girls bitched and moaned about the lack of quality tricks. Everything was being trampled in my generation's version of the Great Depression. As bad as it was, many financial gurus and experts feared it was only going to get worse. Consumer confidence was plunging. Americans who invested heavily in the stock market lost anywhere from one-third to half of their retirement funds. Homeowners saw the value of their property plummet as much as 50 percent. The Nevada housing market fell right into the toilet, leading the nation in foreclosures.

The gambling Mecca that used to be impervious to the outside world suddenly changed. The international and domestic woes hit Las Vegas hard. Casinos laid off thousands of workers. Fewer visitors also meant less gaming revenue. The stock prices for Las Vegas Sands, Wynn Resorts, and Boyd Gaming lost from 70 to 95 percent in value. Boyd scrapped plans to build its multi-billion dollar Echelon project on the north end of The Strip that was supposed to rival the CityCenter project. Billionaire Kirk Kerkorian (majority owner of the MGM Mirage group) envisioned an extravagant CityCenter development as a city within a city, housing a massive luxury casino and resort, two smaller boutique hotels, and two towers filled with condos. All of these lofty plans and more were set in motion during the boom years. Amid the credit crunch, the project ran past the deadline and went over budget with construction costs ballooning in excess of $8 billion. The CityCenter almost became a black hole in the middle of The Strip, before it was miraculously rescued by oil money from Middle East luminaries when DubaiWorld bought into the CityCenter project as an investment partner.

Despite the callous downturn, Las Vegas will eventually return to its glory days. Over the next 50 years, the city's prominence will rise and fall once again. Booms and busts. The time will eventually come when the Bellagio and Venetian structures are imploded and new casinos are constructed on their ruins, much like the Dunes and the Sands were before them. The cycle will continue. Birth. Death. Rebirth. Build. Tear down. Rebuild.

No matter how bad things get, I believe that Las Vegas will always survive. Despite the downswing, dreamers continue to fly into Las

Vegas. From my hotel room, I watched the line of planes on approach to McCarran, the lucky ones who were able to land despite the inclement weather. I could almost feel the new batch of passengers on each plane bubbling over with exuberance. They wait weeks and months until their vacation days kick in so they can answer the voices inside their heads. The planes keep landing every few minutes to unload their cargos of walking ATMs. Some were misunderstood souls trying to fulfill their destiny, while others were running away from their realities and running toward lubricious life-size blow-up dolls named Amber, Cinnamon, Raven, Summer, Mercedes, Layla, Crystal, Sierra, Lavender, and Sable.

The party animals run together in drooling packs under the resplendent lights during four-day binges that make John Belushi's fiercest bender look like a circle of girl scouts roasting marshmallows. Post-modern Las Vegas orgies are fueled by neverending flows of Red Bull, fistfuls of Adderall, and enough cheap blow to choke a giraffe. The fiends know this and can't get there fast enough. Even the chemical-free citizens are no less high, and inebriated on the ecstatic possibility of becoming the biggest and baddest muthafuckin' baller in town. The possibility always exists on that next hand of blackjack, the next toss of the dice, the next turn of the roulette wheel, and the next basketball game.

False hope is as easy as it is cheap.

The first whiff of casino air ignites a spark in your soul as it jumps right out of your intestines and knocks back eight consecutive glasses of Champagne while you sit next to a slippery pimp with bling the size of bowling balls and a stable of girls with the elasticity of Romanian gymnasts. The $500 an hour working girls carry around bottles of KY and a range of STDs as they lay in wait for their prey. Those scornful tramps drench themselves in poorly cloned perfumes to try and hide the smell of tube steak on their breath. They hone in on sexually maladroit poker players who haven't seen daylight, let alone the pink parts of a vagina in months. Their orange eyeballs radiate envy, sloth, greed, wrath, gluttony, lust, and pride. They drain the life out of anyone walking within five feet of their tortured karmas.

Weekend warriors hope to obtain a long-overdue hummer from their wives after an expensive dinner followed up by a show at the latest Cirque du Soleil production, or worse, listening to outdated comics recycle dead hooker jokes to a half-empty room of crocked Baby Boomers. Young girls in black cocktail dresses and high heels glide across the casino floor in search of true love or at least a fulfilling one-night stand with Mr. Right Now. Sprinting valets dodge pothead limo drivers. Grieving wives walk out of little white chapels, holding back tears after their shotgun weddings. They know it's the beginning of an era and the end of the rest of their lives.

The delusional slot addicts keep their fingers punching away at the machines that gobble up their money. The invisible causalities, who you and I choose not to see most of the time, feed their last $33 into the slots hoping to win back 5 percent of their losses. Sometimes they play long enough to get a free drink, a free buffet, a free room, maybe even a free show that they have no desire to see in the first place. A win is a win. It doesn't matter if it's an octogenarian snagging a big score at the penny slots, or if it's a Norwegian poker prodigy dragging a *monsterpotten.* Their veins burst with excitement and the same avalanche of endorphins flood their bloodstream.

The glimmering lights of The Strip reflect a kaleidoscope of colors onto the sizzling pavement where your Aunt Maudie from Oklahoma walks on glistening gems, but the brightness blinds the populace and hides the opposite end of the Las Vegas spectrum where vampires lurk in dimly lit parking lots and siphon the blood of conventioneers from Houston. Chalk it up to the sadistic cycle of addiction that continues every second of every day in the city of sinners where the Ten Commandments are brazenly frowned upon as lunatics run rampant down Las Vegas Boulevard trying to fuck anything that moves.

Vegas cabbies angrily clutch their steering wheels and secretly wish they could mow down the herd of vile pedestrians.

"This place used to be wonderful," a bald cabbie with a thick Brooklyn accent once told me. "It is from the outside, but on the inside it's loathsome and full of addicts."

Angels have to dart in and out of traffic on Las Vegas Boulevard trying to scrape the fallen ones off the scorching pavement. The angels assigned to Nevada are the loneliest ones in the universe. Their halos have withered in the heat. Many of them wander into the Rhino and sit in the VIP section for hours on end hoping to have the grittiness of the day wear off with an intense session of dry humping from coked-up Ukrainian girls.

The guilt-ridden sinners hide from the sneers of God and become the wayward refugees that pious little Mormon children pray for every night. Thousands of citizens with good reputations, solid marriages, and impeccable criminal records become shattered casualties in hazy weekends of Dionysian decadence while holed up in a room at the Stratosphere shooting pharmaceutical cocaine into the veins of their feet with a 21-year-old from Boise who moved to Vegas to become a blackjack dealer but ended up on the pole. After she orders $500 in room service and clogs up the toilet with a nasty case of diarrhea, another sucker realizes that he should have waited to sober up before slurring marital vows in front of a fat and sweaty Elvis at the Graceland Wedding Chapel.

IRAs, 401Ks, college savings, housing payments, credit card advances – all are fleeced to support the habitual self-inflicted terror. If you're ever feeling sorry for yourself, head to a Gamblers' Anonymous meeting at the Rescue Mission. The mainstream media loves to paint a picture of glitzy Vegas, but they should include audio excerpts of testimonials from AA, GA, and NA meetings. The masses seem to forget about the omnipresent evil. What happens in Vegas gets discussed in AA meetings.

"The only way to get clean is to sweat it out," mused an old humble junkie who spoke to a group of a dozen lifelong losers.

Security guards haul away those who cannot be saved – the fools caked in vomit and shriveled up in the shit-stained bathroom stalls and the dilettantes slumped over at the end of the bar grasping their souvenir cups.

Want to take a ride in a time machine? Play in the midnight poker tournament at Binion's where it smells like a third-rate nursing home on a tobacco farm. The sickening aroma of sour urine wafts everywhere around Fremont Street where corruption and corporate scumbags trashed what used to be the jewel of Las Vegas and moved on. No one actually goes Downtown to get shanked by a pimple-faced guy with no teeth, but, it sure does happen. In the 1960s and 70s, high rollers in Stetsons drove through Downtown in convertibles. Now you can't drive anywhere near there in an open-air vehicle without worrying about getting clipped in a drive-by or getting carjacked by an angry mob of hoodlums behaving like the diseased cockroaches that used to swarm my kitchen floor at the Redneck Riviera. Downtown now resembles an old Parisian whore who still smuggles cock to remind herself that she's still alive.

Often, I wonder how much of the approaching downfall of modern Western civilization will be traced back to all-you-can-eat-buffets. Menageries of swine stuffing their faces with prime rib are oblivious to the millions of others dying a slow death from starvation. Flies crash-land on their swollen, protruding bellies while we grin and give ours a hearty rub. With every extra plate of pasta or every scoop of gelato our society takes another step toward Hell's front door.

The hustlers, the pimps, the suits, the grifters – they all wake up every day with only one goal in mind – to steal every dollar in your pocket. Our brainwashed bodies are easy to rob because we firmly believe

238

the TV when it tells us "What happens in Vegas, stays in Vegas." Alas, those credit card bills never stay in Las Vegas. Neither does that itchy infestation of crabs that follows you back home to Boston where you attempted to pull off the biggest bluff since Moneymaker duped Sammy Farha and explain to your six-months pregnant wife the real reason you shaved your pubic hair and applied ointment to your balls three times a day. It would break her heart if she found out that you drank too much top-shelf tequila and succumbed to a threesome with Austrian honeymooners named Karl and Freda who stole your cell phone, credit cards, and your entire poker bankroll.

Why do some of us live and why do some of us die? Why do some leave Las Vegas as winners while the rest leave utterly hungover, violated, and broke? I've been seeking answers since my first visit in 1995. As the years pass, I only have more questions and never any answers. Ghosts wander the hotel corridors in hopes of running into desperate people, because they are the only ones who will actually talk to them. I saw one. I saw many. But the wispy apparitions never answered my questions about human frailty.

Grubby once told me a story that epitomizes the most depressing and depraved display of gambling addiction that I've ever heard: "I went to the Mirage and sat down at a Mr. Cashman slot machine. I was like, what the hell is this? The seat was wet. It was drenched in urine. Someone pissed themselves. They refused to get up for a bathroom break and kept gambling. I guess they finally left when they ran out of money. And it's not the first time that it's happened to me."

That's an ugly, rancid secret that the casinos don't want you to know. Right now, some nasty fucker is sitting in his own shit chasing a jackpot in hopes of finding a path to salvation.

After almost four years of living on and off in the shadows and suburbs of Sin City, I love Las Vegas despite all of my negative musings about it. I've glimpsed the true heart of darkness and watched friends and their fortunes fade into oblivion in the hopeless pursuit of fame and prosperity. The majestic poker boom has come and gone and I continue gathering as many crumbs as I can before fleeing once again.

Las Vegas is a magical destination filled with spectacular memory burns. The city is also a hub of many gratifying milestones in my life.

Las Vegas is where I strengthened a bond with my brother and where I crossed paths for the first time with people who would become friends for life.

Las Vegas is where I fell in love with the woman of my dreams, my girlfriend Nicky, who spares no expense of effort in carefully steering me away from the more self-destructive aspects of my nature.

Las Vegas is where I acquired a small fortune on a couple of websites with a father and son duo in Flipchip and the Poker Prof.

Las Vegas is where I finally made a name for myself as a scribe after a decade of desperation.

Las Vegas is also where I learned about the tragic consequences of living life on the edge 24 hours a day. Southern Comfort. Corona. Red Stripe. Makers Mark. Greyhounds. Marijuana. Vicodin. Percocet. Valium. Xanax. Lortabs. Sudafed. Oxycontin. Adderall. Redbull. Ecstasy. Molly. Cocaine. Ketamine. Mushrooms. LSD. DMT. Spearmint Rhino. Cheetah's. Crazy Horse Too. Sapphire. Olympic Garden. The Tilted Kilt. The Hooker Bar. All-you-can-eat-sushi. Pai Gow. The WSOP. Sports betting on the World Cup, NFL, NBA, NHL, and college basketball. Keno. Craps. Blackjack. Beer bowling. Lime Tossing.

After a 24-hour snow delay in Las Vegas, we were finally on our journey home. I know that I've had enough of Vegas when I start missing the plastic hills of Hollyweird. Nicky drove the first leg and raced out of town on an empty freeway. I was stunned by the empty roads and lack of traffic as we left the Las Vegas city limits. Nicky was enamored by the thin layer of snow that blanketed the surrounding desert. I had never seen a cactus covered in a crystalline skeleton of ice and snow before.

"Bags of money," I said, pointing up to the cavalcade of aircraft waiting to land at McCarran.

Chicago, New York City, San Francisco, Dallas, Denver, Atlanta, Minneapolis, Portland, Toronto, London, and Miami. All flights eventually land in Las Vegas to unload more suckers with bags and bags of money. They foolishly think they can tame the lost paradise. I know, because I'm one of them.

Acknowledgements

Thanks to my brother, Derek McGuire, for the unwavering support. I am here today because of my brother's unselfishness.

Many friends from college stuck by me through many of the dark years, and I have to thank David Sheer, Jerry Engel, Dave Simanoff, Jon Schanzer, Armando Huerta, Bob Chencinski, and Brad Singer. My freshman year roommate, Dave Simanoff, encouraged me to start blogging in 2002. I took his advice and the rest is history.

My girlfriend "Nicky" has been incredibly understanding and patient throughout the entire process, often putting her work on hold to help me out. She's a sincere inspiration and I love her dearly.

I would never have achieved any semblance of success without the help of Flipchip and the Poker Prof from LasVegasVegas.com. They are like family to me and I would have never survived my first year in Las Vegas without them. The Prof gave me my first big break in the poker industry and I'm eternally grateful.

Thanks to Grubby for letting me live with him in Henderson and letting me tag along with him on all of those wild adventures. He's one of a kind.

Thanks to Jeremiah Schupbach a.k.a. The German Butcher for saving my ass when I was drowning and stuck. He helped me trim all of the fat from the behemoth first draft.

I have to give credit to my group of editors and proofreaders which include Dr. Ken Friedman, Jeremiah Schupbach, Nicky, Derek, Benjamin Gallen, Rachel Schupbach, Neil Fontenot, and Jessica Lapidus. Your contributions are priceless. I can never thank you enough for your time and effort.

Thanks to Jerome Schmidt from Inculte Publishing for taking a bold leap of faith with me and agreeing to publish the French version of *Lost Vegas* without reading a single word.

Thanks to Benjamin "Benjo" Gallen for talking sense into me one night with Satre's lobster.

Thanks to Kat Goodale for helping me with the cover art.

Thanks to Otis for putting up with my shit every summer and for being my friend.

Thanks to John Caldwell for believing in me.

Thanks to Dan Michalski for many late night discussions about writing, life, and trying to stay sane.

Thanks to Tom Sexton for the Archie Karas research.

Thanks to Wil Wheaton for all of the advice, inspiration, and guidance over the years.

Special thanks to everyone at PokerStars including Brad Willis, Jeffrey Haas, Simon Young, Mad Harper, Howard Swains, Stephen Bartley, Thomas Koo, and Sarne Lightman.

Thanks to all of the organizations who hired me over the years to write for them, particularly: LasVegasVegas.com, Poker News, Poker Player Newspaper, Fox Sports, PokerStars Blog, Bluff Magazine, U.K./Europe Poker News Magazine, Poker Pro, Massive Impact Productions, the OnGame Zone, and the Borgata Casino in Atlantic City. I especially want to thank some of the people who hired me or signed my paychecks including Stan Sludikoff, Brad Willis, John Caldwell, Tony G, Damon Rasheed, Matt Parvis, Simon Young, Wilko, Kim Lund, Mickey, Michael Friedman, Ray Stefanelli, Trey Leurssen, Eric Morris, Eddy Kleid, Lance Bradley, Lou Kreiger, Haley Hintze, Garry Gates, Amy Calistri, Scott Gallant, Ilya Gorodetskiy, Marco Esquandoles, and Sean & Brent from Lord Admiral Radio.

Thanks to Jeffrey Pollack for letting me speak my mind at the WSOP. Thanks to Nolan Dalla, the WSOP media director, and a hearty thanks to Harrah's especially Gary Thompson, Seth Palansky, Dave Curley, Alan Fowler, and Ty Stewart. Thanks to all the dealers and the entire tournament staff at the WSOP (past, present, and future) especially Steve Frezer, Charlie Ciresi, Johnny Grooms, and Jack Effel.

Thanks to the gang from the Blue Parrot home game back in New York City (Ferrari, Rick, Ugarte, Coach, Swish, F-Train, and Joel), where I honed my reporting skills writing up recaps of our Monday night home games.

Thanks to all of the bloggers out there, especially those who sent me traffic over the years: Iggy, Aaron Gleeman, Wicked Chops Poker, and Shane "Shaniac" Schleger.

Special thanks to Jonno Pittock and the entire staff at the Crown Casino in Melbourne, Australia. I also have to thank Conrad Brunner, Warren Lush, Liz Lieu, Gaz Edwards, Human Head, Justin from Paradise Poker, Kym Bracken, Johnny Walker, Jason "Spaceman" Kirk, Charlie Tuttle, Snoopy, Steve Preiss, Brian Cooley, Colin Coley, Barry Greenstein, Linda Geenen, Brian Balsbaugh, Poker Royalty, Dr. Tim Lavalli, AlCantHang, BJ Nemeth, Matt Savage, Felicia Lee, Gene Bromberg,

Henry Wasserman, Jen Creason, Andy Bloch, Matt Maranz, Dave Swartz, 441 Productions, Andrew Feldman, Johnny Hughes, Ali Lightman, Neil Stoddart, Dave King, Jen Mason, Jen Leo, Lara Miller, Heather Borowinski, Poker Road, Joe Sebok, Scott Huff, Poker Listings (Matt, Marty, Arthur, Owen, Rod, et al.), Joe Giron, Ryan Kallberg, Adam Stormwind, Jeremiah Smith, Martin Harris, Lori the dealer, Jesse, Tiffany Michelle, Michael Craig, Oliver Tse, Rob Gracie, Gail Smith, Bruce Cohen, Regis High School, Blogger.com, the Hooker Bar, the Tilted Kilt, and Professional Keno Player Neil Fontenot.

Justin Shronk, a former colleague of mine at Poker News and a producer at Poker Road, passed away during the writing of this book. RIP, brother.

I have to express my sincere thanks to Dr. Ken Friedman for helping me become a better writer.

I'm sure I missed a lot of folks, and I apologize if you were not mentioned. So here's a general thanks to **all of my friends** for all of your love, cash, and friendship over the years. Lastly, I want to thank you, the reader, for your support over the years. Lost Vegas would never have been possible without your help.

Paul McGuire

(Las Vegas, May 2010)

If you would like to read more of my work, visit…

Tao of Pauly – taopauly.com
Tao of Poker – taopoker.com
Truckin' – mcgtruckin.blogspot.com
Coventry Music – phish-coventry.com
Tao of Bacon – taobacon.blogspot.com

For future news and updates about *Lost Vegas*, visit lostvegasbook.com. You can also follow **@LostVegasBook** on Twitter.

Made in the USA
Lexington, KY
09 February 2011